CULTURES
I·N C·O·N·T·A·C·T

The Impact of European Contacts on
Native American Cultural Institutions
A.D. 1000–1800

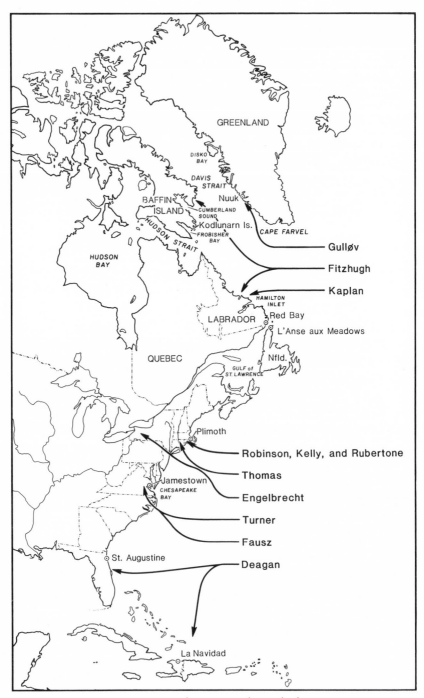

Eastern North America and Greenland

C U L T U R E S

I·N C·O·N·T·A·C·T

The Impact of European Contacts on
Native American Cultural Institutions
A.D. 1000–1800

Edited & with commentary by

WILLIAM W. FITZHUGH

Anthropological Society of Washington Series

SMITHSONIAN INSTITUTION PRESS

WASHINGTON & LONDON

1 9 8 5

The Smithsonian Institution Press publishes a series of significant volumes
in anthropology edited by the Anthropological Society of Washington.
The Society, the oldest continuously functioning anthropological association
in the United States, was founded at the Smithsonian Institution in 1879.
Each volume in the series collects essays by leading scholars
on aspects of a central topic, originating in a program of lectures
sponsored by the Society.

Library of Congress Cataloging-in-Publication Data

Main entry under title:
Cultures in Contact.

(Anthropological Society of Washington series)
Bibliography: p.
1. Indians of North America—Cultural assimilation—
Addresses, essays, lectures.   2. Indians of North America—
History—Colonial period, ca. 1600–1775—Addresses, essays,
lectures.   3. Indians of North America—First contact with
Occidental civilization—Addresses, essays, lectures.   4. Indians
of North America—Foreign influences—Addresses, essays,
lectures.   I. Fitzhugh, William W., 1943– .   II. Series.
E98.C89G74   1985   973'.0497   85–22173
ISBN 0-87474-438-5

The paper used in this publication meets the minimum requirements
of the American National Standard for Permanence of Paper
for Printed Library Materials Z39.48-1984.

Designed by Maria Epes

C O N T E N T S

Introduction
William W. Fitzhugh   1

P A R T   I :

The Arctic Sector:
Inuit Responses to Explorers, Whalers, Traders, and Missionaries

Commentary on Part I
  William W. Fitzhugh   19
Early Contacts North of Newfoundland before A.D. 1600:
A Review
  William W. Fitzhugh   23
European Goods and Socio-Economic Change in Early Labrador
Inuit Society
  Susan A. Kaplan   45
Whales, Whalers, And Eskimos: The Impact of European Whaling
on the Demography and Economy of Eskimo Society in
West Greenland
  Hans Christian Gulløv   71

P A R T   I I :

New England—the Move Inland:
Land, Politics, and Disease

Commentary on Part II
  William W. Fitzhugh   99

Preliminary Biocultural Interpretations from a Seventeenth-
Century Narragansett Indian Cemetery in Rhode Island
    Paul A. Robinson, Marc A. Kelley, and Patricia E. Rubertone   107

Cultural Change on the Southern New England Frontier,
1630–1665
    Peter A. Thomas   131

New York Iroquois Political Development
    William Engelbrecht   163

P A R T   I I I :

The Chesapeake: Two Views— Anthropology and History

Commentary on Part III
    William W. Fitzhugh   187

Socio-Political Organization within the Powhatan Chiefdom
and the Effects of European Contact, A.D. 1607–1646
    E. Randolph Turner   193

Patterns of Anglo-Indian Aggression and Accommodation
along the Mid-Atlantic Coast, 1584–1634
    Frederick J. Fausz   225

P A R T   I V :

The South—Labor, Tribute, and Social Policy: The Spanish Legacy

Commentary on Part IV
    William W. Fitzhugh   271

Spanish-Indian Interaction in Sixteenth-Century Florida
and Hispaniola
    Kathleen A. Deagan   281

Contributors   319

INTRODUCTION

William W. Fitzhugh

One of the major responsibilities of the president of the Anthropological Society of Washington (ASW)—and by far the most interesting one—is to develop a series of monthly programs on some theme of scholarly importance to the membership of this august body, whose founder (in 1880) was John Wesley Powell and whose principal offspring (in 1888) was the American Anthropological Association. It was my privilege to undertake this task during the society's 1981–82 season, for its proudly announced meetings numbers 1010 through 1017. In this task I was ably assisted by Alison Brooks and Mark Leone. In view of our own interests and the socio-cultural themes of recent program series, we decided that the topic should be archeological. Our selection was influenced by a number of factors, including geographic relevance to our membership, potential for research development, availability of speakers, and financial feasibility. The latter constraint resulted from the Anthropological Society of Washington having just been "pushed from the nest" of societies managed by the American Anthropological Association. Independent but managerially naive, we planned to produce a captivating program without threatening the exchequer.

In due course we announced a theme: Native American Adaptations to Early European Contact: Greenland to Florida. We hoped this subject would fulfill our goals and attract speakers with research projects bordering on history, ethnology, and archeology. The ASW Board was generous in its support of the proposal, at the same time admonishing us to avoid budget-busting. Fortunately, we were able to impose on the generosity of our speakers, most of whom agreed to pay their own way to Washington in return for dinner and hospitality *à la maison*. For some, these speaking engagements proved quite eventful. Hans Christian Gulløv came from

Copenhagen "masked" as a courier for the Smithsonian Travelling Exhibition Service, bearing a specimen to be installed in the Smithsonian's Inua exhibition. Randolph Turner spent a morning broken down on Interstate 95 in the midst of the ice storm that resulted in our having to cancel the ASW mid-winter symposium. And Kathleen Deagan had some memorable moments in a late-night standoff with a burglar through my living room window. For these and other inconveniences endured, as well as for the authors' hard work in preparing their manuscripts for publication, I am most grateful.

Selection of the program topic was inspired by recent advances in research on the early historical period of Indian and Eskimo (Inuit) cultures in eastern North America, ca. 1500–1750. During this period native groups encountered a technological and social order profoundly different from any that had existed previously in this region, and were presented with strong material and social incentives for interacting with European groups. The impact of these contacts is documented amply in historical sources (Morison 1971; Quinn 1977, 1979), but for reasons noted below archeological attention to this period has been almost non-existent. What work has been done has a strong artifact-centered orientation, with the result that little is known of the impact of European contact on the cultural institutions that governed these native societies. It is here that a great deal of useful anthropological work could be done, for these contact situations covered a variety of native cultures which exhibited different levels of socio-economic organization and came from a vast geographic region having varied ecological potentials. These contacts were made within a relatively brief period of time by a variety of European groups with relatively similar kinds of technology and organization but diverse purposes and methods. Hence, for the study of culture process, the early East Coast contact horizon affords a wide panorama of acculturation case studies in addition to presenting an opportunity for better understanding of the specific culture histories of the native groups themselves.

Although neglected for many years, studies of contact-period culture history have now begun to interest increasing numbers of archeologists. The difficulty of adequately identifying processes and causes of culture change in prehistoric archeology has attracted some archeologists to the historic period, with its ethnographic and documentary sources, in search of insights and methods that would lead to advances in prehistoric interpretation. Equally important to archeologists is the knowledge gained through historical research about the relevance of various data fields, the conditions under which such data might be preserved archeologically, and the recovery methods that might be most productive. It is instructive, therefore, to note a shift in orientation among anthropologically trained archeologists toward ethnography, history, and a variety of new data sources, including paintings and illustrations, ledgers, diaries, and municipal records. Although these trends have necessitated training and research outside the traditional areas of archeology and anthropology (Adams 1974; Axtell 1979), they have substantially expanded the potential of historical archeology.

Although shifts toward the historic period of native American culture history are providing new sources of data and new interpretations for both prehistoric and historic studies, the field of "historical archeology" in eastern North America has remained largely descriptive and unanthropological. Its most manifest goal, as evidenced in major research efforts, has been re-creation of colonial America. Plimoth Plantation, Jamestown, Williamsburg, and St. Mary's City are admirable and highly professional programs, but their emphasis has been on European enterprises in America and the internal workings of those small-scale societies. Forts, battlegrounds, villages, plantations, trading posts, kilns, and outhouses have been excavated, reported, and presented to the public at great expense and with great effort. In these projects relatively little attention has been given to the fact that many of these communities or enterprises were closely articulated with native American cultures. Reference to Indian life associated with these settlements has been minimal. Only in a few cases, such as David Hurst Thomas's St. Catherines Island project (Thomas *et al.* 1978, 1984) and Kathleen Deagan's work in Florida (Deagan 1978, 1983), have European and native relationships been a continuing theme in historic-period archeology on the East Coast. Otherwise, information on native life as it influenced colonial societies is often derived from European literature; rarely has it come from contemporary records, and almost never from data excavated at archeological sites. Fundamentally, the paucity of Native American archeological data of the historic period reflects the simple fact that few contact sites have been professionally excavated and reported. Today, the archeologist interested in historic-period Indian cultures is in the same situation as the ethnologist studying the material culture of the eastern Indians. For both, life begins west of the Mississippi insofar as availability of documented collections is concerned. Despite a longer period of contact, more archeological sites, and documentary data, research in the eastern United States is just beginning to take advantage of this untapped resource.

There are many good and justifiable reasons why this situation has arisen: shortage of personnel and funding, lack of training in history among prehistoric archeologists, boundary zones in discipline-based research, site destruction, and others. But in the final analysis, the fundamental cause has been the absence of a strong tradition of historically oriented anthropological archeology in this country. This is one of the few liabilities of the anthropological orientation of American archeological study. In Europe, where history and archeology are closely linked, for both intellectual and ethnic reasons, this problem does not exist. The lack of archeological information on contact-period Indian cultures is only one side of the coin, for archeological attention to the more mundane aspects of rural colonial life has been equally deficient. The most notorious case illustrating the effects of this condition is the recent controversy as to whether the Vermont stone chambers and their purported Ogam inscriptions were the work of sea-faring Celts or Phoenicians from the Iberian Peninsula and Mediterranean in the first millenium B.C. (Fell 1976; see also Cook 1978), or root cellars dating to a little-known period of early New England pioneer life (Neudorfer 1979).

At this pivotal point in the re-orientation of American archeology toward research on historic period and European contact studies, we face a variety of critical questions. How and in what areas can the interface between native American and European society be studied in the East, where it is of great importance and yet so little known? What methods are appropriate? Where are the data and how can connections be made across disciplinary lines? Is the paucity of archeological data really attributable to site destruction from colonial land-use practice, village and urban sprawl, and dam and highway construction, or is this frequently heard claim just a rationalization for neglect? Must this chapter of history remain an archeological version of the "dark and bloody ground" which refers to the silent demise of Indian tribes between the Piedmont and the Mississippi River (Silverberg 1968)? Somehow this seems too pessimistic a view; more likely we are simply faced with a dearth of evidence caused by our own failure to pursue research on this important subject.

An underlying impediment to research has been the view that archeological cultures, like their ethnographic counterparts, were tightly organized, spatially discrete entities with clearly defined boundaries separating one group from another. Rooted in the conceptions of early anthropologists and biological theory which equated "cultures" with "species," these views have produced stereotypic "Indian" culture types that are only slightly more real than the cigar-store Indian and other images of Indian society that continue to play to national audiences in the media and to a measurable degree in museum displays. To the public, the eastern Indian, like the Eskimo, has become a stock figure whose historical reality has been abstracted from the European viewpoint. Where is a more objective view of the "real" American to be found?

The beginnings of an answer can be seen in historical ethnography being conducted by anthropologists and historians in western and northern parts of the continent (e.g., Bailey 1937; Bishop 1974; Burch 1979; Dobyns 1966; Hoffman 1961; Kaplan 1983; Ray 1974; Tanner 1979; Trigger 1976; Trudel 1981; Weinstein 1983). In addition, interesting work has been done on East Coast subjects (e.g., Axtell 1981; Bragdon 1979, 1981; Brasser 1971; Fenton 1957; Grumet 1978; Lurie 1959; Salisbury 1982). These works employ an interactive socio-economic view in which individual motives and intercultural dynamics are important components of the study of social and historical processes and of the definition of cultural and societal entities.

Little attention, however, has been given to archeological studies of early contact from the native point of view (cf. Binford 1964; Brain 1979; Ceci 1977, 1980; Deagan 1983; Jordan and Kaplan 1980; Kaplan 1983, 1984; Ramsden 1978; Salwen 1978; Simmons 1970; Thomas 1979; Trigger 1980, 1982). For the ASW program we decided therefore to attempt an archeological perspective on the earliest period of contact—primarily the sixteenth and seventeenth centuries—and to concentrate not on changing material culture and technology per se, but rather on the effects of European contact on the institutions that organized native societies. By doing so, we hoped to identify structural change in the organization of these groups and to relate changes in economic and social organization, religious beliefs, settlement patterns, subsistence, land use, and other systems to various contact and acculturation phenomena. Archeologically extracted material forms were to be used to illuminate changes in native societies under varying degrees of adaptation and influence from centers of European contact ranging from ship-based interaction to special-purpose posts and seasonal or permanent settlements. In each case we hoped to explore an early contact situation in which a native American society was undergoing initial acculturation or adaptation to changes from pre-contact conditions. Such a program would contribute to the field of early contact archeological studies and would also present a variety of type cases instructive in terms of acculturation theory and studies of historical processes.

Because of the diversity of these goals we decided to select early contact situations spanning the entire geographic sweep of eastern North America from the arctic to the tropics. Preference was given to coastal locations of contact because they were the settings for the earliest European encounters. Unfortunately, our decision to limit the papers to early coastal studies was difficult to fulfill given the patchwork of current research and available data, and compromises had to be made. Also, we would have liked to expand the lecture series to provide more synoptic coverage, but time, publication commitments, and financial constraints made a more grandiose presentation unworkable. Nevertheless, it was deemed important to consider the effect of European contacts as they were influenced by geography as well as by native cultural variability.

Another reason for selecting study cases from a wide range of geographic regions along the Eastern Seaboard was to facilitate comparison of changes observed in native lifeways resulting from differences in the European groups involved. Too frequently it is assumed that European contacts produced similar effects on native American societies irrespective of geography, native culture type, and the specific nature of the European group—its size, composition, national and cultural origin, religious denomination, economic orientation, and general motivation. One reason why these factors have often been overlooked, especially by archeologists, is that contact period material culture often consists of the same types of European artifacts, but in fact the similarity of contact goods dispersed among different Indian cultures in widely separated regions is largely irrelevant to the individual histories of the groups involved. These objects reveal relatively little unless they are examined in terms of context, function, and the manner in which they were obtained, modified, and distributed within various societies. Archeologists studying Indian sites are only just beginning to take this necessary step in the analysis of introduced European material culture.

Too frequently, also, we have based our views of early European interactions with native Americans on the erroneous assumption of a monolithic European influence governed by some common strategy and unified set of goals. In fact, the European groups interacting with Amerindian societies along the East Coast were tremendously varied in their own cultural backgrounds and in their motivations and capabilities. Historians have long been aware of this diversity, which was especially great in the sixteenth and seventeenth centuries. The major nationalities involved—French, English, Dutch, Basque, Spanish, and Scandinavian—subsumed a variety of religious affiliations and a far greater array of commercial or special interest groups which, in various combinations, had different and frequently competitive goals and motivations. Furthermore, the logistics by which these groups were supported in the New World and the means by which their contacts with native groups were managed produced a highly diverse set of agendas. These variables must be considered in assessing the types of European contacts and influences experienced by native Americans, the reactions of these groups to these contacts, and the influence of contacts on their relationships with other native populations.

The implications for such interactive complexity in understanding the reactions of native groups to European encounters are important in drawing anthropological conclusions about patterns of cultural interactions and change and about the organizing principles that govern such behavior. The welter of contact variables in the early centuries of the colonial era, for which historical and acheological records are less precise than they are for later periods, makes the task even more difficult. Are data and interpretations from the eighteenth- and nineteenth-century subarctic fur trade analogous to cultural processes involved in sixteenth- and seventeenth-century eastern North America? Does the earlier date and different historical situation, to say nothing of different geography and ecology of the eastern case, render such comparisons inappropriate? Similar kinds of questions pertain to analogies drawn between eighteenth- and nineteenth-century contacts in northwestern North America and those of sixteenth- and seventeenth-century West Greenland, Labrador, and Newfoundland. In another geographically relevant parallel, what useful conclusions can be drawn between Spanish and Indian contact histories in eighteenth- and nineteenth-century California compared with sixteenth- and seventeenth-century Spanish-Indian contacts in the eastern Caribbean and southeastern North America?

The diversity of the cast of characters in the contact history of the Eastern Seaboard produced a complexity that was probably greater than that which existed (or exists) in any other part of the New World. The papers presented in this series of essays provide both a small sample of this diverse field and a basis for comparing different contact situations with respect to geographic location, types of native cultures, and European agents. In addition they explore the various native and European institutional structures that underlie these interactions.

Certain themes recur throughout these papers as key components in the European-native interactions. Among them are: European attitudes or policies regarding economic resources; the kinds of technologies and methods used for harvesting resources, including the use of native peoples; European attitudes and policies toward native religious beliefs; military and strategic policy toward Indians and other Europeans; kinds of involvement with native village life; intensity and duration of contacts; and potential for competition, whether for non-renewable (minerals, oil, land) or renewable (food, fur) resources. Also notable are differences in datelines, rates of contact, and acculturation stages between different regions, but especially between arctic/ subarctic and subtropical regions; different organizational levels and subsistence bases of the native societies, ranging from small hunting bands to complex chiefdoms; different population levels and densities; different resistance, resilience and isolation from European diseases; and differing capabilities to resist or regulate European contacts through native institutions.

Toward an Archeology of History

The relationship between Europeans and native Americans has interested both students of culture and history and the wider public for more than two centuries. During this period several conflicting conceptions have been advanced and to varying degrees accepted by European, European-descended, and native groups.

Early European explorers and observers viewed Indian and Inuit peoples as uncivilized savages who might with moral impunity be ignored, treated as curiosities, or manipulated as needed to meet the goals of businessmen, clerics, scientists, or politicians. Civil interaction with native peoples was pursued insofar as it was critical to the success of such European ventures as the procurement of gold, silver, and fur, but when westward expansion was the primary goal, expulsion or isolation of native groups was frequently the policy of choice. These exploitive or antagonistic relationships with native groups arose from ethnocentric attitudes which to some degree persist to the present in both public and private arenas.

More recently, a growing awareness of native life and history has led to the view that the virtual annihilation of many of these cultures and their people is attributable to the merciless and unconscionable economic, military, political, and spiritual exploitation of native American groups by European explorers and colonists competing for nationalistic and mercantile dominance in the

New World. This view holds that Indian groups were unwitting witnesses to their own destruction or, at best, ineffectual defenders of their rights in the face of broken treaties and unfavorably balanced transactions. History supports the validity of many elements of this perspective.

Yet another view of native Americans—one perpetuated in history books, museum displays, and many other educational forums—is that of the romanticized "noble savage." American Indians are envisioned as dressed in animal skins rather than the European clothing they more frequently wore (Hansen 1982), heroic in defense of tribal territory, possessed of high philisophical ideals, and delicately attuned to their natural surroundings (Martin 1978 [but see Krech 1981]) and to neighboring Indian groups, if not to European settlers. Such "Pocahantas" and "Squanto" images are rarely tempered by a sense of historical reality, and much of the general public remains content with the myth of an eastern Indian race that mysteriously vanished in a kind of morally neutral process of natural selection that included barter, treaty, and war.

Although these three dramatically conflicting concepts may all seem simplistic to thoughtful people, the history of Indian-white relations has not yet advanced to the point of offering a well-documented objective view, and scholarly attention has only recently been turned to this neglected field. This collection of essays advances this cause by presenting a series of case studies documenting the effects of European contacts on native cultural institutions during the first two and a half centuries of European-native interaction in eastern North America and Greenland. Perhaps more than demonstrating what is known, the scope of these essays provides some small measure of the great volume of work that remains to be done in the anthropology of European contact.

I will close by noting that, as stated in the early part of this introduction, these lectures were planned to explore the potential of studying changes in cultural institutions of societies undergoing early contact with Europeans in eastern North America. Despite my optimism in 1981 and my encouragement to the speakers to adduce archeological data where it was available, it is obvious from the content of these essays that the speakers' early reservations about the adequacy of this database were valid. Much of what appears here is derived from historical sources and ethnographic evidence rather than from archeological data. This project, then, demonstrates the need for more archeological attention to this important gap in our knowledge and to the urgency of addressing it while the physical evidence is still available.

Organization of This Volume

The order of paper presentation in this volume is from north to south, from Greenland to the Caribbean. This arrangement was chosen on the premise that geography is a determinant of the kinds of interactions that have taken place between Europeans and American Indian and Eskimo (Inuit) peoples, as well as the effects of these interactions.

Arctic contacts, presented as Part I of this volume, began with the Norse voyages and colonization of the New World in A.D. 985. These contacts continued on a sporadic basis in Greenland, Baffin Island, Labrador, and Newfoundland for nearly five hundred years. Following a brief interlude, contacts were re-initiated in the sixteenth century by explorers, whalers, and fishermen, and later by missionaries. Despite the large area in which these contacts occurred, their effects on native cultures were relatively similar—in some cases, strikingly so, as will be demonstrated in the case of communal house development in Labrador and Greenland. However, in addition to cultural homogeneity, the Eastern Arctic had similar geographic features and animal resources, and its various regions were united still further by a shared history of European interaction and resources exploitation. For these reasons and because these contacts persisted over a long period of time, they constitute a distinct set within the larger group of contact situations reported here.

Part II concerns the effects of European contact on cultures whose economies had the advantage of food cultivation in addition to hunting, gathering, and fishing. Situated in a more temperate environment, the cultures involved—the Narragansett, the middle Connecticut River valley Indian tribes, and the Iroquois—are examined at a time when expanding European settlements resulted in direct and indirect competition for native lands, resources, and services. These papers discuss the development of institutionalized trade, the introduction of disease, and changes in settlement patterns, land tenure, mortuary beliefs, and tribal organization—changes which reflect a deeper and more significant level of interaction than that which prevailed in arctic regions during this period. In addition, these northeastern examples demonstrate how societies occupying relatively similar environments have developed in different directions, in contrast to the more convergent patterns exhibited in arctic regions.

Part III presents two views of early contact in the Chesapeake Bay region. At issue here is the manner of European involvement in the Powhatan chiefdom and neighboring tribes seen from two different perspectives, that of the anthropologist and that of the historian. These contacts occurred in the late 1500s and early 1600s, just after the establishment of the first European posts, when traders and farmers were beginning to expand westward into Indian territory. In addition to providing a contrast between anthropological and historical approaches, these papers provide insight into the role of individuals as agents of inter-cultural contact and change, a focus not represented in other papers in this volume. The Powhatan chiefdom also provides us with an example of the effects of European contact on one of the most socio-politically complex societies on the Eastern Seaboard.

Finally, in Part IV we present a comparative case of European-Indian contact in Florida and Hispaniola. In these examples we see the effects of Spanish policy on very different cultures occupying different environmental regions. These cases not only demonstrate regional diversity, they also show the effects of different national goals, methods, and policies as they relate to English and Spanish exploitation and occupation of these lands. Of particular note is the rapid rate at which these changes occurred in the Caribbean compared to Florida, and the different effects on native groups in these areas. From a biogeographic point of view the rapid cultural disintegration caused by European conquest, disease, and subjugation in the Caribbean also contrasts strongly with the more mitigated effect of contact on temperate mainland cultures and others in arctic settings. Despite differences in economy and socio-political organization, cultures in these latter areas were afforded a degree of insulation from European contact not available in the Caribbean, by virtue of having larger territories, larger populations, greater economic flexibility, or longer periods in which to adjust to changing conditions.

REFERENCES CITED

Adams, Robert McC.
    1974 Anthropological Perspectives on Ancient Trade. Current Anthropology 15(3):239–258.

Axtell, James
    1979 Ethnohistory: an Historian's Viewpoint. Ethnohistory 26(1):1–13.
    1981 The European and the Indian. London: Oxford University Press.

Bailey, A. G.
    1937 The Conflict of European and Eastern Algonkian Cultures, 1504–1700. St. John: New Brunswick Museum.

Binford, Lewis R.
  1964 Archaeological and Ethnohistorical Investigation of Cultural Diversity and Progressive Development Among Aboriginal Cultures of Coastal Virginia and North Carolina. Ph.D. dissertation, University of Michigan.

Bishop, Charles
  1974 The Northern Ojibwa and the Fur Trade: an Historical and Ecological Study. Toronto: Holt, Rinehart, and Winston.

Bragdon, Kathleen
  1979 Probate Records as a Source for Early Algonquian Ethnohistory. Papers of the Tenth Algonquian Conference. William Cowan, ed. Ottawa: Carleton University Press.
  1981 Another Tongue Brought In: An Ethnohistorical Study of Native Writings in Massachusetts. Ph.D. dissertation, Department of Anthropology, Brown University.

Brain, Jeffrey
  1979 Tunica Treasure. Cambridge: Peabody Museum of Archaeology and Ethnology, Harvard University.

Brasser, Theodore J.
  1971 The Coastal Algonkians: People of the First Frontier. In: North American Indians in Historical Perspective. Eleanor B. Leacock and Nancy O. Lurie, eds. pp. 64–91. New York: Random House.

Burch, Ernest S.
  1979 Caribou Eskimo Origins: An Old Problem Reconsidered. Arctic Anthropology 15(1):1–35.

Ceci, Lynn
  1977 The Effect of European Contact and Trade on the Settlement Pattern of Indians in Coastal New York, 1524–1655: The Archaeological and Documentary Evidence. Ph.D. dissertation, City University of New York.
  1980 Locational Analysis of Historic Algonquian Sites in Coastal New York: A Preliminary Study. Proceedings of the Conference on Northeastern Archaeology. Research Reports 19, James A. Moore, ed. pp. 71–91. Amherst: University of Massachusetts.

Cook, Warren L., ed.
  1978 Ancient Vermont. Proceedings of the Castleton Conference, Castleton State College. Castleton, Vermont: Academy Books.

Deagan, Kathleen A.
  1978 Cultures in Transition: Assimilation and Fusion Among the Eastern Timu-

cua. *In:* Tacachale. J. T. Milanich and S. Proctor, eds. pp. 89–119. Gainesville: University Presses of Florida.
1983 Spanish St. Augustine: the Archaeology of a Colonial Creole Community. New York: Academic Press.

Dobyns, H. F.
1966 Estimating Aboriginal American Population. Current Anthropology 7:395–416.

Fell, Howard B.
1976 America B.C.: Ancient Settlers in the New World. New York: Quadrangle/The New York Times.

Fenton, William N.
1957 American Indian and White Relations to 1830. Chapel Hill: The University of North Carolina Press.

Grumet, Robert S.
1978 An Analysis of Upper Delawaran Land Sales in Northern New Jersey, 1630–1758. *In:* Papers of the Ninth Algonquian Conference. William Cowan, ed. pp. 25–35.

Hacquebord, Louwrens
1984 The History of Early Dutch Whaling: a Study from the Ecological Angle. *In:* Arctic Whaling: Proceedings of the International Symposium on Arctic Whaling, February 1983. H. K. Jacob, K. Snoeijing and R. Vaughan, eds. pp. 135–148. Groningen: University of Groningen.

Hanson, James A.
1982 Laced Coats and Leather Jackets: The Great Plains Intercultural Clothing Exchange. *In:* Plains Indian Studies: A Collection of Essays in Honor of John C. Ewers and Waldo R. Wedel. Smithsonian Contributions to Anthropology 30. Douglas H. Ubelaker and Herman J. Viola, eds. pp. 105–117.

Hoffman, B. G.
1961 Cabot to Cartier: Sources for a Historical Ethnography of Northeastern North America, 1497–1550. Toronto: University of Toronto Press.

Jordan, Richard H. and Susan A. Kaplan
1980 An Archaeological View of the Inuit/European Contact Period in Central Labrador. Etudes/Inuit/Studies 4(1–2):35–45.

Kaplan, Susan A.
1983 Economic and Social Change in Labrador Neo-Eskimo Culture. Ph.D. dissertation, Department of Anthropology, Bryn Mawr College.
1984 Eskimo-European Contact Archaeology in Labrador, Canada. *In* Comparative Colonialism. British Archaeological Reports. Stephen Dyson, ed.

Krech, Shepard III, ed.
1981 Indians, Animals, and the Fur Trade: a Critique of Keepers of the Game. Athens: The University of Georgia Press.

Lurie, Nancy O.
1959 Indian Cultural Adjustment to European Civilization. *In:* Seventeenth-Century America. J.M. Smith, ed. pp. 3–60. Chapel Hill: University of North Carolina Press.

Martin, Calvin
1978 Keepers of the Game: Indian-animal Relationships and the Fur Trade. Berkeley: University of California Press.

Morison, Samuel Eliot
1971 The Discovery of North America: The Northern Voyages, A.D. 500–1600. New York: Oxford University Press.

Neudorfer, Giovanna
1979 Vermont's Stone Chambers: Their Myth and Their History. Vermont History 47(2):79–146.

Quinn, David B.
1977 North America from Earliest Discovery to First Settlements: The Norse Voyages to 1612. New York: Harper and Row.
1979 New American World: A Documentary History of North America to 1612. 5 vols. David B. Quinn, Alison M. Quinn, and Susan Hillier, eds. New York: Arno Press and Hector Bye, Inc.

Ramsden, Peter G.
1978 An Hypothesis Concerning the Effects of Early European Trade Among Some Ontario Iroquois. Canadian Journal of Archaeology 2:101–106.

Ray, Arthur J.
1974 Indians in the Fur Trade: Their Role as Trappers, Hunters, and Middlemen in the Lands Southwest of Hudson Bay, 1660–1870. Toronto/Buffalo: University of Toronto Press.

Salisbury, Neal
1982 Manitou and Providence: Indians, Europeans, and the Making of New England, 1500–1643. New York: Oxford University Press.

Salwen, Bert
1978 Indians of Southern New England and Long Island: Early Period. *In:* Handbook of North American Indians: Northeast, 15. Bruce G. Trigger, ed. pp. 160–176. Washington, D.C.: Smithsonian Institution.

Silverberg, Robert
1968 Mound Builders of Ancient America: the Archaeology of a Myth. Greenwich: New York Graphic Society.

Simmons, William S.
1970 Cautantowwit's House, an Indian Burial Ground on the Island of Conanicut in Narragansett Bay. Providence: Brown University Press.

Tanner, Adrian
1979 Bringing Home Animals: Religious Ideology and Production of the Mistassini Cree Hunters. New York: St. Martin's Press.

Thomas, Peter
1979 In the Maelstrom of Change: The Indian Trade and Cultural Process in the Middle Connecticut Valley, 1635–1665. Ph.D. dissertation, University of Massachusetts at Amherst.

Thomas, David Hurst, Grant D. Jones, Roger S. Durham, and Clark S. Larsen
1978 The Anthropology of St. Catherines Island. Vol. 1. Natural and Culture History. Anthropological Papers of the American Museum of Natural History 55(2).

1984 Spanish Santa Catalina: Archaeology in the Active Voice. Paper delivered to the Anthropological Society of Washington, December 18, 1984. Washington, D.C.: Anthropological Society of Washington/Smithsonian Institution.

Trigger, Bruce G.
1976 The Children of Aataentsic: a History of the Huron People to 1660. 2 vols. Montreal: McGill-Queen's University Press.
1980 Archaeology and the Image of the American Indian. American Antiquity 45(4):662–676.
1982 Response of Native Peoples to European Contact. *In:* Early European Settlement and Exploitation in Atlantic Canada: Selected Papers. G. M. Story, ed. pp. 129–155. St. John's: Memorial University of Newfoundland.

Trudel, Francois
1981 Inuit, Amerindians and Europeans: A Study of Interethnic Economic Relations on the Canadian Southeastern Seaboard (1500–1800). Ph.D. Dissertation, University of Connecticut.

Weinstein, Laurie L.
1983 Survival Strategies: the Seventeenth-Century Wampanoag and the European Legal System. Man in the Northeast 26:81–86.

PART I

The Arctic Sector:
Inuit Responses to Explorers, Whalers, Traders,
and Missionaries

Commentary on Part I

William W. Fitzhugh

European involvement with Inuit cultures of the Eastern Arctic and Greenland began in A.D. 982, exactly a thousand years before this lecture series
was launched. The arrival of Norse explorers and colonists brought Europe
and the Americas into an historical process that continues to unfold today as
Danish Greenland celebrates the inauguration of Home Rule and Inuit people
in the American and Canadian Arctic prepare to exercise an increasing measure of self-government and cultural autonomy. Not only have Inuit language, culture, and population survived; Inuit people also continue to occupy
their territorial homeland. This persistence is extraordinary in view of the
long record of Inuit-European contact. Such was not to be the destiny of
many other eastern North American groups, like the extinct Beothuck Indians of Newfoundland and other cultures whose identities became lost in the
tangled ethnic and demographic realignments dating to this period. For
northern peoples, this initial phase of Inuit-European contact began with the
Norse voyages and lasted until the middle of the eighteenth century, when it
became possible for missionary and commercial posts to gain permanent
footholds in Greenland and Labrador. The process by which early contacts
progressed from first contact to this later stage of sustained interaction is
reviewed in the papers that follow.

The essential features characterizing European-native interaction in this
zone need a brief summary. First, the culture and physical geography of the
Eastern Arctic played a key role in shaping contact history (see Kaplan, this
volume, figure 1). Second, the presence of a relatively homogeneous Inuit
culture whose economy was limited by the environment to hunting, fishing,
and gathering and whose low population density presented little possibility of
complex political organization ruled out certain kinds of interaction, such as

sustained warfare. Geographical isolation insured that the arena of contact was occupied only by the principal actors themselves, making reinforcement and political alliances rarely possible. A third feature is that the Europeans who made the contacts usually were based on ships rather than on land. These meetings were frequently random rather than planned events; they were sporadic and unpredictable, especially in the early periods, and could not be counted upon by native peoples as a source of regularly needed commodities. Therefore, raw materials and artifacts obtained from Europeans supplemented rather than replaced materials available in existing native exchange systems. But because European materials had social as well as technological value, their presence altered Inuit socio-economic organization. Finally, Inuit and European groups had a mutual interest in maintaining friendly relationships, for reasons of economy and survival.

The contacts that took place in the Atlantic region of the Eastern Arctic fall roughly into four chronological stages between A.D. 982 and 1750. The first of these might be termed the "exploration" period, A.D. 982–1550, when contact took place as discrete events rather than as a continuing process of interaction. Except for the Norse settlement of southwestern Greenland, this period is characterized by encounter events in which Inuit "mined" European contacts and sites for metal, wood, cloth, and other material goods. The entrance of these rare commodities into Inuit society enhanced the prestige of individuals who could obtain them as much as they contributed to increased technological efficiency. We have no direct evidence that European contact resulted in major changes in Inuit cultural institutions during this period.

The second phase of contact, characterized by Inuit raiding of posts and travelling trade, began with the introduction of whaling as a major economic activity after A.D. 1550. Basque whaling was established in Newfoundland and southern Labrador at this time, followed in the 1600s by Dutch and English trading and whaling along the coasts of Labrador, in Davis Strait, and in West Greenland. This activity broadened the geography of Inuit access to European goods and produced changes in Inuit social and economic structures.

When whale populations declined in the later 1600s, whalers adopted part-time trading roles, their vessels becoming trading posts where natives could exchange ivory, baleen, and oil for a wide range of European goods. This activity had the effect of partially shifting production of oil and baleen from vessel crews to the native people, who could take advantage of the presence of whales at times when the whalers were not present, especially late fall. This "floater" exchange persisted until shore-based European trading posts and Moravian mission stations began to be established in the eighteenth century, after which the "post and mission" period produced a more diverse set of contact conditions ranging from full-time association in areas where these stations existed to a continuance of floater trade in the outlying regions, throughout the eighteenth and nineteenth centuries.

The effects of these contact stages on Inuit culture are discussed in the following papers. The first paper reviews the geographical and historical background of the region and the effects of the Norse and other early exploration-period contacts. Little evidence is found for changes in Inuit cultural systems during this period. Susan Kaplan's paper concentrates on the second and third phases of contact as it occurred in Labrador, using historical, ethnographic, and archeological evidence. Significant changes in Inuit social and economic organization are noted, in addition to changes in demography, settlement patterns, and residence forms, leading to the advent of the "communal house period." Gulløv, writing primarily from the perspective of historical records, presents a reconstruction of West Greenland Inuit regional economy and settlement pattern changes that illuminates strong parallels with changes observed in Labrador, but emphasizes migration rather than socio-economic factors as the mechanism of change. The most visible archeological result of the parallel developments in Labrador and Greenland is the appearance of large multi-family dwellings at approximately the same time (the late seventeenth or early eighteenth century) in both places. At present, no suitable explanation is available for the simultaneous appearance of this residence pattern in these widely separated regions, or for its absence from intervening areas.

The riddle of communal house origins and their regional relationships, now in its second generation of research, is only one of many interesting problems of cultural processes that have arisen as archeologists and historians work to narrow the "proto-history" gap in the Eastern Arctic. While many obstacles remain in conducting research on these questions in arctic regions, it is at least reassuring that many of the sites needed to solve these problems are known and accessible, unlike so many early contact sites in other areas of eastern North America.

Early Contacts North of Newfoundland
before A.D. 1600: A Review

William W. Fitzhugh

A B S T R A C T

Peoples of the Eastern Arctic were in sporadic contact with the Norse for nearly half a millenium following A.D. 1000. After a brief quiescent period, the voyages of Martin Frobisher and John Davis renewed European contact in the late 1500s. Historical and archeological evidence suggests that although scarce European materials and implements entered and perhaps stimulated the regional exchange system and Eskimo people must have become familiar with the interests, technologies, and vulnerabilities of chance European visitors, contact did not alter other aspects of native life until after A.D. 1600.

Northern peoples are generally thought to have been isolated from European contacts by their remote geographic location until the latter half of the nineteenth century. While this is true for portions of northern Greenland and the western Canadian Arctic and Alaska, peoples of the Davis Strait and the Newfoundland-Labrador regions have been in contact with European groups for at least a thousand years. It is reasonable to suppose that these contacts had some effect on the development of these cultures, not only during the period of intensive contact that began after the growth of the northern whaling industry in the 1600s, but in earlier periods as well. This paper reviews evidence of European interactions with native peoples between ca. A.D. 1000 and 1600 and discusses the effects and probable effects of these contacts.

1. Geography and Cultural Setting

Native cultures north of Newfoundland have been strongly influenced by similar conditions of geography, ecology, and culture history, and by historical European contacts. Foremost among these features are similarities in geography and environment. West Greenland, eastern Ellesmere and Baffin islands, Labrador, and Newfoundland bound two-thirds of the Davis Strait and Labrador Sea. Although the vegetation and topography of the region are diverse, ranging from tundra-clad or glaciated high arctic regions to lowland subarctic forest coasts, these lands share a common ecological base that includes many of the same animal resources. Caribou and char or trout, the most important land foods, are found throughout most of this area. But similarities in marine ecology, created by the influence of the East Greenland and Labrador currents, have had the greatest impact on human adaptations. These currents bring cold, nutrient-rich arctic waters, seasonal pack ice, and arctic marine fauna south of the Arctic Circle and into contact with warmer Atlantic waters, producing an unusually rich marine system. The arctic marine fauna of this region includes several species of seals and whales, walrus, polar bear, fish, and avifauna whose north-south migratory movements makes them available to people throughout the region.

As a partial response to similar environmental conditions these lands have had a relatively unified history of cultural development that extends from prehistoric times into the modern era. Originally, the Eastern Arctic was occupied by Paleoeskimo peoples who arrived there from the Western Arctic about four thousand years ago (McGhee 1978; Maxwell 1980). However, the cultural similarities in Canadian and Greenland Eskimo culture stem from the appearance in North America about a thousand years ago of a new people bearing a Neoeskimo cultural tradition which, like the preceding Paleoeskimo tradition, also moved into the Eastern Arctic from the west. These Neoeskimo people belonged to the Thule culture. During the next few hundred years Thule culture, by a process of either replacement or amalgamation, or both, supplanted resident Dorset Paleoeskimos and became dominant throughout the region. Despite the wide spatial distribution of Thule sites, rapid transportation techniques, including the use of dog traction and large skin boats known as *umiaks,* enabled Thule and later Neoeskimo peoples to maintain contact with their neighbors so that they preserved their common language and cultural traditions. For this reason the cultural geography at A.D. 1500 was that of a single relatively homogeneous culture area extending from northern Greenland to central Labrador. Further south, the coasts of Labrador and Newfoundland were occupied in the summer season by Montagnais-Naskapi and Beothuck Indians, whose cultures differed from Eskimo culture in nearly all respects, although these differences frequently went unnoticed by early European visitors.

1.1. Prehistoric Cultural Landscape

Prior to A.D. 1500 the cultural landscape of the area was considerably different, and far more diverse. Although Norse accounts describe native peoples met in Greenland and other regions of North America universally as *skraelings*, in fact several different cultural groups occupied these regions between A.D. 1000 and 1500 (Fitzhugh 1972, 1977). In Newfoundland, Dorset culture—a late Paleoeskimo culture that inhabited the Eastern Arctic from ca. 800 B.C. to A.D. 1400—had become extinct locally and was replaced by an Indian culture ancestral to Beothuck Indians (Pastore 1984; Tuck 1976). Like their ethnographic descendants, these proto-Beothuck people would have had a coastal adaptation during the summer. It is probable that these Indians were the skraelings described by Norse in the Vinland sagas (Fitzhugh 1978:170; McGhee 1984:13).

In Labrador the disposition of native groups was more complex during the Norse period. Southern and central Labrador was occupied by the Point Revenge culture, which was probably closely related to proto-Beothuck culture in Newfoundland. Point Revenge peoples, whose artifacts are found at many sites dating from A.D. 800 to 1500 (Fitzhugh 1978:166; Loring 1983), probably spoke a variety of Algonquian language, used canoes rather than kayaks, painted their bodies and tools with red ocher, and hunted caribou in the interior during the winter and caught fish, birds, and seals on the coast during the summer.

Although Point Revenge people lacked the specialized techniques for winter ice hunting used by Dorset and Thule Eskimos, the distribution of Point Revenge sites from inner bays to outer islands demonstrates an ability for coastal transportation. Perhaps most revealing in this regard is that Point Revenge peoples utilized Ramah chert for making stone tools. The geological source of this chert is in Ramah Bay, northern Labrador, fifty miles north of the coastal forest boundary and more than a hundred miles north of the northern limit of most Point Revenge settlements. Although other stone materials were occasionally used, especially during the early periods, by A.D.

1000 Ramah chert dominated Point Revenge assemblages on the central Labrador coast. It was also traded to the south, appearing as preforms and finished tools in caches and sites dating to this period in the Strait of Belle Isle and as isolated finds in sites as far south as Nova Scotia, New Brunswick, and New England (Fitzhugh 1978:171). Point Revenge people continued to occupy the central Labrador coast until they were displaced by southward-moving Thule and historic Labrador Inuit in the sixteenth century. The ultimate fate of Point Revenge culture and its peoples is not known at present. They may have become extinct in the squeeze between advancing Inuit groups and eastward-moving Laurentian Iroquois or southern Montagnais, or, they may have abandoned their coastal life, seeking refuge from Eskimo pressure in the Labrador-Quebec interior, to become the ancestors of the modern Montagnais-Naskapi (Fitzhugh 1978:172).

North of the Point Revenge settlement areas in Labrador one finds evidence of a large and well-established Late Dorset Eskimo culture occupying coastal locations between A.D. 900 and 1400 (Cox 1978:111; Fitzhugh 1980:600; 1981:43). Late Dorset peoples inhabited coastal locations throughout the year and made use of the entire northern coast, including the region around Ramah Bay. Like Point Revenge people, their lithic tools were made of Ramah chert. Their boats were probably skin kayaks like those of later Eskimos, and they had rich shamanistic and secular art traditions (Jordan 1979/80; Thomson and Thomson 1981). Dorset culture disappeared in Labrador about A.D. 1400, toward the end of the Norse era, at a time when Thule culture began to advance south into northern Labrador (Fitzhugh 1980:601; Kaplan 1983, and this volume). As in the case of the Point Revenge disappearance, we do not know if Late Dorset people were absorbed by the advancing Thule wave, were physically exterminated, or shifted west into Ungava Bay. Oral traditions among nineteenth-century Inuit speaking of a race called Tunit, widely thought to be Dorset people, describe ethnic differences and conflicts between Tunit and Eskimo peoples that may provide clues about the fate of the Dorset culture. In Quebec, it may have survived after A.D. 1400 (Harp 1974/75; Plumet 1979), and some archeologists see a continuance of Dorset traditions in Sadlermiut sites in northern Hudson Bay (Taylor 1959).

North of Hudson Strait on eastern Baffin Island, Dorset people may have been present during the early period of the Norse era, but few Late Dorset sites have been excavated in this area (Maxwell 1973). Shortly after A.D. 1000, however, Thule culture replaced Dorset culture and adapted productively to the rich marine ecology of this region. Similar events occurred in northern Baffin Island, in Ellesmere Island, and in northwestern Greenland. Subsequently, Thule culture expanded to Peary Land in North Greenland and south into the Upernavik and Disko Bay regions of West Greenland, where a regional variant known as Inugsuk culture developed after A.D. 1300 and later moved into South and East Greenland (Jordan 1979; Mathiassen 1930; Meldgaard 1977).

This review demonstrates that the Norse period was one of considerable cultural diversity and dynamism in the Davis Strait-Labrador region. Indian cultures had within a few centuries of A.D. 1000 replaced Dorset culure in Newfoundland and Labrador; Late Dorset groups, maintaining a foothold in northern Labrador, Hudson Strait, and probably in Hudson Bay, were being pressed and would soon be replaced by advancing Indian groups from the south as well as by Thule people from the north; and Thule peoples were engaged in a rapid expansion which resulted, by A.D. 1500, in their taking possession of most areas of the Eastern Arctic and Greenland, including those formerly occupied by Norse colonies.

2. Norse Contacts with Native Peoples

The details of historical and archeological evidence supporting Norse contacts with native cultures in Greenland and northeastern North America are too voluminous to be detailed here, and in any case are available in a number of other publications (Gad 1971; Jones 1964; Jordan 1979; McGhee 1982; McGovern 1979, 1980). The most recent and comprehensive treatment of Canadian Arctic Norse contacts is that of McGhee (1984). Nevertheless, it is useful to summarize the salient points as they relate to culture change and ethnic interactions in this area before the advent of renewed European interest in the sixteenth century. This summary follows the path from Newfoundland to Greenland outlined in the previous discussion.

2.1. Vinland and Southern Voyages: Exploration, Colonization, and Wood Procurement

The only evidence of a Norse site in North America is at L'Anse aux Meadows, located at the tip of the Great Northern Peninsula in Newfoundland (Ingstad 1977). As the probable location of Vinland itself, this site is of both historical and symbolic significance. The impact of this colony on native

Indian cultures of Newfoundland and adjacent regions probably is as yet archeologically undetectable, however, because of its short period of occupation—probably less than a year—and the apparent infrequency of native contacts. Literary accounts of the Vinland contacts with native peoples describe a number of volatile encounters that, in the best of times, included trade, but these chance meetings were so sporadic and unstructured that each side had more to lose than to gain from them. The result was that after a number of voyages and explorations just before and after A.D. 1000, the Norse ceased trying to establish colonies west of Greenland, and concentrated instead on such enterprises as trade and wood procurement from this area. It is widely believed that interference and opposition from native peoples caused the failure of the Vinland colonization effort, with native peoples having gained the upper hand by virtue of their larger populations, the tenuous Norse lines of support, the relative equivalence of offensive weapons on both sides, and the natives' superior homeland knowledge and survival skills. However, the Vinland experience of opportunistic trade and sporadic conflict initiated a pattern of social intercourse that was to continue with few changes in the Eastern Arctic for the next seven hundred years.

Outside of Norse saga accounts, only two pieces of archeological evidence exist to suggest the nature of Norse contacts south of Hudson Strait. The first is a Norse penny minted between A.D. 1065 and 1080 which was found in the Middle Woodland component of the Goddard site in coastal Maine (Skaare 1979; Bourque and Cox 1981). Since this component also contained Ramah chert and a fragment of a Dorset burin-like tool, it is likely that the coin, which had been perforated for use as a pendant, was obtained by Indians or Eskimos through contact with Norse north of the Gulf of St. Lawrence long after the documented Vinland voyages and reached its final destination through Indian trade networks. The other find, a Late Dorset-style soapstone lamp found in the smithy at L'Anse aux Meadows (Ingstad 1977:87–92), must have been obtained by Norse trading with Dorset people or scavenging their sites in northern Labrador, for Late Dorset culture disappeared in Newfoundland and southern Labrador several hundred years before the Vinland voyages began (Fitzhugh 1980:30). These finds confirm that Norse voyages to Labrador occurred occasionally from the eleventh through the fourteenth centuries, either as accidents, when boats were blown off course to or from Greenland, or as trading, exploring, or wood collecting expeditions. The latter was the cause of a particular visit to Markland recorded for A.D. 1347 (Gad 1971:140). While these finds do support some degree of

Norse contact with Indian and Eskimo groups, absence of Norse remains from several Point Revenge and Late Dorset sites excavated in Labrador suggest that contacts here probably were brief and had little effect on native peoples.

2.2. Eastern Arctic Contact: Trade and Diffusion

The Central and Eastern Arctic north and west of Hudson Strait has a better record of Norse archeological finds than does Labrador (McGhee 1984:14–20). Despite the discovery of a pendant fashioned from Norse copper in a Dorset site in Hudson Bay (Harp 1974), such finds do not substantiate direct contact between Norse and Dorset cultures in Canada, for this material could have been traded from Greenland through Dorset or Thule culture intermediaries. However, artifacts like a native-made wooden figurine showing details of Norse clothing style from a excavated Thule site in southern Baffin Island (Sabo and Sabo 1978) reflect direct local contact between Eskimos and Norsemen. Other Norse-derived materials, such as smelted iron rivets, knife blades, chain mail fragments, a bronze bowl, European hardwoods, woolen cloth, and other materials found at a widening circle of Thule culture sites (McCartney and Mack 1973; Schledermann 1980; Schledermann and McCullough 1980) have forced a reappraisal of the previous model emphasizing unplanned and infrequent Eskimo interaction with Norse explorers. The growing number of new finds, epitomized by the recovery of a bronze balance arm from a High Arctic Thule site, suggest that trade with Canadian Eskimo groups provided a significant incentive for Norse voyages west of Greenland (McGhee 1984:21).

In addition to stimulating native demand for European commodities, these contacts would have acquainted native peoples with Norse nautical skills, logistical capabilities, and trading and military tactics. Undoubtedly, this knowledge became part of native oral tradition and was put to use in contact situations.

2.3. Greenland: Sustained Interaction or Competition?

While the Vinland colony was small and of brief duration, the Greenland settlements, which were established in unoccupied lands, flourished. The "Eastern Settlement" at Narssaq and Julianehaab was the largest and may have had between four and eight thousand inhabitants during its heyday, while the smaller "Western Settlement" near present-day Nuuk attained a peak population of between one thousand and seventeen hundred (McGovern 1980:246). Benefitting from a significant climatic optimum that facilitated regular ship communication with Europe, these settlements were so productive that a bishop was appointed from Norway and a cathedral was even built at Gardar in the Eastern Settlement. Unlike the more sporadic contact in the Canadian Arctic described above, Norse and Inuit contact in Greenland occurred more frequently—perhaps in a sustained manner at times—and probably made a significant impact on both cultures.

Norse contact with Eskimos in Greenland began after A.D. 1050, when Norse ivory and fur hunters encountered and probably traded with Thule culture people immigrating southward into the Nordrsetur, the Disko Bay region used until that time exclusively by Norse expeditionary hunters to generate exchange for the European trade. Later, the Thule/Inugsuk culture, expanding south of Disko Bay, is thought to have competed economically with the Western Settlement, and perhaps contributed to its downfall about A.D. 1350. In a similar vein, continued southward expansion may also have played a role in the disappearance of the Eastern Settlement after A.D. 1450 (Jones 1964; Gad 1971; McGovern 1980:265).

Various models have been proposed to explain the nature of Norse-Eskimo interaction in Greenland (McGovern 1979). In simplest terms they emphasize Eskimo invasion, Norse acculturation, Eskimo acculturation, and mutual isolation. Each of these models has strong and weak points. Archeological evidence does not clearly establish the legitimacy of any one, but available data (Meldgaard, personnel communication to McGovern 1977; Jordan 1978) suggest Eskimo acquisition of Norse material goods without noticeable changes in cultural institutions or beliefs. Archeological studies of this problem are still in their infancy. However, it appears likely that Eskimo attraction to Norse materials can be tied to their first contacts with Norse in the Nordrsetur and were partially responsible for Eskimo advance into southwest Greenland and the subsequent plundering of abandoned Norse sites.

3. Effects of Norse Contacts on Northern Peoples

The historical and archeological data reviewed above demonstrate clearly that the Greenland Norse, and perhaps Norse voyagers from Iceland and Norway, interacted in a variety of ways with North American and Greenland natives for nearly five hundred years between A.D. 982 and 1450. Although historical documentation and a growing body of archeological data substantiate both this contact and the diffusion of Norse materials to Eskimo groups in surrounding regions, the evidence does not permit any substantial understanding of the impact of these contacts on native cultures. These contacts ranged from peaceful trade (perhaps prolonged trade in Greenland) to bloody battles and skirmishes for profit and territory, as well as the scavenging of abandoned sites. The Norse were vulnerable except in their strongholds in Greenland. They travelled in small parties in small boats, and their weapons were only marginally superior to those of native groups. Because the Norse had more to lose in terms of boats, men, and scarce wood and iron goods, we may deduce that their preference was for cautious, controlled interaction. However, their trips probably always were unpredictable in outcome, as is suggested by the presence of precious items—ones not likely to have been traded—like the bronze balance arm, chain mail, and broadcloth at Thule sites in Canada and Greenland.

Since Norse voyages west of Greenland were probably not undertaken frequently, they may have had little effect on Eskimo or Indian cultures beyond introducing small amounts of European technology into native inventories and trade networks and acquainting natives with European interests and capabilities. Apparently the most potentially important aspect of Norse technology—the smelting of iron from bog and other ores—was never revealed to native peoples; if it was, it was never adopted, perhaps due to a shortage of firewood for making charcoal in regions north of Hudson Strait.

These contacts stimulated native interest in European technology, probably resulted in development of strategies of opportunistic contact, and may have resulted in shifts in native seasonal settlement patterns, or more significantly, changes in cultural distributions. Although archeological data do not yet substantiate any case of Norse-induced territorial change, it is a suspected cause of the southern movement of Thule people in Greenland, and has been suggested as a possible factor in the northward movement of Point Revenge Indians (Fitzhugh 1978:178) and the eastern movement of Thule Eskimos, who may have back-tracked iron trade in Canadian Dorset culture from Alaska to Greenland (McGhee 1984:22). In this regard it is interesting to note that the Western Eskimo term for iron, *savik,* is a Greenlandic rather than a Siberian term (Murdock 1892:157). Beyond these speculative ideas, the question of whether Eskimo or Indian cultural institutions or beliefs were seriously influenced by Norse contacts remains a matter for future archeological investigation.

4. Renewed European Contacts in the Sixteenth Century

4.1. Basque Whaling in the Strait of Belle Isle

Although European contacts may have persisted in the form of Norse interactions in Greenland in the fourteenth and fifteenth centuries, Norse influence on Eskimo Indian cultures on the North American mainland at this time probably diminished or disappeared. In these areas a new and far more important phase of development began with Cabot's voyages and the installation of commercial enterprises north of the Gulf of St. Lawrence after A.D. 1500. Especially important for northern cultures was the Basque whale fishery that began in the Strait of Belle Isle in 1543 (Barkham 1980, 1982; Kaplan, this volume; Tuck 1982). Each summer this operation brought large numbers of ships and larger numbers of whaleboats (shallops) into harbors where whales were hunted, blubber was rendered, and—at the end of the whaling season, in late fall or early winter—casks were prepared for shipment to Europe. Although native groups seem not to have been present in the Strait of Belle Isle region at the beginning of this enterprise, Indians—and later Eskimos—soon were attracted by the possibilities of trade, and, following the departure of the crews in the fall, the European stations were frequently plundered for iron, shallops, and other items. As Kaplan's paper points out, these incentives probably contributed to the expansion of Thule culture from northern Labrador into the central coast region, which served as the base for raiding and trading ventures into the Strait. The success of these ventures is attested to by the presence of Basque artifacts in sixteenth-century Eskimo sites in Hamilton Inlet. Some Eskimos may even have moved permanently or semi-permanently into southern Labrador, Quebec, and New-foundland to enter into closer ties with Europeans there.

These contacts had a significant impact on native cultures. For the first time European materials became available to Eskimo and Indian groups on an annual basis from fixed geographic locations in southern Labrador. In addition to promoting the expansion of Eskimos into Indian territory on the central Labrador coast, the availability of European goods caused social and economic changes in Inuit cultures as these European materials moved back north through a form of Inuit "down-the-line" trade. This form of single-point entry for European goods roughly parallels both that of Thule/Inugsuk culture contacts with the Norse settlements in Greenland in the twelfth and thirteenth centuries described above and that in Greenland during the seventeenth-century English and Dutch whaling period, as documented by Gulløv (this volume).

4.2. The Frobisher and Davis Voyages: Sources of European Goods and Early Ethnography

While Basque contacts were taking place in southern Labrador, the more isolated regions of northern Labrador and Baffin Island were exposed to exploration and commercial ventures of a different sort, the voyages of Englishmen Martin Frobisher (1576–78) and John Davis (1585–87). Their importance lies not only in their being the first known post-Norse explorers encountered by Eskimos north of southern Labrador but also in the high quality of the documentation they amassed, which contains the first objective descriptions of Inuit (the preferred term for historic period Eskimo) culture in Western literature (Collinson 1867; Quinn 1979; Stefansson 1938; Taylor 1959).

Frobisher led three expeditions to the Eastern Arctic. The first voyage was to search for a route to Cathay via the fabled "Northwest Passage." The second and third voyages were essentially commercial enterprises financed by Queen Elizabeth and a group of investors on the strength of an assay on a sample of "gold" ore from the 1576 voyage that later turned out to be worthless.

During the first summer, the party of three vessels and some fifty men were in repeated contact with a small group of Inuit in the Frobisher Bay region. As in the case of the Norse encounters with skraelings, these encounters were initially peaceful, and items of interest were eagerly exchanged by both parties. However, Inuit curiosity and acquisitiveness soon resulted in skirmishes that culminated in the loss of the ship's only tender and its crew, and the erection of fortifications on Kodlunarn Island. From the accounts it appears that iron and boats were the principal items desired by the Inuit. Frobisher noted that some of their arrows were tipped with blades of iron, which could have been derived either from the Cape York meteor fall in northwest Greenland or from Norse or later unrecorded European contacts. One Inuk wore a copper or bronze ornament which he said had come from the west, which Frobisher took to mean Cathay.

At the end of the first season, Frobisher cached some equipment and supplies at his base camp on Kodlunarn Island. Upon his return the next year he found the caches broken open and the materials gone. That summer, 1577, an uneasy truce existed between the two groups as Frobisher's men explored the inner reaches of Frobisher Bay for a passage to the west, searched for more ore, and quarried "gold-bearing" rock for the financiers. There were no serious incidents, and the Inuit kept their distance.

The final voyage, in 1578, brought the largest expedition into the Canadian Arctic that was to be mounted for the next three hundred years: sixteen ships with more than a hundred miners, including supplies of iron, lumber, mortar, charcoal, weapons, mining tools, and food for establishing a full-fledged colony equipped for winter settlement. Fortunately for the miners, who probably would not have survived, a storm dispersed the flotilla early in the summer, and in the ensuing confusion and loss of cargo plans for the colony were scuttled. However, an experiment in arctic architectural and social engineering was conducted with the building of a mortared stone dwelling structure at the crest of Kodlunarn Island. In this house, which Frobisher presumed might lead the Inuit to contemplate the advantages of civilized life, he left several loaves of bread. It was his intention to return the next year, and he again cached a large supply of materials on the island. But when Frobisher arrived in England the recognition that his "gold" was worthless brought him scorn and financial disaster.

Frobisher's legacy in arctic studies has been reviewed in a number of publications (Cheshire *et al.* 1980; Hall 1865; Kenyon 1975, 1981; Stefansson 1938), and reports have been issued on aspects of his expeditions and on relics recovered from Kodlunarn Island by Hall, Kenyon, and the Smithsonian (see Hall 1865; Klingelhofer 1976; Roy 1937; Sayre *et al.* 1982; Stefansson 1938). From the anthropological point of view, the importance of the Frobisher voyages lies in the description of a mid-sixteenth-century Inuit group in greater detail than any that would be produced for the next two hundred years. Frobisher's reports show a cohesive band of hunters who were already familiar with European materials and who knew how to take advantage, by trade and thievery, of the presence of a large, well-equipped expedition. Once the pattern of hostility closed their peaceful access to these materials, Inuit avoided contact and took their opportunities as they could, stealing when possible and scavenging the European sites after each successive departure.

Undoubtedly, a large amount of English material culture entered Baffin Island Inuit culture during these few years in the middle 1570s, and a portion of these goods were probably exchanged with Inuit groups elsewhere. In 1981 a Smithsonian research team found evidence of the local use of red-fired rooftiles and bricks in Inuit campsites on Kodlunarn Island. Evidence of Inuit dispersal of Frobisher materials, especially iron, in the Frobisher Bay environs has also been noted (Hall 1865:437). In addition to amplifying knowledge about the Frobisher voyages, future archeological research in this region promises to yield information on the impact of Frobisher's voyages on native populations. One of the interesting discoveries is that the results of radiocarbon analysis of smelted iron ingots (known as "blooms") collected from Kodlunarn Island by Charles Francis Hall in 1861 and the Smithsonian in 1981 produced dates in the early twelfth and thirteenth centuries, while the iron itself was excavated from sixteenth-century Frobisher context (Sayre *et al.* 1982). The explanation for this discrepancy has not yet been determined, but it raises complex issues concerning where and how these blooms were produced, and what their relationship is to the Frobisher artifacts found with them.

Ten years after Frobisher's departure, John Davis spent three summers (1585–87) exploring the coasts of Labrador and eastern Baffin Island. Like Frobisher, Davis was a careful observer, and his reports contain extensive commentary on Inuit clothing, tools, customs, and behavior (Quinn 1979:228–251). His most detailed observations come from the Cumberland Sound region north of Frobisher Bay, where he was met by a hundred Inuit kayaks—an astonishing number indicating a large Inuit population in this region. Like Frobisher, Davis found people using copper and iron-tipped weapons. In the summer, the Inuit economy was based on whaling, fishing, and seal hunting, for the success of which numerous charms were carried. Davis described religious observances and handed out iron knives and other goods which he had brought expressly as friendship gifts. As they had in Frobisher's case, however, wrestling matches, games, and friendly trading gave way to increasingly serious pilfering, culminating in a bold attempt to steal the ship's anchor and boats by severing the ship's mooring. At this point Davis decided to depart for safer waters. During this voyage Davis also met Eskimos in Greenland and either Inuit or Indians in Labrador.

5. Conclusion

This brief overview of late sixteenth-century contacts with the Baffin Island Inuits reveals a pattern of interaction similar to that suggested for Norse activities in the Canadian Arctic and Greenland. These encounters began with expressions of friendship and joy by the Inuits, followed by trading and entertainment. Soon the Europeans lost important materials, precipitating the breakdown of the trade and peaceful social contact. Finally, reciprocal raiding and stealing and stealth prevailed as each side strived to gain an upper hand by strength of arms or by captive-taking and negotiation. Inuit desire for metal and European tools and weapons accounts for much of this activity. The materials obtained in these encounters entered a regional exchange system involving other Inuit groups outside the area of direct contact.

It would appear that early European contacts beginning with the Norse and ending in the late sixteenth century produced recognizable changes in Eskimo and Inuit life in the Eastern Arctic and Greenland. Apart from the suggestion that Thule culture may have been attracted to the Eastern Arctic from Alaska by the prospect of acquiring Norse metal (McGhee 1984:22), the most obvious impact was technological: the modification and use of European materials, especially metals and hardwoods, as substitutes for stone, bone, ivory, and other local traditional products. Most of these European materials were modified into artifacts like knife and weapon blades, drills, engraving tools, axes, and wooden utensils which retained their traditional Eskimo forms and were used in traditional ways. No radically new technologies, such as iron smelting or new forms of transportation, seem to have been adopted. However, the presence of Norse wool shears, coopered tubs, gamesmen, spindle whorls, baleen saws, and cooking pots—in addition to items such as those mentioned above—in Thule/Inugsuk sites in Greenland suggests that a limited amount of cultural borrowing did occur in areas adjacent to Norse settlements. Most of these items reflect interest in acquiring articles for subsistence and utilitarian needs rather than for social or religious purposes. A similar pattern in the use of European raw materials has been noted in the development of Labrador Inuit culture in the 1600s (Jordan and Kaplan 1980).

These material introductions probably did not result in major changes in Inuit culture because they did not alter the economic or subsistence systems in a major way. However, they almost certainly had an impact on socioeconomic organization. Acquisition of metal, hardwood, ceramics, cloth, and other materials as a desirable social goal would have affected individual and group behavior. Before European contact, Eskimos obtained many of the materials they needed for making implements—soapstone for lamps and pots, jadeite and slate for points and knives, etc.—through long-distance travel or regional exchange systems. The appearance of Europeans provided new and closer sources of exotic materials, changing the geography of acquisition and distribution and calling for different methods of procurement. Bravado and the ability to organize people and to manipulate social and economic affairs would have been important personal characteristics in successful dealing with European contact. Unfortunately, descriptions of trading encounters are not specific with respect to the role of native leadership, but they do not indicate centralized control of the trading process or of the distribution of the trade goods obtained. Most accounts suggest diffuse political organization much like that of nineteenth-century Inuit of this area and unlike that of the more centralized, hierarchically controlled groups observed in the Western Arctic by Franklin and others at this same period.

Nevertheless, the introduction of large (by comparison with previous standards) amounts of precious new materials into groups with access to Europeans would have required changes in the methods by which such goods were distributed within the local community and within regional exchange systems. When such materials were made available to Inuit groups in Labrador in the sixteenth and seventeenth centuries, control seems to have become vested in powerful trader-traveler-shamans who channelled the movement of Inuit-produced products (primarily oil, ivory, and baleen) into European hands while serving also as the conduit for redistribution of European goods into their villages and to Inuit groups located farther from the European sources (Jordan and Kaplan 1980; Kaplan, this volume; Taylor 1976). Similar, though diminished, effects were probably occurring among Inuit groups in Norse Greenland and perhaps also in adjacent areas of the Canadian Arctic. In addition to heightening local competition for prestige and authority and enhancing the status of the most aggressive individuals and kin groups, the ability of powerful leaders to distribute European materials outside the local group would have influenced the development of regional political and economic organizations by making these goods available through an Eskimo trader's preferred social networks. Although there is no evidence yet that such changes occurred outside of Labrador and possibly in Greenland, the wide distribution of Norse and other early European materials provides a means for investigating socio-economic questions of this type.

Related to this issue is the question of demographic and territorial shifts that may have been stimulated by European activity. Seasonal movements may well have been adjusted to place Inuit camps in areas that were likely to be frequented by European vessels or in places established by custom for trade contacts. This seems likely because vessel captains tended to follow sailing directions that brought them to land that had been previously explored, were considered safe harbors, and provided opportunity for adventitious contact with familiar people. As the pace of European contact quickened, the existence of such ports of convenience for repeated visits, such as Frobisher's at Kodlunarn Island and Davis's farther north in Baffin Island, would have become widely known to native peoples, who would have tended to congregate in these areas during the summer navigation season. Summer settlement patterns probably also were shifted to outer coastal locations to provide greater access to European vessels. This may explain the large size of the group met by Davis. Such changes would be immediately visible in archeological data and have been detected, in numerous instances, in Labrador (Kaplan 1983, and this volume). It is also possible that contact introduced European diseases into native societies, which would have had a serious impact on later Inuit history, but there are no data on this subject before A.D. 1600.

This paper therefore concludes on a speculative note, as befits its focus on a relatively unstudied problem in a youthful field. Clearly, European-native contact in the Eastern Arctic between A.D. 982 and 1600 is poorly known today but has considerable archeological promise in conjunction with historical records and ethnography. Unfortunately, so few data are available from excavated sites that discussion of contacts and the effects of contacts on native peoples is short on facts and long on guesswork. Beyond the obvious conclusions—native familiarization with European materials, technology, interests, capabilities, and tactics, and possibly the development of native methods to take advantage of sporadic contact opportunities—little more can be said at present. Certainly native peoples defended their interests successfully and managed to acquire much of what they wanted from visiting Europeans without greatly endangering their lives or up-rooting established cultural traditions. European contacts took place, after all, for only a few days in late July or August and on a very sporadic basis chronologically. Inuit societies continued to flourish in the Eastern Arctic throughout this period of sporadic contact, which lasted for more than five hundred years in Labrador and longer in Greenland and other regions. The conditions of this type of contact, primarily for raw materials acquisition, did not change until systematic contacts began after A.D. 1600, first with ship-based exploitation and trade, and later with installation of seasonal and finally permanent posts and missions which brought Inuit culture into more intimate social, economic, and religious contact with European society, altering its nature in a more profound way.

R E F E R E N C E S   C I T E D

Barkham, Selma

1980 A Note on the Strait of Belle Isle During the Period of Basque Contact with Indians and Inuit. Etudes/Inuit/Studies 4(1–2):51–58.

1982 Documentary Evidence for Basque Whaling Ships in the Strait of Belle Isle. *In:* Early European Settlement and Exploration in Atlantic Canada. G. M. Story, ed. pp. 53–96. St. John's: Memorial University of Newfoundland.

Bourque, Bruce J. and Steven L. Cox

1981 Maine State Museum Investigation of the Goddard Site, 1979. Man in the Northeast 22:3–27.

Cheshire, Neal, Tony Waldron, Alison Quinn, and David Quinn

1980 Frobisher's Eskimos in England. Archivaria 10:23–50.

Collinson, Richard

1867 The Three Voyages of Martin Frobisher. London: Hakluyt Society Series One.

Cox, Stephen

1978 Paleo-Eskimo Occupations of the North Labrador Coast. Arctic Anthropology 15(2):96–118.

Fitzhugh, William

1972 Environmental Archeology and Cultural Systems in Hamilton Inlet, Labrador. Smithsonian Contributions to Anthropology 16.

1977 Indian and Eskimo/Inuit Settlement History in Labrador: An Archaeological View. *In:* Our Footprints are Everywhere: Inuit Land Use and Occupancy in Labrador. Carol Brice-Bennett, ed. pp. 1–41. Nain, Labrador: Labrador Inuit Association.

1978 Winter Cove 4 and the Point Revenge Occupation of the Central Labrador Coast. Arctic Anthropology 15(2):146–174.

1980 Preliminary Report on the Torngat Archaeological Project Arctic 33(3):585–606.

1981 Smithsonian Archeological Surveys in Central and Northern Labrador, 1980. *In:* Archaeology in Newfoundland and Labrador—1980. Annual Report no. 1. Jane Sproull Thomson and Callum Thomson, eds. pp. 26–47. St. John's: Historic Resources Division, Government of Newfoundland and Labrador.

Gad, Finn

1971 The History of Greenland (I). London: Hurst and Co.

Hall, Charles Francis

1865 Arctic Researches and Life Among the Esquimaux. London: Samson Low, Son, and Marson.

Harp, Elmer Jr.
1974 A Late Dorset Copper Amulet from Southeastern Hudson Bay. Folk 16:33–44.

Ingstad, Anne Stine
1977 The Discovery of a Norse Settlement in North America. Oslo: Universitetsforlaget.

Jones, Gwyn
1964 The Norse Atlantic Saga. London: Oxford University Press.

Jordan, Richard H.
1979 Inugsuk Revisited: An Alternative View of Neo-Eskimo Chronology and Culture Change in Greenland. In: Thule Eskimo Culture: An Anthropological Perspective. Allen P. McCarthy, ed. pp. 149–170. Mercury Series. Archaeological Survey of Canada Paper 88.
1979 Dorset Art from Labrador. Folk 21–22:397–418.

Jordan, Richard H. and Susan A. Kaplan
1980 An Archaeological View of the Inuit/European Contact Period in Central Labrador. Etudes/Inuit/Studies 4(1–2):35–45.

Kaplan, Susan A.
1983 Economic and Social Change in Labrador Neoeskimo Society. Ph.D. dissertation, Department of Anthropology, Bryn Mawr College.

Kenyon, Walter A.
1975 Tokens of Possession. The Northern Voyages of Martin Frobisher. Toronto: Royal Ontario Museum.
1981 The Canadian Arctic Journal of Captain Edward Fenton, 1578. Archivaria 11:171–203.

Klingelhoffer, Eric
1976 Three Lost Ceramic Artifacts from Frobisher's Colony, 1578. Historical Archaeology 10:131–134.

Loring, Stephen
1983 An Archaeological Survey of the Inner Bay Region between Nain and Davis Inlet, Labrador: A Report of the 1982 Field Season. In: Archaeology in Newfoundland and Labrador—1982. Annual Report no. 3. Jane Sproull Thomson and Callum Thomson, eds. pp. 32–56. St. John's: Historic Resources Division, Government of Newfoundland and Labrador.

Mathiassen, Therkel
1930 Inugsuk, a Mediaeval Eskimo Settlement in Upernavik District, West Greenland. Meddelelser om Grønland 77(4).

Maxwell, Moreau
   1973 Archeology of the Lake Harbor District. Mercury Series. Archaeological
        Survey of Canada Paper 6.
   1980 Archaeology of the Arctic and Subarctic Zones. Annual Review of Anthro-
        pology 9:161–185.

McCartney, Allen P. and D. J. Mack
   1973 Iron Utilization by Thule Eskimos of Central Canada. American Antiquity
        38:328–339.

McGhee, Robert
   1978 Canadian Arctic Prehistory. Toronto: Van Nostrand Reinhold.
   1982 Possible Norse-Eskimo Contacts in the Eastern Arctic. *In:* Early European
        Settlement and Exploration in Arctic Canada. G. M. Story, ed. pp. 31–40.
        St. John's Memorial University of Newfoundland.
   1984 Contact Between Native North Americans and the Medieval Norse. Ameri-
        can Antiquity 49(1):4–26.

McGovern, Thomas H.
   1979 Thule-Norse Interaction in Southwest Greenland: A Speculative Model. *In:*
        Thule Eskimo Culture: An Anthropological Perspective, Allen P. McCart-
        ney, ed. pp. 171–188. Mercury Series. Archaeological Survey of Canada
        Paper 88.
   1980 Cows, Harp Seals, and Churchbells: Adaptation and Extinction in Norse
        Greenland. Human Ecology 8(2):245–275.

Meldgaard, Jørgen
   1977 Continuity and Discontinuity in the Unit Culture of Greenland. *In:* Dan-
        ish-Netherlands Symposium on Developments in Greenlandic Arctic Cul-
        ture. Hans P. Kydstra, ed. pp. 1–52. Groningen: University of Groningen.

Pastore, Ralph T.
   1984 Excavations at Boyd's Cove, Notre Dame Bay—1983. *In:* Archaeology in
        Newfoundland and Labrador—1983. Annual Report no. 4. Jane Sproull
        Thomson and Callum Thomson, eds. pp. 98–105. St. John's: Historic
        Resources Division, Government of Newfoundland and Labrador.

Plumet, Patrick
   1979 Thuléen et Dorsetiens dans L'Ungava (Nouveau-Quebec). *In:* Thule
        Eskimo Culture: An Anthropological Retrospective. A. P. McCartney, ed.
        pp. 110–112. Mercury Series. Archaeological Survey of Canada 88.

Quinn, David B.
   1979 Newfoundland From Fishery to Colony. Northwest Passage Searches, Vol.
        IV. *In:* New American World. A Documentary History of North America

to 1612. David B. Quinn, Alison M. Quinn, and Susan Hillier, eds. New York: Arno Press and Hector Bye, Inc.

Roy, Sharat K.
1937 The History and Petrology of Frobisher's "Gold Ore." Geological Series of the Field Museum of Natural History (2):21–38.

Sabo, Deborah and George Sabo
1978 A Possible Carving of a Viking from Baffin Island, N.W.T. Canadian Journal of Archaeology 2:33–42.

Sayre, Edward V., Garman Harbottle, Raymond Stoenner, Wilcomb Washburn, Jacqueline S. Olin, and William Fitzhugh
1982 The Carbon-14 Dating of an Iron Bloom Associated with the Voyages of Sir Martin Frobisher. *In:* Nuclear and Chemical Dating Techniques: Interpreting the Environmental Record, Lloyd A. Currie, ed. pp. 441–451. Washington D.C.: American Chemical Society.

Schledermann, Peter
1980 Notes on Norse Finds from the East Coast of Ellesmere Island, N.W.T. Arctic 33:454–463.

Schledermann, Peter and Karen McCullough
1980 Western Elements in Early Thule Culture of the Eastern High Arctic. Arctic 3:833–841.

Skaare, Kolbjørn
1979 An Eleventh Century Norwegian Penny Found on the Coast of Maine. Meddelelser fra Norsk Numismatisk Forening 2:12–17. Oslo: Norwegian Numismatic Society.

Stefansson, Vilhjalmur
1938 The Three Voyages of Martin Frobisher in Search of a Passage to Cathay and India by the Northwest, A.D. 1576–8. From the Original Text of George Best. London: Argonaut Press.

Taylor, E. G. R., ed.
1959 The Troublesome Voyage of Captain Edward Fenton, 1582–83. Second Series, Volume 113. London: The Hakluyt Society.

Taylor, J. Garth
1976 The Inuit Middleman in the Labrador Baleen Trade. Paper presented at 75th Annual Meeting of the American Anthropological Association, November 1976.
1980 The Inuit of Southern Quebec-Labrador: Reviewing the Evidence. Etudes/Inuit/Studies 4(1–2):185–194.

Taylor, William E., Jr.
1959 The Mysterious Sadlermint. The Beaver 290:26–33.

Thomson, Jane Sproull, and Callum Thomson
1981 Spirits of Earth and Water. Canadian Collector 16(2):39–42.

Tuck, James A.

1976 Newfoundland and Labrador Prehistory. Ottawa: Archaeological Survey of Canada.

1982 A Sixteenth Century Whaling Station at Red Bay, Labrador. *In:* Early European Settlement and Exploration in Atlantic Canada. G. M. Story, ed. pp. 41–52.

European Goods and Socio-Economic Change in Early Labrador Inuit Society

Susan A. Kaplan

A B S T R A C T

Over a 600-year period the Labrador Inuit culture underwent repeated and rapid changes in social, economic, and political organization. Using archaeological, ethnohistorical, ecological, and demographic data, this paper examines the Labrador Inuit population's responses to ecological changes and five hundred years of European contact.

The rugged mountainous coastline of Labrador (figure 1) has been occupied since 7000 B.P. (Fitzhugh 1977:4, 1978a:89). Maritime Archaic Indians; Pre-Dorset Eskimos; Intermediate Period Indians; Early, Middle, and Late Dorset Eskimos; Point Revenge Indians; Thule Eskimos; Labrador Inuit; Montagnais-Naskapi Indians; and Euro-Canadians have all called Labrador home. Each of these groups has adapted to the land, its highly seasonal resources, and one another in slightly different ways. This paper examines the Neoeskimo colonization of Labrador, their adaptation strategies, and their responses to contact with other native Americans and to Europeans.

In the fifteenth century A.D., when Neoeskimos (the combined term for Thule and historic Labrador Inuit) began settling Labrador, they entered an occupied land. Late Dorset Eskimos and Point Revenge Indians were then living along Labrador's east coast. The Late Dorset Eskimos exploited the marine and terrestrial resources between Killinek and Nain, while the Point Revenge Indians harvested marine and terrestrial resources between Nain and the Strait of Belle Isle (Fitzhugh 1978b; Loring 1983; figure 2). Both the Point Revenge Indians and the Late Dorset Eskimos fashioned chipped stone

Figure 1. *The Labrador-Davis Strait Region*

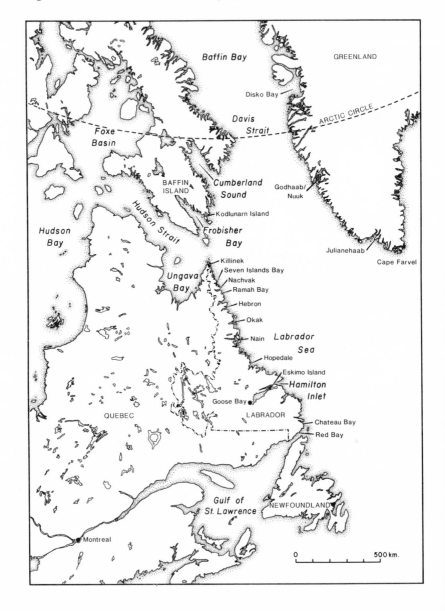

Figure 2. *Late Dorset Eskimo, Point Revenge, and Neoeskimo Sites*

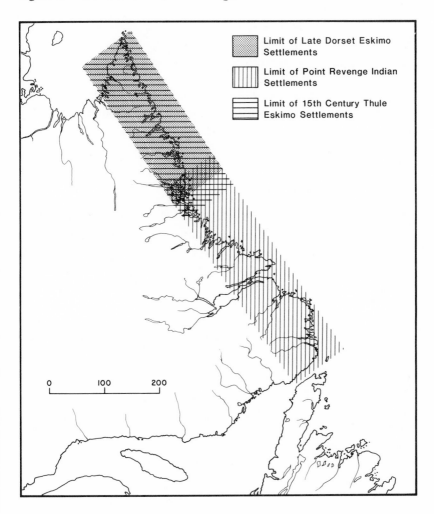

implements and weapons out of Ramah chert, a translucent grey quartzite available only in the vicinity of Ramah Bay, in northern Labrador, well within Dorset-occupied territory. Whether the Point Revenge Indians made forays north into Late Dorset Eskimo territory to quarry this material themselves or acquired it through trade with Late Dorset people is not known. A few stray Point Revenge Indian implements have been found north of Hebron, suggesting northern procurement journeys on the part of the Indians, but Point Revenge people may also have obtained this material by trade. However, archaeological data suggest that the contacts between Point Revenge Indians and Late Dorset Eskimos were limited. The two groups had only marginally overlapping settlement spheres; their dwelling forms were distinct from one another; and there were no similarities in their lithic technologies other than their use of the same raw materials.

The Eskimos who began settling Labrador in the fifteenth century were descendants of Thule culture groups (an early component of the Neoeskimo tradition) that had migrated east from Alaska ca. A.D. 1000. They practiced a modified maritime adaptation (Fitzhugh 1972:161), focussing much of their attention on the procurement of large marine mammals, particularly bowhead whales. Thule people probably were not surprised to find other people in Labrador, for they had already encountered Late Dorset Eskimos in the Central Arctic (Bielawski 1979; Jordan 1979; Plumet 1979; Thomson 1981a, 1981b). Whether through conflict or acculturation, or by means of both processes, Thule culture dominated the north Labrador coast by the end of the fifteenth century. By this time Late Dorset Eskimo culture appears to have disappeared in Labrador and from much of the Eastern Arctic. However, Neoeskimo and Dorset harpoon head forms, and Neoeskimo myths describing earlier peoples, called Tunits, suggest some degree of cultural exchange.

1. Neoeskimo Pioneers

Thule people were superbly equipped to exploit Labrador's highly seasonal resources and to deal with its difficult environment. The newcomers arrived with dog-drawn sleds, large skin boats (*umiaks*), and single-man skin boats (*kayaks*). With this equipment people and heavy gear could be transported long distances with speed. Also, the newcomers were able to negotiate mountainous terrain, snow, ice, and open water with relative ease. The early Neoeskimos used the toggling harpoon, the bow and arrow, dogs, and a number of different kinds of spears, enabling them to exploit marine and terrestrial animals under a variety of conditions. Indeed, Thule people had access to the full range of Labrador's resources due to the versatility of their technology and the flexibility of their hunting strategies.

Precontact sod house villages found between Killinek and Nain (Cox 1977:124, 184; Kaplan 1980, 1983:216; Schledermann 1972:34, 1976a) reveal that a fifteenth-century Thule culture fall-winter house was a small semisubterranean structure built out of sod, wood, stone, and whale bone. Two house forms are now recognized to have been used, although their temporal relationship is not yet known. One house form consisted of a sub-rectangular or square structure with a raised sleeping platform along the back wall of the house. The other form consisted of a main sub-rectangular or square room with a secondary alcove adjoining it. In some cases these houses had several alcoves, giving the structure a clover leaf shape. Sleeping platforms with vertically set slab retaining walls sometimes were placed at these alcoves. The houses had interior kitchens and storage areas and neatly paved floors and entrance passages.

The shallow middens and the small sizes of prehistoric Neoeskimo settlements suggest that the original Labrador Thule population was small. Indeed, a number of settlements found along the coast may have been built by the same group of people moving south exploring the various merits of Labrador's fjord and island regions. House cluster patterns within village sites suggest that between one and three extended families, living in three to five houses, comprised a typical settlement. Probably, sod houses were occupied in the late fall, winter, and early spring. Snow knives recovered in Thule sites suggest that snowhouses were used as temporary winter and spring shelters as well. During the warmer months of the year people lived in boulder-walled, hide-covered rectangular and oval structures.

Sod house settlements were built in outer island locations next to winter ice-free zones (*polynyas*). Temporary structures were erected on outer and inner islands, and in bays. In all likelihood, winter fishing and fall caribou hunting lured people to the interior as well. However, the early Thule people focused their attention on the procurement of bowhead whales, walrus, white whales, seals, and birds, all of which were primarily available in outer island environments. Subsistence activities were cooperative endeavors. The skills and the manpower of a number of settlements may have been pooled during the whaling season. Walrus hunting was most efficiently done when a number of men helped kill and butcher the animals. Fall caribou hunting, using fences and drives, and spring fishing at stone weirs required the involvement of an entire settlement.

Lithics recovered from prehistoric Thule sites in Labrador suggest that the newcomers brought fine-grained slates, nephrite, and possibly soapstone with them. Once in Labrador, people probably began searching for local sources of these materials. Tool inventories from sites in Nachvak and Seven Islands Bay indicate that people residing there began using a coarse-grained grey slate, probably collected in neighboring Ramah Bay. People must have started exploiting the soapstone outcrops found throughout Labrador as well. Indeed, some of these soapstone sources may have been easy to locate due to the quarrying efforts of earlier Dorset groups. Whether Neoeskimos continued importing fine-grained slates and nephrite or found local sources of these materials is not known.

The Thule population established settlements as far south as Nain's outer island, while Point Revenge Indians continued to occupy the inner islands in this region. The nature of interaction between these two groups is not yet understood. Possibly, for most of the year the groups did not see each other. However, they must have met during times such as the fall caribou hunting season, when hunters from both groups would have gone to inner bays and into the interior in search of game. Unfortunately, there is no archaeological data upon which to judge whether the relations between these two groups consisted of mutual tolerance, general avoidance, or outright hostility.

2. Neoeskimo Settlement Expansion

Nain was not to remain the limit of the Neoeskimo's domain. By the late 1500s or early 1600s at least three sod house settlements were established in Hopedale, and a single settlement was begun on Eskimo Island, a small island in the "Narrows" of Hamilton Inlet and Groswater Bay (figure 3). Neoeskimo expansion to Hopedale is not hard to explain. The area was one of the most productive sea mammal hunting locales along the Labrador coast, the climate was less severe than along the northern coast; and there were a number of places suitable for the construction of sod house settlements. By the eighteenth century one of the largest of Labrador's Neoeskimo populations flourished in Hopedale. However, the establishment of a settlement on Eskimo Island is not as easy to explain. While the waters surrounding the island supported an abundance of seals, fish, and waterfowl, the immediate site area lacked walrus and large whales, which were a significant part of the

Figure 3. *Early Inuit and Basque Sites*

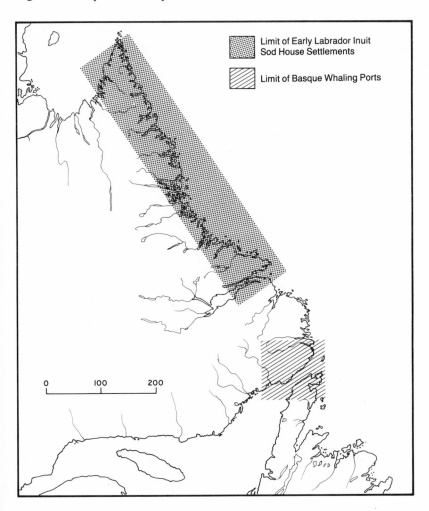

Limit of Early Labrador Inuit Sod House Settlements

Limit of Basque Whaling Ports

0   100   200

diet of Neoeskimos and their dogs, and probably an important component of religious life as well. The Eskimo Island settlement was in Indian territory and was vulnerable to attack from that quarter. Finally, the distance from Eskimo Island to the closest Eskimo settlement at Hopedale was so great that the Eskimo Islanders lacked any kind of neighborly support. Why, then, was this settlement established, and why did it continue to thrive?

Excavation of late sixteenth- and early seventeenth-century houses on Eskimo Island (Jordan 1974, 1977; Jordan and Kaplan 1980; Kaplan 1980, 1983:216, 230) indicate that the sod houses on the island were architecturally identical to those inhabited by the fifteenth-century Thule population in northern Labrador. The dwellings were small; they had long entrance passages, and a single sleeping platform ran along the back wall of each house. However, in addition to traditional Thule material culture, archaeologists recovered European-made goods in these houses and associated middens. Eskimo Island 3 (Houses 3 and 4) yielded European hardwoods, metal spikes, an anchor prong, glass beads, tiny fragments of Venetian-like glass, glazed ceramic sherds, red roofing tiles, and a badly corroded gun mechanism. The hardwoods were fashioned into float plugs; the spikes show evidence of having been cold hammered into knife blades, scrapers, and harpoon heads; and many of the tile fragments bear signs of having been ground, suggesting that they were used as whetstones or as a source of red pigment.

While the houses excavated at Eskimo Island 3 have produced the largest quantity of sixteenth-century European-made materials (and are the most thoroughly excavated Early Neoeskimo houses in Labrador), other Neoeskimo sites along the east coast have yielded exotic European goods as well. Houses and strata dating to the late 1500s and early 1600s in Hopedale, Nain, Hebron, Okak, and Killinek (Bird 1945; Jordan and Kaplan 1980; Kaplan 1980, 1983) have yielded traditional technologies along with occasional pieces of European-made goods—principally spikes, miscellaneous fragments of metal, and glass beads.

3. European Visitors

3.1. Martin Frobisher

While the Neoeskimo population was establishing itself along the coast of Labrador, equally dramatic activities were taking place on Baffin Island and along the southern Labrador-Newfoundland coast. Thule culture Neoeskimos probably did not occupy Labrador during the Norse period. However, Martin Frobisher, at first seeking a northern route to China and later on a quest for gold, established temporary stations on Kodlunarn Island, in what is now Frobisher Bay, in 1576, 1577, and 1578. During the three years of activity in this part of the New World, the Frobisher parties camped near Baffin Island Inuits, (the preferred term for historic period Eskimos), and had occasion to interact with them. The Baffin Islanders gained access to European materials through trade with the Englishmen, by scavenging through the Englishmen's abandoned camp, and possibly by salvaging the wrecks of some of Frobisher's ships (Fitzhugh, this volume). A number of Inuits living in the Frobisher Bay area must have had face-to-face contact with the Englishmen. However, an even larger number of people in the Eastern Arctic must have heard about the strangers and gained access to European-made goods through traditional long-distance trade networks. Quite possibly, Inuits living in northern Labrador were among this group.

3.2. Basque Whaling

Further south, Basque whalers spent six months of the year pursuing bowhead whales in Newfoundland waters, while Frenchmen developed a cod fishery south of them. Unlike Frobisher's short-lived enterprise, the Spanish Basque whale fishery flourished for fifty years. According to Selma Barkham, who discovered a wealth of insurance documents, wills, and court records referring to the sixteenth- and seventeenth-century Basque fishery in Spanish archives, whaling vessels left Spain for "Terranova" in mid-June (Barkham 1978a:11, 1977b, 1977c, 1978b, 1980; Tuck and Grenier 1981). By the time these vessels reached the Labrador coast the winter pack ice had broken up enough for crews to maneuver their ships into harbors such as those at Red Bay and Chateau Bay (Barkham 1977b:12). Having anchored their large ships, the Basques used small boats to pursue bowhead whales. But harpooned whales did not always die immediately, leading to ownership disputes between crews who happened upon the dead animals; hence some of the court records discovered by Barkham. Once a whale was dead, it was towed to a shore station to be butchered. The whale's blubber was cut into strips that were placed in large cast-iron caldrons for rendering into oil. The rendered oil was stored in casks that had been assembled on shore, and the casks were loaded onto the mother ship. The coopers who built the casks and the men who rendered the oil carried out their tasks under shelter. Thus, among the cargo brought to the New World were metal hoops and wood for the construction of the casks; nails, wood, and roofing tiles for the building of the shelters; and iron and other materials used to repair ships, boats, and whaling gear (Barkham 1973:93; 1978a:9, 11).

Whaling crews remained in Newfoundland-Labrador waters until mid-January. After approximately six months of whaling, and before freeze-up, the Basques left for Europe. Initially the whalers sailed directly to cities such as London, where they sold their oil and later also baleen. Later, however, the Spanish Basques learned to make a better profit by distributing their New World commodities from Spain (Barkham 1977c:577, 1978a:9).

During a single season twenty to thirty ships operated in Newfoundland and Labrador waters. The larger ships carried approximately two thousand barrels of oil, each barrel having a 400-pound capacity. The fishery involved approximately two thousand men each season (Barkham 1978a:10). However, this fishery was viewed strictly as a seasonal enterprise. Crews did not usually live ashore, and they expected to be back in Europe when winter set in. In the winters of 1574–75 and 1576–77, however, ships were caught in the New World by an early freeze-up. The men on those ships overwintered in Labrador, suffered greatly, and some of them died (Barkham 1977c:579).

Ice problems, hunting accidents, and occasionally the sinking of ships, such as the *San Juan,* now being excavated by an underwater archaeology Parks Canada team (Tuck and Grenier 1981), did not discourage the Basques, who enjoyed a monopoly on whale oil until the late 1580s. At this time the Basque fishery began to flounder, for ships once destined for the New World were being diverted for use in the Spanish war against England. The final blow to the Basque whaling enterprise came in the 1590s, when the Spitzbergen whale population was discovered, and the British and Dutch began whaling (Barkham 1977a, 1977b). Initially the English and Dutch employed the Basques, who were the only people with whaling technology and skills. When by closely observing their employees the northern Europeans learned Basque whaling techniques, however, the Spanish Basque whaling era came to an end.

3.3. Dutch Traders

In the early seventeenth century a new European presence, that of independent Dutch traders, was felt along the length of the Labrador coast. Evidence of Dutch activities has come to light as a result of Jan Kupp and Simon Hart's examination of Dutch archival records. According to Kupp and Hart (1976:10), in the seventeenth century, while the Dutch and English whalers were hunting whales in Spitzbergen waters and competing with one another for the world oil and baleen market, a class of small Dutch vessels operated by traders regularly sailed for Davis Strait waters. The exact destinations of these ships were never specified, probably as a measure of protection against competition. Kupp and Hart argue that the independent traders were going to West Greenland, Baffin Island, and Labrador, where they acquired baleen, skins, and ivory.

Kupp and Hart's conclusion that the Dutch were trading in the eastern High Arctic and in Labrador seems reasonable, particularly when certain later documents which make reference to earlier experiences are examined. Zorgdrager (1728, in Kupp and Hart 1976:12) noted that the fishing and trading opportunities of "West Greenland" and "Davis Strait" were excellent, but cautioned that the natives in these lands were aggressive and should not be given firearms. The "Society of Strait of Davis Trade and Fishery," established in 1720, issued instructions for fishermen in 1733. Included in these instructions was a statement urging crews to sail along the Labrador coast after the fishing season in order to trade with the natives but cautioning that this trade could be dangerous and detailing accounts of Dutch-Inuit altercations (Kupp and Hart 1976:17).

Like the Europeans who arrived before them, the Dutch never established permanent settlements in this part of the New World; indeed, they never established shore stations in Baffin Island or Labrador as far as is known today. Unlike the Basques, they did not linger in any one place for long. In all likelihood, contacts between Dutch and Inuit were of short duration, and the motivations for the contact were purely economic.

4. Early Labrador Inuit-European Relations

Seventeenth-century Neoeskimo (known as Labrador Inuit in historic periods) settlements have been located along the length of the Labrador coast from Killinek to Hamilton Inlet. The sod house villages continued to be built in outer island regions, and there appears to have been a shift in the population distribution, with the greater density of settlements appearing on the central coast rather than on the north coast of Labrador. Assuming that seventeenth-century contact period sites have been accurately identified (differentiating them from precontact Neoeskimo sites without extensive excavation is difficult), three processes may account for this change in population distribution. First, the greater food and wood resources and the milder climate of the central coast may have attracted people to this area; second, populations along the north coast, indeed along the length of the coast, may have suffered a decline in numbers due to the introduction of European diseases, causing depopulation of northern settlement pockets; and finally, since Newfoundland and southern Labrador continued to be a predictable source of European goods, people may have shifted their settlements south to gain easier access to these desirable exotic materials.

Archeological data suggest that the immediate impact of European activities on the Labrador Inuit population was not great. The Inuit continued to focus their hunting efforts on procurement of large marine mammals; their house forms did not change; and despite the presence of some exotic materials, their technology remained unchanged. Burials from the precontact and early contact periods suggest little differentiation in the treatment of the dead. While little is known about the religious life of Labrador Inuit, in all probability it remained unchanged during this period.

Diagnostic European-made artifacts recovered from late sixteenth- and early seventeenth-century sites in northern Labrador are few in number. Therefore, comparison of these European-made items and those recovered from Frobisher-related sites on Baffin Island is not meaningful. Until more archaelogy is done in northern Labrador and on Baffin Island, it will not be possible to determine if northern Labrador people were recipients of these materials. However, a preliminary comparison of European-made objects recovered from Eskimo Island 3 and those found in Basque shore sites in Red Bay (Tuck 1982) suggest that the Eskimo Island 3 materials were carried to the New World by the Basques. These collections do not suggest that a formal Inuit-Basque exchange system was in operation. Rather, both parties may have engaged in opportunistic trade or these early Labrador Inuit may have simply raided untended caches and shelters during the winter, and not encountered any Basques at all.

The broadest outlines of native American and Basque relations are not yet understood. According to Barkham (1980), Basques were in contact with "Indians" as early as 1537. Hostile "Eskimos" were first mentioned in a 1625 document. Inuit may have first learned of the Basque presence when a Basque ship strayed north of the Strait of Belle Isle, or they may have encountered Basques or their shelters and caches during southern hunting forays. Archeological and ethnohistorical data are not likely to provide information on exactly where and when the groups became aware of each other. If their relationship amounted to more than chance encounters, however, archival papers may provide clues as to its nature.

The idea that Eskimo Island 3 was established with access to European goods rather than natural resources as the primary consideration initially may seem extraordinary. However, when this southern expansion is seen in the context of past Neoeskimo history, the suggestion is reasonable. While the Thule culture Neoeskimos who settled in Labrador may never have set eyes on Europeans, oral tradition and past experiences with other native Americans would have prepared them for such meetings. First, Eskimo myths and legends probably contained descriptions of Eskimo and Dorset contacts with Norsemen. Regardless of how accurate or fanciful these stories may have been, they would have acquainted people with the fact that foreigners had repeatedly visited America's northern shores and might do so again. The Inuit involved in this initial contact with Basques had secured their homes in Labrador at the expense of Late Dorset Eskimo and Point Revenge Indian peoples; they were not strangers to altercations and were used to getting what they wanted.

The Europeans travelling in this section of the Arctic in the sixteenth and seventeenth centuries had as their missions exploitation of the area's resources. None of them settled among the native Americans, and while they were interested in the Inuit trade, they had no plans to alter the natives' lifestyles. While archeological data regarding sixteenth- and seventeenth-century settlements indicate that throughout this period Inuit culture remained largely unchanged, archeological and ethnohistorical data relating to the eighteenth century suggest an entirely different scenario. These data suggest that the cumulative impact of European visits to Labrador during the 1700s was great. European goods became objects of great prestige. People appear to have gone to great lengths to own them, and to control other peoples' access to them. These developments had social, economic, and political implications.

5. Eighteenth-Century European and Inuit Societies

5.1. French Contacts

The Newfoundland cod fishing grounds had been harvested by the French beginning in the sixteenth century (Innis 1940; Trudel 1978:100). Initially, the French limited their activities to northwestern and southern Newfoundland waters, avoiding Labrador altogether. However, when the Treaty of Utrecht was signed in 1713, the French lost the rights to base their fishing fleets in Newfoundland and were forced to turn their attention to the Labrador coast.

The French approached Labrador quite differently than did the European groups that had been there previously. The French allocated individuals tracts of land and encouraged the establishment of year-round residences in the New World. The permanant residents of Labrador were to become involved in the seal fishery and to search to mineral resources. Arrangements were also made for a seasonal fishery. Finally, the French suggested that the seasonal visitors and year-round residents of Labrador establish relations with the Labrador Eskimos, who had baleen, oil, and skins, all valuable commodities in the European market (Trudel 1978:103–104).

The plans set forth by the French did not work out as anticipated. Residents and seasonal visitors quarrelled over the rights to the more productive fishing grounds. More serious were problems between the Europeans and the Inuit. While individuals such as Louis Fornel had managed to establish and maintain trade relations with some Inuit groups in the mid-1700s, the overall relations between the Europeans and natives were not good, and they degenerated steadily through the eighteenth century (Zimmerly 1975). The reason for this decline involved the unanticipated and aggressive demand by Inuit for European commodities.

In the early 1700s, 150 years after the Basques' arrival, flotillas of up to a hundred Inuit boats travelled south from the central and northern Labrador coast to visit the Europeans. The visitors traded with the Europeans during the day and raided their caches and settlements at night, stealing the very items they had traded and anything else that they could move. They returned to the north with wooden boats, metal tools, and quantitites of other valuable items. At their worst the Inuit descended on isolated French fishing communities and ransacked the caches and cabins, killing people in the process. The French, seeing all Inuit as potential murderers and thieves, killed them on sight. In addition, Inuit lost their lives in boating accidents and by contracting European diseases (Trudel 1978:114–116).

5.2. Changes in Inuit Society

Why were the Inuit after European goods? One of the earliest indications that Neoeskimo culture had undergone a fundamental change is a 1680 description of a new kind of sod house referred to as a multifamily house (Jolliet 1694, in Clermont 1980:152), but there is also evidence of dramatic changes in Inuit life in archaeological and ethnohistorical sources. Sod house settlements dating to the eighteenth century have been located between Killinek and Hamilton Inlet. In addition, Cartwright reported the existence of sod houses in Sandwich Bay, south of Hamilton Inlet (Taylor 1977:51). Surveys along the coast between Sandwich Bay and the Strait of Belle Isle have not produced evidence of more southern settlements, but this area has not been thoroughly surveyed (Fitzhugh 1982).

Archaeological remains indicate that eighteenth-century sod houses were quite different from the Thule culture houses described above. These later Labrador Inuit dwellings were still made of wood, stone, sod, and whale bone but they were large rectangular buildings with long entrance passages. Houses ranged in size from 7 by 6 meters to 16 by 6 meters. Each house had two or three stone-walled sleeping platforms that ran along the back and side walls of the house. In addition, each had multiple lamp stands, one for each of the family units residing therein (Bird 1945:128; Jordan 1974, 1977, 1978; Jordan and Kaplan 1980, 1983; Schledermann 1972, 1976b; Leechman 1950).

The slate and nephrite tools used by prehistoric Eskimos had by this time been replaced by metal implements, some of them manufactured by Europeans and others fashioned out of spikes by Inuit. Excavations of houses at Eskimo Island 1 and Eskimo Island 2 reveal that the Eskimo Island houses in particular contained huge quantities of European goods. One house produced five French clasp knives, over eight thousand trade beads, hundreds of spikes and nails, musket balls, gunflints, gun parts, kaolin pipe fragments, spoons, buttons, glass, and ceramic sherds. The array and quantity of goods recovered from these Eskimo Island houses suggest that the Eskimo Islanders were amassing European-made materials for trade to their northern neighbors as well as for their own use.

The large eighteenth-century Inuit sod house has been the focus of much of the work done in Labrador. People have tried to explain why the Inuit adopted this house form, and since it has no obvious antecedents, archaeologists have wondered whether it developed in Labrador or was an idea imported from elsewhere. Scholars have been intrigued to find that the large house was also used by the West Greenland Neoeskimo population during roughly the same period.

The large eighteenth-century house has been called a "communal house" (Taylor 1974; Schledermann 1972, 1976a, 1976b; Jordan 1974, 1977, 1978; Jordan and Kaplan 1980; Kaplan 1980), a "long house" (Petersen 1974;

Gulløv 1982a, 1982b), and a "common house" (Petersen 1974). Bird (1945:179) suggested that the Inuit built such structures as a means of defense against Europeans. Petersen (1974) and Schledermann (1976a) have suggested climatic change as the reason for the adoption of this house form. Jordan (1978) and Taylor (1976) have argued that the house developed in response to external contacts with Europeans. Gulløv (1982a, 1982b) has linked the house form to developments in East Greenland, while he and Taylor (1976) have also associated the large house with long-distance trade networks.

The Moravian missionaries who established stations among the Labrador Inuit beginning in 1771 left a wealth of descriptions of Inuit life. According to the analyses of these documents by J. Garth Taylor (1974), the nuclear family was the basic social unit among the eighteenth-century Inuit. Unlike other eastern Arctic Inuit people, however, the Labrador men often had two or three wives. Men, their wives (often sisters), and close relatives all tended to live under the same roof. Often, a household was composed of the families of the father and his married sons, or those of a father and his son-in-law.

According to Taylor, the father or husband was the authority figure in the house. He was recognized as such on the basis of both his kinship position and his abilities. Married brothers were competitive for such positions of authority and rarely resided under the same roof without their father being present. The head of the household owned at least one umiak or, in later periods, a European-made wooden whaleboat or sloop. This critical piece of equipment was used for whaling, moving the household, and trading. A man needed a network of support in order to make, maintain, and use these large boats.

Analyses of demographic trends and subsistence settlement patterns (Kaplan 1983) reveal that by the eighteenth century the Inuit population had grown considerably, to perhaps six times the size of the fifteenth-century Thule population. Settlement pattern studies show that by the eighteenth century far outer island settlements had been abandoned in favor of settlements in inner island regions. Possibly, Inuit experiencing growth in their numbers found that they could not support this larger population while maintaining a strong outer-island focus. The new, more centrally located settlements permitted hunters to exploit a greater variety of resource zones among outer islands, inner islands and bays, and the interior. Indeed, the large eighteenth-century population may have started to rely on fish and caribou to supplement their marine mammal diet, as did the nineteenth-century population (Kaplan 1983).

The increase in population size led to a growth in the number of settle-ments simultaneously inhabited in the eighteenth century. The demographic trends also resulted in an increase in the size and a change in the makeup of an eighteenth-century settlement. Previously, an outer-island settlement proba-bly consisted of four or five dwellings, each housing an average of five people. At most, thirty people lived in a settlement and joined in cooperative hunting ventures. An average of twenty people lived in an eighteenth-century house (Taylor 1974:11). Indeed, in many ways an eighteenth-century house was the equivalent of a fifteenth- or sixteenth-century settlement. An eighteenth-century settlement of only three houses was twice the size of a fifteenth-century community. While Taylor records instances of cooperation among settlements, he has also described the poor relations that existed between households and between settlements. According to the Moravian accounts, blood feuds were common; further, there appears to have been no means of resolving conflicts that extended beyond the household level of organization.

5.3. Inuit Enterpreneurs

In fifteenth- and sixteenth-century Neoeskimo society, an excellent hunter would probably have been in a position of leadership within a settlement. A powerful shaman also would have assumed a position of authority. An indi-vidual who was both an excellent hunter and a shaman would have been even more powerful, although his power would not have extended beyond the settlement level. A careful reading of descriptions of eighteenth-century activities reveals that not all households were of equal size, suggesting that some were wealthier than others. Moravians and other travellers referred to certain men as "chief person," "captain," and "king." Kohlmeister and Kmoch (1814) noted that important men were given special burials atop prominent points of land.

The names and life histories of some of these important late eighteenth-century men are beginning to be known. Mitsuk (Taylor 1974:81), a man from Okak whose household consisted of thirty-seven people, owned two boats and travelled along the north Labrador coast. Tuglavina (Taylor 1974:81, 1983, 1984) was from Nain. He owned a two-masted sloop, and his trading activities and influence ranged from Nain to the Strait of Belle Isle. In addition to being a trader he was a recognized shaman. Kapik, a shaman and a leader among the Hopedale people, was a major force opposing the Mora-vian missionaries (Kleivan 1966:73). Semigak presided over the north coast in the nineteenth century (Kaplan 1983). Seguilla spent most of his time in southern Labrador (Lysaght 1971).

By the eighteenth century people along the length of the Labrador coast had European goods and wanted more of them. While there were instances when northerners could acquire goods directly from Europeans, such as when the Dutch plied Labrador waters, for the most part the only consistent source of European goods was in the south. Inuit settlements were distributed in a line down the length of the Labrador coast. This geographic arrangement and the southern point of entry of desired commodities shaped the economic development that followed (figure 4).

European goods entered the Inuit system in a number of ways. First, there were the traditional trade routes. By the mid-seventeenth century it was clear that Europeans desired to trade for baleen, oil, and skins. When the French finally formalized the trade, feathers and ivory were added to the list. By the eighteenth century a long-distance trade network linking settlements along the length of the Labrador coast was in full operation (Taylor 1976). Baleen, oil, feathers, ivory, and sealskins were traded south, the European market being their ultimate destination. European goods were traded north, becoming rarer and more costly as they entered the northern regions.

A number of entrepreneurs saw opportunity in this development. The men mentioned above became interregional traders, regional suppliers, and brokers, activating their household and settlement networks, but also establishing and maintaining interregional networks. In all likelihood such individuals assumed this new trading role from established positions of power as respected hunters and shamans and, perhaps, the relatives of older trader-travellers. The entrepreneurial activities of these few men resulted in the forging of interregional relations between households and settlements. As the interregional traders became more wealthy, their status and power increased. These men, exploring an ill-defined level of Eskimo social and political organization, bound the disparate households and settlements into individual economic units. As the trade networks became routes to wealth and power, so the household and settlement units, supporting and being cared for by these traders, were strengthened and grew in size.

6. Conclusion

The 1763 Treaty of Paris granted England rule over Labrador. This development initially had little impact on Labrador life. The Eskimos continued to

Figure 4. *Long-Distance Trade Networks in Labrador*

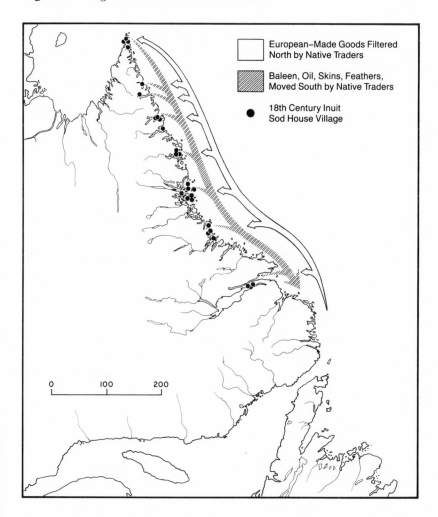

European–Made Goods Filtered
North by Native Traders

Baleen, Oil, Skins, Feathers,
Moved South by Native Traders

● 18th Century Inuit
Sod House Village

0   100   200

trade and fight with the French and British. However, the warlike state began to depress the British fishery, so the government took steps to alleviate the situation: to reduce the vulnerability of British fishermen while at the same time eliminating the French competition by announcing that year-round occupation of Labrador by Europeans was to be forbidden. This decree, however, had little effect on events in Labrador.

One element in this policy was to contain the Inuit in northern Labrador and keep them from interfering in the fishery in the south. For this reason, in 1771 the first year-round European settlement to be located north of Hamilton Inlet was established by Moravian missionaries, under arrangement with the British government. The Moravians, with previous experience among the Greenland Inuit, agreed to shift the Inuit limit of activities north of European fishing establishments if, in exchange, they were allowed sole access to the native population so that they could Christianize it (Whiteley 1964). To carry out their goals they also secured permission to operate trading posts at their stations, a move intended to attract Inuit to their establishments and eliminate the Inuit's need to travel south to European settlements and posts (Hiller 1971a, 1971b, 1977:83; Whiteley 1964:33).

The Moravians' establishment of a station in Nain in 1771 marked the first time in over two hundred years of contact that a group of Europeans went to Labrador specifically to alter Inuit lifeways. The Moravians perceived the roots of eighteenth-century Eskimo society and developed economic strategies to undermine the activities of Labrador's powerful men and the long-distance trade networks. Eventually, the missionaries were aided by the collapse of the European baleen market, the depletion of whale and walrus stocks in Labrador waters, and the effects of introduced technologies such as the rifle, the fishnet, and the animal trap, which undercut the need for cooperative hunting efforts (Kaplan 1983).

During the first three hundred years of their occupation of Labrador Neoeskimos showed themselves to be an aggressive and opportunistic people ready, able, and willing to exploit all resources and situations that were of interest to them. Initially, the social and economic organization of this egalitarian society was structured around ecological considerations and subsistence concerns. By the eighteenth century, in response to rapid population growth and the continued presence of Europeans in southern Labrador and Newfoundland, Inuit life had changed. Settlement locations were moved, hunting strategies and priorities were altered, and the acquisition and control of European goods, considered to be prestige items, became key aspects of

Inuit life. Households and settlements along the length of the Labrador coast became economically linked by long-distance trade networks controlled by a class of powerful men who had heightened political, social, and economic status.

Major factors contributing to the cultural changes discussed in this paper include the linear distribution of settlements along the Labrador coast, demographic trends, and a long history of European contact which did not involve European settlement in Inuit territory. The cultural developments in Labrador can now be seen in a broad framework of social, economic, and demographic changes. Interestingly, the geography, ecology, and contact history of West Greenland closely parallel those of Labrador. Future research in these two areas of the Arctic should result in a clearer understanding of the developments discussed here, and may produce a classic example of parallel cultural evolution.

REFERENCES CITED

Barkham, Selma
  1973   Building Materials for Canada in 1566. Association for Preservation Technology, Bulletin 5(4):93–94.
  1977a Guipuzcoan Shipping in 1571 with Particular Reference to the Decline of Transatlantic Fishing Industry. *In*: Anglo-American Contributions to Basque Studies: Essays in Honor of Jon Bilbao. Desert Research Institute Publications on the Social Sciences, No. 13, pp. 73–81.
  1977b The Identification of Labrador Ports in Spanish 16th Century Documents. Canadian Cartographer 14(1):1–19.
  1977c The First Will and Testament on the Labrador Coast. Geographical Magazine 49(9):574–581.
  1978a The Basques: Filling a Gap in Our History Between Jacques Cartier and Champlain. Canadian Geographical Journal 49(1):8–19.
  1978b The Unlikelihood of Prolonged Basque-Eskimo Contact in the Sixteenth Century. Paper presented at the First Inuit Conference, Laval University, Quebec.
  1980   A Note on the Strait of Belle Isle During the Period of Basque Contact with Indians and Inuit. Etudes/Inuit/Studies 4(1–2):51–58.

Bielawski, Ellen
  1979   Contactual Transformation: The Dorset-Thule Succession. *In*: Thule Eskimo Culture: An Anthropological Retrospective. Allen B. McCartney, ed. pp. 100–109. Mercury Series. Archaeological Survey of Canada 88.

Bird, Junius B.
1945 Archaeology of the Hopedale Area, Labrador. Anthropological Papers of the American Museum of Natural History 39(2).

Clermont, Norman
1980 Les Inuit du Labrador Meridional avant Cartwright. Etudes/Inuit/Studies 4(1–2):147–166.

Cox, Stephen L.
1977 Prehistoric Settlement and Culture Change at Okak, Labrador. Ph.D. dissertation, Department of Anthropology, Harvard University.

Fitzhugh, William W.
1972 Environmental Archaeology and Cultural Systems in Hamilton Inlet, Labrador. Smithsonian Contributions to Anthropology 16.
1977 Indian and Eskimo/Inuit Settlement History in Labrador: An Archaeological View. *In*: Our Footprints are Everywhere. Carol Brice-Bennett, ed. pp. 1–41. Nain, Labrador: Labrador Inuit Association.
1978a Maritime Archaic Cultures of the Central and Northern Labrador Coast. Arctic Anthropology 15(2):61–95.
1978b Winter Cove 4 and the Point Revenge Occupation of the Central Labrador Coast. Arctic Anthropology 15(2):146–174.
1980 A Review of Paleo-Eskimo Culture History in Southern Quebec-Labrador and Newfoundland. Etudes/Inuit/Studies 4(1–2):21–31.
1982 Smithsonian Surveys in Central and Southern Labrador in 1981. *In*: Archaeology in Newfoundland and Labrador 1981. Jane Sproull Thomson and Callum Thomson, eds. pp. 32–55. St. John's: Historic Resources Division, Government of Newfoundland and Labrador.

Gulløv, Hans Christian
1982a European Contact with the Eskimos in Greenland: Archaeological Investigations in West Greenland During the 1970s. Paper presented to the Anthropological Society of Washington, March 1982.
1982b Migration et diffusion—peuplement Inuit de Quest du Groenland à l'epoque post-medievale. Etudies/Inuit/Studies 6(2):3–20.

Hiller, James
1971a Early Patrons of the Labrador Eskimos: The Moravian Mission in Labrador 1764–1805. *In*: Patrons and Brokers in the Eastern Arctic. Robert Paine, ed. pp. 74–97. Newfoundland Social and Economic Papers, No. 2. St. John's: Memorial University of Newfoundland.
1971b The Moravians in Labrador 1771–1805. The Polar Record 15(99):839–854.
1977 Moravian Land Holdings on the Labrador Coast: A Brief History. *In*: Our

Footprints are Everywhere. Carol Brice-Bennett, ed. pp. 83–94. Nain, Labrador: Labrador Inuit Association.

Innis, Harold A.
1940　The Cod Fisheries: The History of an International Economy. New Haven: Yale University Press.

Jordan, Richard H.
1974　Preliminary Report on Archaeological Investigations of the Labrador Eskimo in Hamilton Inlet in 1973. Man in the Northeast 8:77–89.
1977　Inuit Occupation of the Central Labrador Coast Since 1600 A.D. *In*: Our Footprints are Everywhere. Carol Brice-Bennett, ed. pp. 43–48. Nain, Labrador: Labrador Inuit Association.
1978　Archaeological Investigations of the Hamilton Inlet Labrador Eskimo: Social and Economic Response to European Contact. Arctic Anthropology 15(2):175–185.
1979　Inugsuk Revisited: An Alternative View of Neo-Eskimo Chronology and Culture Change in Greenland. *In*: Thule Eskimo Culture: An Anthropological Retrospective. Allen B. McCartney, ed. pp. 149–170. Mercury Series. Archaeological Survey of Canada 88.

Jordan, Richard H. and Susan A. Kaplan
1980　An Archaeological View of the Inuit/European Contact in Central Labrador. Etudes/Inuit/Studies 4(1–2):35-45.

Kaplan, Susan A.
1980　Neo-Eskimo Occupations of the Northern Labrador Coast. Arctic 33(3):646–658.
1983　Economic and Social Change in Labrador Neo-Eskimo Culture. Ph.D. dissertation, Department of Anthropology, Bryn Mawr College.

Kleivan, Helge
1966　The Eskimos of Northeast Labrador: A History of Eskimo-White Relations 1771–1955. Norsk Polarinstitutt Skrifter 139.

Kohlmeister, B. and G. Kmoch
1814　Journal of a Voyage from Okak on the Coast of Labrador to Ungava Bay, Westward of Cape Chudleigh. London: W.M. McDowall.

Kupp, Jan and Simon Hart
1976　The Dutch in the Strait of Davis and Labrador During the 17th and 18th Centuries. Man in the Northeast 11:3–20.

Leechman, Douglas
1950　Eskimo Summer. Toronto: Museum Press.

Loring, Stephen
1983 An Archaeological Survey of the Inner Bay Region Between Nain and Davis Inlet, Labrador: A Report of 1982 Fieldwork. *In*: Archaeology in Newfoundland and Labrador 1982. Annual Report No. 3. Jane Sproull Thomson and Callum Thomson, eds. pp. 32–56. St. John's: Historic Resources Division, Government of Newfoundland and Labrador.

Lysaght, A.M.
1971 Joseph Banks in Newfoundland and Labrador, 1766. His Diary, Manuscripts, and Collections. London: Faber and Faber.

Petersen, Robert
1974 Some Considerations Concerning the Greenland Longhouse. Folk 16–17:171–188.

Plumet, Patrick
1979 Thuleèns et Dorsètiens dans l'Ungava (Nouveau-Quebec). *In:* Thule Eskimo Culture: An Anthropological Retrospective. Allen B. McCartney, ed. pp. 110–121. Mercury Series. Archaeological Survey of Canada 88.

Schledermann, Peter
1972 The Thule Tradition in Northern Labrador. M.A. thesis, Department of Anthropology, Memorial University of Newfoundland.
1976a The Effect of Climatic/Ecological Changes on the Style of Thule Culture Winter Dwellings. Arctic and Alpine Research 8(1):37–47.
1976b Thule Culture Communal Houses in Labrador. Arctic 29(1):27–37.

Taylor, J. Garth
1974 Labrador Eskimo Settlements of the Early Contact Period. Publications in Ethnology 9. Canada: National Museum of Man.
1976 The Inuit Middleman in the Labrador Baleen Trade. Paper presented at 75th Annual Meeting of the American Anthropological Association, November 1976.
1977 Traditional Land Use and Occupancy by the Labrador Inuit. *In*: Our Footprints are Everywhere. Carol Brice-Bennett, ed. pp. 49–58. Nain, Labrador: Labrador Inuit Association.
1983 The Two Worlds of Mikak. Part I. The Beaver 314(3):4–13.
1984 The Two Worlds of Mikak. Part II. The Beaver 314(4):18–25.

Thomson, Callum
1981a Preliminary Archaeological Findings from Shuldham Island, Labrador, 1980. *In*: Archaeology in Newfoundland and Labrador 1980. Annual Report No. 1. Jane Sproull Thomson and Callum Thomson, eds. pp. 5–19. St. John's: Historic Resources Division, Government of Newfoundland and Labrador.

1981b Archaeological Findings from Saglek Bay, 1981. *In:* Archaeology in New-
       foundland and Labrador 1981. Annual Report no. 2. Jane Sproull Thomson
       and Callum Thomson, eds. pp. 5–31. St. John's: Historic Resources Divi-
       sion, Government of Newfoundland and Labrador.

Trudel, Francois
   1978 The Inuit of Southern Labrador and the Development of French Sedentary
         Fisheries (1700–1760). *In:* Papers from the Fourth Annual Congress, 1977.
         Richard J. Preston, ed. pp. 99–121. Mercury Series. Canadian Ethnology
         Service 40.

Tuck, James A.
   1982 A Sixteenth Century Whaling Station at Red Bay, Labrador. *In:* Early
         European Settlement and Exploitation in Atlantic Canada. G.M. Story, ed.
         pp. 41–52. St. John's: Memorial University of Newfoundland.
   1983 Excavations at Red Bay, Labrador–1982. *In:* Archaeology of Newfoundland
         and Labrador 1982. Annual Report no. 3. Jane Sproull Thomson and
         Callum Thomson, eds. pp. 95–117. St. John's: Historical Resources Divi-
         sion, Government of Newfoundland and Labrador.

Tuck, James A. and Robert Grenier
   1981 A 16th Century Basque Whaling Station in Labrador. Scientific American
         245(5):180–190.

Whiteley, W.H.
   1964 The Establishment of the Moravian Mission in Labrador and British Policy
         1763–83. Canadian Historical Review 45(1):29–50.

Zimmerly, David W.
   1975 Cain's Land Revisited: Culture Change in Central Labrador. Newfound-
         land Social and Economic Studies 16. St. John's: Memorial University of
         Newfoundland.

Whales, Whalers, and Eskimos: The Impact of European Whaling on the Demography and Economy of Eskimo Society in West Greenland

Hans Christian Gulløv

A B S T R A C T

After the colonization of Greenland by Moravian missionaries in 1721, the historical source material dealing with the Eskimo population increased appreciably. Aided by this written documentation, by archaeological excavations, and by settlement pattern data, this article explains the role that European colonization and Dutch whaling played in changes in the exchange economy of the Eskimo of Southwest Greenland. The critical features of this system were the travels of the South Greenlanders north along the west coast to the whaling areas at 67 degrees north latitude and at Disko Bay, to obtain whale products missing in the Kap Farvel region. These travels ceased after colonization due to the influence of the Mission, which induced a more settled life for the Eskimos of this area.

1. Introduction

Greenland was the first place in the Arctic to be settled by Europeans. In the southernmost part of West Greenland, Vikings from the Icelandic Free State founded two colonies, the Eastern and Western Settlements (figure 1). For half a millennium, from A.D. 982 to 1500, the Norse maintained a farming and fishing economy in this arctic outpost. Around A.D. 1400 the Western Settlement was abandoned, and a century later the Norse in the Eastern Settlement disappeared from Greenland and from history. The Norsemen's disappearance has fascinated historians for hundreds of years and is still a mystery today (Gad 1970:153–182).

At the same time that Norse settled in South Greenland, Eskimos were moving into North Greenland from the Canadian archipelago. These were

Figure 1 *Location of West Greenland Place Names Mentioned in the Text*

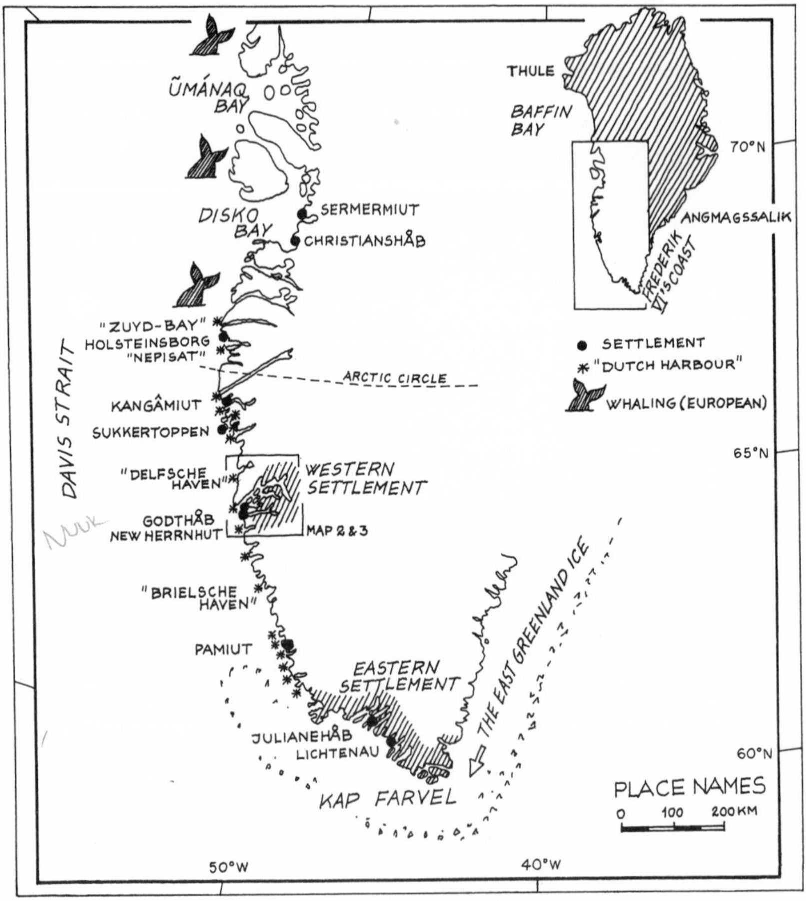

people of the Thule culture. According to radiocarbon dates, they migrated into Greenland in the tenth century A.D. Two centuries later Thule people reached Disko Bay on the central west coast, and in the early 1300s they settled in the Western Settlement, probably at a time when the Norse were still living there (Gulløv 1982a). From evidence found in South Greenland we know of the Eskimo discovery of the Eastern Settlement. The Icelandic Accounts for the year 1379 mention an attack by Eskimos (*skraelings*), but we do not have any information as to where these Eskimos came from (Gulløv 1982b).

In the post-Norse period Eskimos spread all along the west coast. We know from archeological investigations (Bandi and Meldgaard 1952) that when the Thule culture reached Northeast Greenland Paleoeskimos of the Dorset culture probably still lived there. However, consideration of the peoples of Greenland's east coast is beyond the scope of this presentation, which concerns changes in the populations, economy, and settlement forms used by West Greenland Eskimos from the time of the disappearance of the Norse settlements to the establishment of the Moravian Mission colony at Nuuk in the 1720s.

Specifically, the purpose of this paper is to reconstruct changes in Eskimo life as they are revealed through a combination of archeological, documentary, and ethnographic sources. Attention will be directed at data describing the traditional exchange economy in which Eskimos from South Greenland travelled north to Nuuk (Godthaab) and Disko Bay, where they exchanged wood for baleen and obtained from Eskimos living in these northern regions the soapstone absent in the south. Sources describing this exchange economy also note cultural differences between the peoples of South and West Greenland that relate to the change from small, round Thule-type houses to the large "communal" house in Nuuk during the time when the South Greenlanders' travels intensified due to the presence of European whaling activities in Disko Bay. Although this paper cannot explain the full origin of the communal house in Greenland, the documentary sources and regional economic relationships described here provide a basis for working toward an explanation of the culture change involved. Finally I will explore the impact of Hans Egede's colony on the local Eskimo population in the Nuuk region, especially on the decline of that population and its absorption by the South Greenlanders who began to resettle permanently in this area.

2. History Begins

In 1585 the English navigator John Davis met Eskimos on the Greenland west coast in what was probably the first such meeting since the disappearance of the Norsemen. This first authoritatively documented post-medieval Eskimo contact in Greenland took place at 64 degrees north latitude. We are told that many people were gathered at this place, that their houses were dug into the earth and built partly of wood, and that large amounts of driftwood were to be found on the islands off shore:

> . . . During the time of our abode among these Islands, we found reasonable quantitie of wood, both firre, spruce and juniper; which whither it came floting any great distance to these places where we found it, or

whither it grew in some great Islands neere the same place by vs not yet discouered, we know not. But wee judge that it groweth there further into the lande then wee were, because the people had great store of darts & oares, which they made none accompt of, but gaue them to vs for small trifles, as poynts and pieces of paper (Hakluyt 1589:778).

In 1605 the Danish King Christian IV equipped an expedition to the arctic waters. Five Eskimos from West Greenland were captured and brought back to Copenhagen where people saw skraellings for the first time since the Norse period (Gad 1970:219). The Danish king sent two more expeditions to Greenland, in 1606 and 1607, but war between Denmark and Sweden soon put an end to these arctic initiatives. In the following century the west coast of Greenland was visited several times by Europeans, and the coast between 64 to 67 degrees north latitude became known as Davis Strait, or "Straat David" on early Dutch maps.

At the time of the Danish-Norwegian colonization in 1721, a large Eskimo population was found at 64 degrees north latitude. In winter these Eskimos lived in large houses containing as many as forty people. The founder of the colony, Hans Egede, a Norwegian missionary, mentioned in his diary that several *umiaks* (women's boats) passed the colony each spring on their way north to the whaling locations in Disko Bay (figure 2). In one instance, forty umiaks, probably containing more than four hundred people, in addition to others in kayaks, were noted (Egede 1925:19, 236–237). On their way north these people rested at the sound immediately north of the colony, where they camped together with people from the local Kangeq area who had left their winter houses to fish for lumpsuckers. At this place Egede observed more than a hundred tents, which he estimated housed about five hundred people (Egede 1925:208). It was customary for the Southerners to remain in the north for a winter, after which they would return south again.

These observations covering a timespan of 140 years, from the 1580s to the 1720s, are not isolated cases. One, in particular, stands out—the account of David Danell. In the year 1654 he also met Eskimos at 64 degrees north latitude and took four persons back to Europe as prisoners (Egede 1925:60; figure 3). Based on observations made two years before this date, he describes their houses as being dug into the ground and shaped like a baker's oven (Bobe 1916:212). This is the last known account of the original Thule-type house from the west coast of Greenland. When Egede arrives in 1721 we hear only about a different type of house known as the "big" (i.e., probably communal) house.

Figure 2   *Greenlanders Engaged in Whaling*
            (From a 1925 printing of Hans Egede's 1741 "Description of Greenland.")

Figure 3 *Greenlanders from the Nuuk Area Captured in 1654*
David Danell painted this group portrait in Bergen, Norway, after his return from Greenland. (Collection of the National Museum of Denmark.)

When Egede left Norway he brought with him Dutch maps and a small book written by a Dutch whaling captain, Lourens Feykes Haan (1720). In his "Description of Straat Davids . . ." Haan mentions:

". . . the lengths of their houses are different from each other, and are built for a number of families, and some houses are dwellings for 3–4 families. In lack of tree, which often occurs, the roofs of the houses were built of whale bones, yet rafters were used where driftwood occurs and are to be placed across the walls as we do, and under each rafter a beam for supporting the roof is erected . . ."

Haan's observations came from decades of whaling (figure 4) in Davis Strait, so we may assume that the changes in Eskimo dwelling forms, from small, round semi-subterranean houses to the larger, rectangular communal house forms, may have appeared in this area between 1650 and 1700.

3. Whales and Whalers

Ever since the Dutchman William Barentz rediscovered the islands of Svalbard and Novaya Zemlya in 1596, Dutch whalers had sailed in the Barents Sea to catch the "Greenland whales." In 1614 the Noordsche Compagnie was founded in Amsterdam and the European whaling competition began. But it is important to emphasize that according to the historical sources, massive whaling in Davis Strait did not begin until 1719 (Zorgdrager 1720; Haan 1720). During the seventeenth century most of the Dutch who went to Greenland went to barter, not to hunt whales (Dekker 1975). Only after the 1670s did whalers from Hamburg and the Frisian Islands began whaling in West Greenland waters (Dekker 1974; Oesau 1955).

The shift in whaling areas from the Barents Sea to the Davis Strait resulted from a seventeenth-century climatic change known as the "Little Ice Age." Special conditions of currents, drift-ice, and biological production in the arctic seas control the distribution of Greenland whales in different places at different times. With the onset of the "Little Ice Age," the increasing advances of drift-ice forced the whales to abandon their former feeding grounds in the northern Atlantic (Vibe 1967:94), and in the search for new whaling grounds some whalers shifted to Davis Strait, where the barter ships already had been operating.

When Egede founded Haabets Coloni in 1721 he was told that no "real" (i.e., baleen) whales were found at this latitude, i.e., 64 degrees north (Egede

Figure 4 *Dutch Whalers*
Painting is Walvisvangst, by Roelof Salm (1688–1765). (Collection of the Zuiderzeemuseum, Enkhuizen, the Netherlands.)

1925:23). Those whales were found at about 67 degrees north latitude, at a place called Nepisat, where the Eskimos hunted them along the winter ice edge. The Dutch whalers anchored there and at Zuyd Bay, a few miles farther north (figure 4). When the ice broke up in April the whales usually migrated to Disko Bay, Umanaq, and Baffin Bay, and the whalers followed (Egede 1925:106).

There were no baleen whales south of Nepisat according to the historical sources. But from an unpublished record we know of harbors where Dutch ships anchored to barter with the Eskimos in Southwest Greenland (Jochimson 1733). Five of these harbors are located in the Kangamiut area, later called the Sukkertoppen District; to the south we know of eleven harbors, of which Delfsche Haven and Brielsche Haven figured prominently as the oldest Dutch place names in West Greenland, dating from an expedition in 1624, and named on a chart (*pascaarte*) from 1634 (Bobe 1944:53).

For bartering with the Eskimos the Dutch in the latter half of the seventeenth century anchored north of the East Greenland Drift-ice from Pamiut north to Zuyd Bay. When European whaling came to Davis Strait about 1700—massively after 1719 (Zorgdrager 1720)—the ships went to Zuyd Bay and Nepisat in April. During the summer they moved on to Disko Bay, returning in the fall to Zuyd Bay and Nepisat, where Eskimos from north and south settled to barter and hunt (Egede 1925:120–121).

We are also told that the Eskimos from South Greenland, the Kap Farvel area, travelled northward to get baleen for fishing lines and for lines used in binding the wooden frames of kayaks and umiaks (Egede 1925:80). In exchange, the northerners obtained "pots and lamps of soapstone . . . because this stone is not to be found in the North." The travel of large numbers of Southerners into the northern regions for the purpose of bartering goods appears to have been an important feature of traditional West Greenland Eskimo culture, about which more will be said below.

The change in the dwelling house form, the travelling of *some* people from South Greenland and to the middle of the west coast and back again after having wintered, and the appearance of European whaling in the Davis Strait date to the period between 1650 and 1700. Catalyzing effects of climatic cooling probably help explain why these changes began when they did; but we remain in the dark as to why they happened. However, an examination of archeological data, in combination with historical sources, provides some understanding of how Europeans influenced West Greenland Eskimo society.

4. Archeological Data

Our knowledge of archeological materials comes from excavation of hundreds of Thule Eskimo winter dwellings, work that began in the 1930s. According to Meldgaard:

the overall picture shows in West Greenland a hunting culture founded on the Thule Culture, but gradually changing character as the people spread south to warmer areas with more open waters. In time sealing from kayak has become more important than whale hunting, and in the area south of Holsteinsborg [Nepisat/Zuyd Bay] certain cultural elements that belong to the arctic snow and ice, such as the snow house and ice-hunting, have become obsolete, and dog-sledge is getting rare. Still the catch of seal at its breathing holes in the ice and at the ice-edge becomes more important in later periods due to climatic changes. Hence even in southernmost West Greenland the large winter settlements of single-family houses are placed at the ice-covered inner fjords during the cold period in the century before the communal houses are built in the skerries of the outer coast around 1650–1700. (Meldgaard 1977:40).

A comparison of all excavated Thule winter houses, which pre-date the use of the communal house type, brings to light some facts not noted in Meldgaard's analysis. On the one hand, circular single- and double-room Thule houses (figure 5, sketches a and c) have been found stratigraphically beneath communal houses (Gulløv and Kapel 1979/80:367–374). On the other hand, some of the objects found while excavating circular Thule-type houses come from contact with whalers in the colonial period after 1721 (Gulløv 1982b:6–10, 1983). Table 1 displays the distribution of various types of European and Eskimo objects according to house form and locality. The archeological materials on which this table is based are housed in the National Museum in Copenhagen and have been described by Mathiassen (1931, 1933, 1934, 1936a, 1936b) and Gulløv (1983).

All the house forms (figure 5) noted in table 1 occur in other areas of the Eastern Arctic except for the oval type (figure 5, sketch d), which is restricted to Disko Bay. Artifacts found in this house type indicate that it post-dates the founding of Christianshaab in 1734. Of the various house forms the circular houses contain the majority of European artifacts. Double houses are found from the Thule district south along the entire west coast. Except for a single case, this house type is not known in East Greenland; nor have artifacts of European origin been found in East Greenland ruins that

Figure 5 *West Greenland House Types*

The plans shown are based on a, *circular and* c, *double house types associated with Thule and early historic periods in West Greenland (Gulløv 1983:27);* b, *multi-family communal house from Julianehaab (Mathiassen 1936: figure 12) and* d, *oval house plan from Disko Bay (Mathiassen 1934: figure 53).*

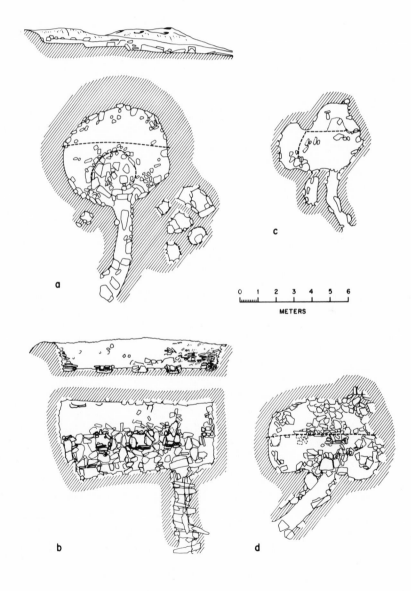

Table 1. *Origin of Artifacts, by Locality and House Form*

Locality / Form / Contents	Disko			Kangamiut		Nuuk		Julianehaab		Frederik VI's Coast		Angmagssalik	Total
	Circular	Double	Oval	Circular	Double	Circular	Double	Circular	Double	Circular	Double	Circular	
No artifacts or only Eskimo artifacts	11	9		9	2	7	1	23	7	8	1	17	95
Artifacts of Norse and Eskimo origin	3				1	2	1	17	1				25
Artifacts of whalers and Eskimo origin			3	4	2	2	1	2					14
Number of houses	14	9	3	13	5	11	3	42	8	8	1	17	134

have been investigated. In West Greenland, communal houses (figure 5, sketch b) contain European artifacts, as do middens and some graves associated with these houses. However, it has been difficult to date middens and to correlate them with particular house forms due to a lack of diagnostic artifacts.

In the absence of more detailed study, it would appear that the original Thule circular and double house forms and the communal houses were in use at the same time in some areas of the west coast, and that the Nuuk and Kangamiut regions of the central west coast were where the greatest amount of contact with whalers took place. Unfortunately, there are no archeological data from Holsteinborg, where Danell (1654) observed circular houses.

This synchroneity between the old Thule house forms (circular and double) and the communal house can be documented further in the Nuuk/Gothaab region (figure 6) as a result of recent archeological surveys and excavations and of historical accounts dating to the founding of the Haabets Coloni in 1721 (Gulløv 1983). Of the thirty-one circular or double houses found in this area, about half have been fully excavated. Materials recovered from these excavations, including bricks and clay pipes (Gulløv 1982b:8), demonstrate European contact. These houses are found both on the outer coast and in the fjords.

The distribution of the communal houses in this region is shown in figure 7. One hundred thirty-five ruins are known, of which forty are found in the fjords and the remainder on the coast. The oldest house so far investigated dates to about 1700 or perhaps slightly earlier, and is located west of Kangeq (Gulløv and Kapel 1979/80). The communal houses for which historical documentation exists are known to have been occupied by South Greenlanders who later belonged to the Moravian Mission established one kilometer south of Nuuk in 1733.

There is a remarkable coincidence between the travels of the South Greenlanders past the colony and the emergence of the communal houses. In fact, one suspects this is not a coincidence. The first entry in Egede's diary about the South Greenlanders traveling into the fjords is dated 1733. Entries for 1735 state, "The southerners went out of the fjord after having cut soapstone for lamps and pots, and travelled southward again" (Egede 1925:267, 292). A smallpox epidemic had ravaged the Nuuk population at that time, and the resources of the region were open for outsiders to exploit. Of two hundred families formerly within twenty-five kilometers of Nuuk, no more than thirty existed at the time of Egede's writing (Egede 1925:283). Forty

Figure 6 *Distribution of Circular and Double Houses in the Nuuk Area*

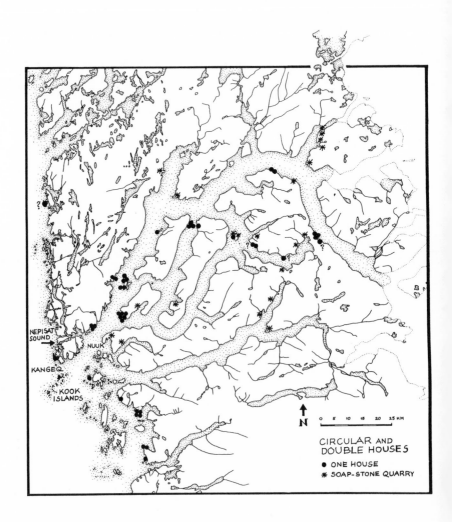

CIRCULAR AND
DOUBLE HOUSES
● ONE HOUSE
✳ SOAP-STONE QUARRY

0 5 10 15 20 25 KM

N

Figure 7   *Distribution of Communal Houses in the Nuuk Area*
These houses first appear in the coastal Kangeq area ca. 1670 and in the fjords
after 1735.

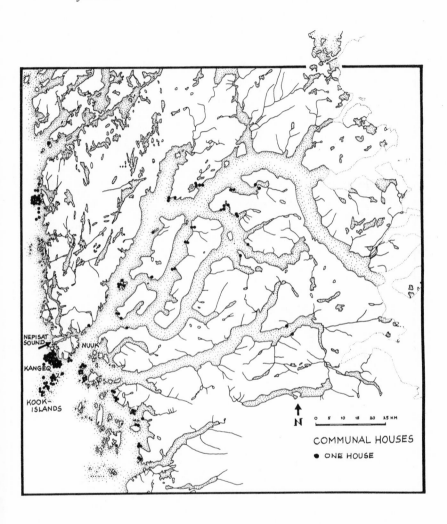

COMMUNAL HOUSES
● ONE HOUSE

years later, in 1774–75, this condition is confirmed by the rural dean Egil Thorhallesen, who wrote that in the Kangeq area "only live Southerners who stay here for a year or more on their way North or South"; he continues "the people at these places [i.e., Kangeq and the Kook Islands] were in former times mostly roaming Southerners, kinsmen of most of the travellers who were to come there afterwards" (Thorhallesen 1914:38–39, 58–59).

Summarizing these observations, we know that the population in the Nuuk region at the start of colonization belonged to two groups: the people in the fjords, many of whom did not come out to the sea (Egede 1925:420), and the people along the coast, who were partly replaced by South Greenlanders enroute to northern locations. Later, particularly after the Moravians became dominant in the missionary work after 1750, we can trace the southerners through the distribution of communal houses in the fjords, judging from the localities where the Moravians settled together with these South Greenlandic proselytes, whom we know lived in communal houses (Cranz 1770).

As we have seen, in the beginning of the eighteenth century the settlement patterns indirectly express a dichotomy in the demographic composition of the Eskimo population of West Greenland, a dichotomy identified because of information on the travels of people from southernmost Greenland northwards to the whaling regions and back again. However, there is as yet no documentation linking the communal house type with the South Greenlanders.

5. South Greenland Ethnography

In 1752 a merchant wrote:

> To comply with certain commodities which more and more Greenlanders want and travel far to get, for example baleen, caribou skin, and soapstone, we could arrange transportation of these commodities from one colony along the coast to another. One example can be given: In the South the Greenlanders themselves use most of the baleen, despite the fact that they have none. Therefore they have to go north to Disko Bay to get it. On their way north they supply the markets with their many fox furs supposedly to the Dutch. In the Disko Bay the Greenlanders need caribou skin and soapstone pots which too are lacking in the South. Therefore the Southerners get these things in the Gothaab area, where it can be found in

large quantity and in the best quarries of the west coast. On their way back again the Southerners get supplies of soapstone in the area for their own use and for exchange among the countrymen in the South (Dalager 1915:87).

Hans Egede travelled in the south in 1723 (1925:92–102), as did the merchant Peder Olsen Walløe between 1749–1753 (Walløe 1927). Cranz (1770) provides information about the south in his "history," and the merchant Anders Olsen (1764) is also very informative in his unpublished work about West Greenland. In these historical sources the south is described as a very rich ecological area inhabited by many Eskimos. Egede refers to Disko Bay and the south as the most densely populated areas of West Greenland (1925:362). Both Egede and Walløe noted a change in dialect between the southern and central west coast regions. In these reports we hear of ringed seals, rose fish, cod, capelin, and halibut in the sea, and of hare, fox, caribou, and ptarmigan on land. Anders Olsen tells of "salmon which in certain places are so big that the Greenlanders have to use the same tools as they use for sealhunting, e.g., harpoon and bladder" (Olsen 1764). This description underlines the richness of the southern resources. But why then travel?

One source provides an account of a specific problem. Storing food for winter use is as important in South Greenland as it is in other regions of the arctic. Fish and seals are particularly important in this regard. As mentioned by Walløe, "it is not the severity of the winter which reduces the hunting and fishing; there are plenty of foods, but the lack of good fishing tools [i.e., baleen for lines and lashings and soapstone for sinkers]" (1927:114). This was the most important restriction on the security of the winter adaptation, for which fish were an important supplement to seals.

In the spring, when the bladder-nose (bearded) seals (*Cystophora cristata*) arrived on the South Greenland coast together with the East Greenland drift-ice, the South Greenlanders gathered on the islands off shore, camping in tents. We are told, according to Walløe, that it was common for some families to go north every second year, later returning to their homeland (1927:110). These travels were made possible by social arrangements between Eskimo families. Going north, southern families gathered with others on the west coast in summer camps, or *aasivik*. Here contacts were established between the two different Eskimo groups through marriage. As noted by the missionary H. C. Glahn, "by marriage between people in the South and on the West Coast, the hate, which occurs between these two groups, could be weakened . . . as the travels brought many people from the South to the North and *vice versa* to stay for one year or more at their kinsfolk, in-laws, and friends" (Glahn 1771:263).

The foregoing observations on demography, archeological materials, settlement patterns, and historical sources put us in a position to suggest a model that helps explain the development of Eskimo exchange systems in a period of climatic change between 1650 and 1750.

6. The West Greenland Exchange Economy

Figure 8 shows the resources included in the exchange system. In the South are found furs—especially fox and caribou—and driftwood; on the central west coast, in the Nuuk/Gothaab area, soapstone, caribou skins, and driftwood; in Disko Bay and southward to the Sisimiut/Holsteinsborg area, whaling products such as baleen, whalebone, and narwhal ivory. The assavik where these exchanges occurred are also shown. Aluk, east of Kap Farvel, is a well-known place where South Greenlanders and East Greenlanders met (Walløe 1927:97–98). Unartoq, west of Kap Farvel, is mentioned as a place where East Greenlanders came in May to fish for capelin (Walløe 1927:87). Nepisat Sound, west of Nuuk/Gothaab, is a famous place for South Greenlanders to have aasivik together with the local Eskimos (Egede 1925). Taseralik, a few miles north of Zuyd Bay, is a place where Eskimos from Disko Bay and Sisimiut/Holsteinsborg fished for halibut, and where the South Greenlanders stopped to participate in various activities before travelling farther north to winter at Sermermiut in Disko Bay (Glahn 1921; Olsen 1764; Egede 1925).

Few source materials describe the exchange system in effect before the South Greenlanders began travelling along the west coast. But to judge from Egede's diary (1925:174) and his "Greenland Description" (1925:329), we can assume the simple exchange model shown in figure 9, in which soapstone is traded for baleen and other whale products. Geographically, the movements of these materials meet at an aasivik, probably one in the Nepisat Sound or somewhere farther north.

The next stage of this model, which describes the situation around 1700, when the South Greenlanders began travelling north directly to the whaling locations, is shown in figure 10. That Dutch whalers entered Davis Strait and contacted the Eskimos is indicated archeologically, but nevertheless, the old Eskimo exchange system continued to function. The travels of the South

Figure 8 *Sources of Southwest Greenland Trade Commodities*
The summer camps shown became regional meeting places for Eskimos partici-
pating in the exchange system between South Greenland and the west coast
(Nuuk and Disko Bay).

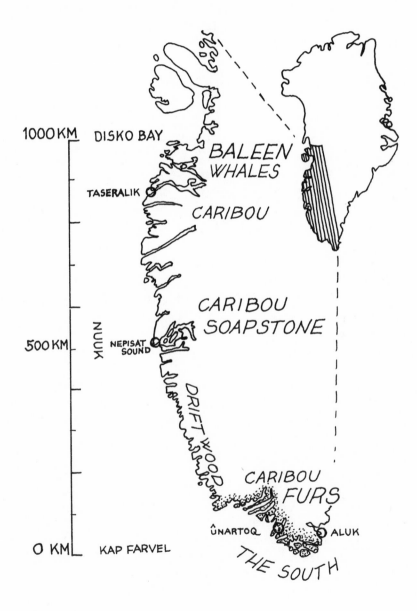

Figure 9 *West Greenland Coastal Exchange System before ca. 1600*

Figure 10 *West Greenland Exchange System, ca. 1700*
The arrows indicate the travel and trade patterns of the South Greenlanders.

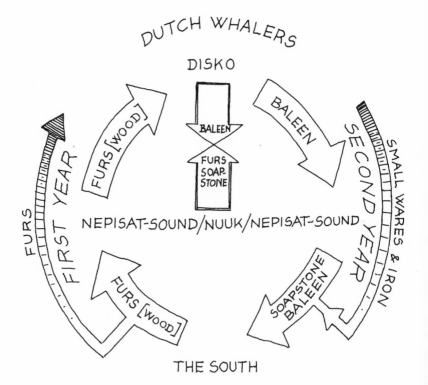

Greenlanders reported by Egede after the colonization in 1721 are illustrated by the four arrows in figure 10. From the South to the assivik in the Nuuk area and further north they brought furs, some of which were bartered to the Dutch, as shown by the small arrow on the left of figure 10. "Wood" (in brackets) indicates building materials needed in the north where no driftwood is found. Egede reports "in the Disko Bay one uses the narwhale teeth as tent poles, and whale bones for rafters and beams in the houses, because of lack of wood. Here are more whales than at Nepisat [at Holsteinsborg]" (1925:159). After wintering in Disko Bay, the South Greenlanders returned with baleen, of which some is exchanged for soapstone at Nuuk. To people in the south they bring back soapstone, baleen, and small wares such as iron, brass, glass beads, and other European materials (arrows to the right in figure 10). To get winter provisions, the families who arrived from the north would convert their goods into food with those who remained behind, as some families went north one year and others the next (Walløe 1927, *op. cit.*).

7. European Impact on West Greenland Eskimo Society

In 1733–34 a smallpox epidemic brought to Greenland from Europe ravaged the Gothaab district. As noted previously, very few families remained alive for many miles around Nuuk. Lars Dalager, a merchant in Nuuk, wrote in 1752 "in former times, some families in the Gothaab district made pots and lamps which they exchanged to people both south and north of the area" (1915:15). As indicated by the comment "in former times," the exchange system illustrated in figure 10 had disappeared. At this time the Southerners went into the fjords to get soapstone themselves, as Egede mentioned in 1735. As figure 11 diagrams, furs and driftwood were brought to the whaling areas and were exchanged for baleen. The latter was brought back to the South together with soapstone from the Nuuk area. In this third and final stage of the exchange economy, the importance of driftwood is again stressed, as Cranz noted that the Southerners exchanged this material for narwhale tusks, whale bones, and baleen (Cranz 1770, I:227). This statement is confirmed by Glahn (1771:261–271).

As an important commodity in the construction of the larger communal houses, driftwood, and its northward exchange, may be closely linked with the appearance of the communal house on the Greenland central west coast. It is logical to assume that the use of driftwood in building communal houses began first in Southern Greenland, where it is abundant, and to see the

Figure 11   *West Greenland Exchange System after 1733*
Only the South Greenlanders continue the exchange system at a time when
European influence is strong.

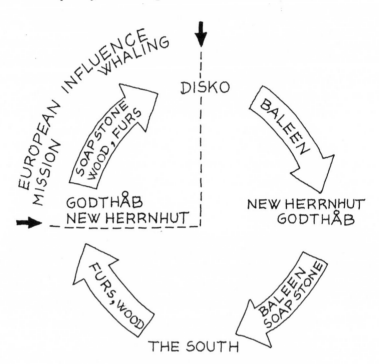

distribution of this dwelling type spreading from south to north along the
coast. At the time of colonization in 1721 no communal houses are reported
in the north, in the Disko Bay area (Egede 1925; Haan 1720). In the 1760s
Glahn mentions the Southerners as big householders who have their cooking
places in the entrance passageways, where they burn wood to conserve
blubber (1771:197). According to an anonymous source from the Kangamiut
area (Mathiassen 1931:50), "big houses" were introduced from the South to
"show the people here in the north how to build houses." The origin of this
house form, therefore, seems to lie to the south, dating to the time when the
first East Greenlanders came around Kap Farvel (Gulløv 1982b), or in the
Kangamiut area when the first Southerners went northwards to barter with
the Dutch whalers. New investigations in history and archeology will be
needed to solve this problem.

In figure 11, the dissolution of the Eskimo exchange system can be seen as resulting from European intervention into the traditional travelling activities of the South Greenlanders (black arrows in upper left half of the model). Intervention came from the Moravians who kept the Greenlanders, i.e., the Southerners, at the mission stations where they were baptised; and "nobody are so scrupulous as the Moravians and, according to this, very pernicious in the country . . ." (Glahn 1771:265). Consequently, the travels were stopped at New Herrnhut in the Gothaab district, and the Southerners no longer went north to the whaling grounds. With travel eliminated, the basic condition of the traditional Eskimo exchange system disappeared. In 1774 a new Danish colony, Julianehaab, was founded in the South, and in the same year the Moravians founded the mission station at Lichtenau, south of Juliane-haab, providing alternative means for the Eskimos of these regions to obtain resources formerly secured by barter in the north.

8. Summary

For one hundred years, from 1650 to 1750, a climatic change known as the "Little Ice Age" gave rise to the displacement of animals, especially whales, in the arctic and neighboring waters. Early historical sources provide information about events taking place in West Greenland during this period.

European whaling began in the Davis Strait at the end of the seventeenth century, and in 1721 Danish-Norwegian colonization began at 64 degrees north on the west coast of Greenland. After the founding of the colony, first-hand accounts on Eskimo society were made on a yearly basis.

The Eskimo population in South Greenland—today the municipalities of Qaqortoq, Narsaq, and Nanortalik—originated from two post-medieval Thule Eskimo groups, the West Greenlanders and the East Greenlanders. The East Greenlandic migration into the former Norse Eastern Settlement can be traced linguistically (Petersen n.d.). During the seventeenth century the subsistence patterns changed in South Greenland and some families travelled northwards along the west coast. The purpose of these travels was not migration away from areas of scarce food resources but to obtain raw materials needed to catch fish for winter use in a region rich in ecological resources. Especially important were the securing of baleen needed for fishing lines and lashing materials, and soapstone for sinkers, pots, and lamps. Social contacts were maintained by marriage arrangements with West Greenland families.

At the same time, a dependence on the European whalers was noticed at the whaling localities, where the Eskimo obtained iron, fish hooks, brass kettles and other goods. These commodities were exchanged primarily for Eskimo fur products.

The missionary activities during the eighteenth century stopped the Eskimo travels first at New Herrnhut. Later on the movements of the Eskimo population were reduced and took place only within the district of the colony itself.

REFERENCES CITED

Bandi, Hans-Georg and Jørgen Meldgaard
  1952 Archaeological Investigations on Clavering Ø/ Northwest Greenland. Meddelelser om Grønland 126(4).

Bobe, Louis
  1916 Christian Lund's Relation til Kong Frederik II om David Danell's tre Rejser til Grønland 1652–54. Danske Magazin 6 (2):202–32.
  1944 Hans Egede, Grønlands Missionaer og Kolonisator, Meddelelser om Grønland 129(1).

Cranz, David
  1770 Historie von Grönland, I–III. Leipzig: Barby.

Dalager, Lars
  1915 Grønlandske Relationer . . . 1752. Louis Bobe, ed. Det grønlandske Selskabs Skrifter 2.

Dekker, P.
  1974 De Amelander valvisvaart. It Beaken 6:206–223.
  1975 De Terschellinger arctische ruilhandel en walvisvangst. De grondleggers van de vaart op Straat Davis door Amsterdamse interesse. It Beaken 3:167–188.

Egede, Hans
  1925 Relationer fra Grønland 1721–36, and Det gamle Grønlands ny Perlustration eller Naturel-Histoire. Louis Bobe, ed. Meddelelser om Grønland 54.

Egede, Niels
  1939 Tredie Continuation of Relationerne . . . 1739 til 1743. Hother Osterman, ed. Meddelelser om Grønland 120.

Gad, Finn
   1970   The History of Greenland, I: Earliest Times to 1700. London: C. Hurst & Company.

Glahn, Henric Christopher
   1771   Anmaerkninger til de tre første Bøger af Hr. David Crantzes Historie om Grønland. Copenhagen.
   1921   Dagbøger for Aarene 1763–64, 1766–67 og 1767–68. Hother Osterman, ed. Det grønlandske Selskabs Skrifter 4.

Gulløv, H. C.
   1982a Eskimoens syn pa europaeeren. Grønland, 226–234. *Also published as:* The Eskimo's View of the European: The So-Called Norse Dolls and Other Questionable Carvings. Arctic Archeology 20(2).
   1982b Migration et diffusion—peuplement inuit de l'Ouest du Groenland a l'epoque post-medievale. Etudes/Inuit/Studies, 6(2):3–20.
   1983   Nuup Kommuneani Qangarnitsanik Eqqaassutit/Fortidsminder i Nuuk kommune. Nuuk.

Gulløv, H. C. and Hans Kapel
   1979/ Legend, History, and Archaeology. A study of the art of Eskimo narratives.
   80   Folk 21–22:347–380.

Haan, Lourens Feykes
   1720   Beschryving van de Straat Davids, benevens des zelven Inwooners, Zede, Gestalte, en Gewoonte, misgaders hunne Visvangst, en andere Handelingen. Amsterdam.

Hakluyt, Richard
   1589   The Principall Navigations Voiages & Discoveries of the English Nation. London.

Jochimson, Mathis
   1733   Anmaerkninger over Det Straet Daviske Cart. Manuscript, Library of the Navy, Copenhagen.

Mathiassen, Therkel
   1931   Ancient Eskimo Settlements in the Kangamiut Area. Meddelelser om Grønland 91.
   1933   Prehistory of the Angmagssalik Eskimos. Meddelelser om Grønland 92.
   1934   Contributions to the Archaeology of Disko Bay. Meddelelser om Grønland 93.
   1936a The former Eskimo Settlements on Frederik VI's Coast. Meddelelser om Grønland 109.

1936b The Eskimo Archaeology of Julianehaab District. Meddelelser om Grønland 118.

Meldgaard, Jørgen
1977 The Prehistoric Cultures in Greenland: Discontinuities in a Marginal Area. *In:* Continuity and Discontinuity in the Inuit Culture of Greenland. Hans P. Kylstra, ed. Groningen: University of Groningen.

Oesau, Wanda
1955 Hamburgs Grönlandfahrt auf Walfischfang und Robbenschlag vom 17.–19. Jahrhundert. Hamburg: Glückstadt-Hamburg.

Olsen, Ander
1764 En kort tabelle. I rubricher forfattet over Fasteland med Fiorden og øer fra Colonien Frederichaab og nordefter . . . Sukkertoppen 1764. Manuscript, Library of the Navy, Copenhagen.

Petersen, Robert
n.d. Some features Common to East and West Greenlandic in the Light of Dialect Relationships and the Latest Migration Theories. Arctic Anthropology XX.

Thorhallesen, Egil
1914 Beskrivelse over Missionerne i Grønlands Søndre Diskrikt . . . 1774–1775. Louis Bobe, ed. Det grønlandske Selskabs Skrifter 1.

Vibe, Christian
1967 Arctic Animals in Relation to Climatic Fluctuations. Meddelelser om Grønland 170(5).

Walløe, Peder Olsen
1927 Dagbøger fra hans Rejser i Grønland 1739–53. Louis Bobe, ed. Det grønlandske Selskabs Skrifter 5.

Zorgdrager, C. G.
1720 Bloyende Opkomst der Aloude en Hedendagsche Gronlansche Vischerey, etc. Amsterdam.

PART II

New England—the Move Inland:
Land, Politics, and Disease

Commentary on Part II

William W. Fitzhugh

South of the Strait of Belle Isle contact history took a different turn. Fundamentally, this resulted from the different environmental parameters involved, for here the land, rather than the waters, offered greater incentive to European enterprises, and communication was not hampered by sea ice, short seasons, and poor harbors. Animals were plentiful, and the larger Indian populations were capable of supplying more fur. And the land was fertile; much of it was cleared and under cultivation when Europeans arrived. In short, the potential of this region, with its more permissive climate and more extensive coast and hinterlands, offered opportunities for European exploitation that never could be realized in arctic regions. As these activities grew, attracting greater numbers of vessels, diverse financial interests, and eventually a wider range of goals, a fundamentally different course of impact evolved, one that would affect native history in ways never experienced by the more dispersed, isolated peoples of the Eastern Arctic.

It is neither possible nor necessary to detail here the geographical and cultural conditions of the Northeast at the time of contact. This has been done in a number of other publications, most notably in the many fine articles contained in the *Handbook of North American Indians* (Trigger 1976). In addition, readers should consult the many works on archeology, early history, ethnohistory, and historical ethnography on this region (e.g. Axtell 1981; Bailey 1969; Biggar 1922–36; Dobyns 1983; Innis 1940; Jennings 1975; Lescarbot 1907–11; Morison 1971; Quinn 1974, 1977, 1979; Salisbury 1982; Snow 1980; Trigger 1976; Trudel 1981; Winthrop 1853; among others). However, a few of the most salient differences will be mentioned in order to understand why the course of European-native contact history was so different here.

In terms of natural environment, the coastal regions south and west of Newfoundland were far more diverse geographically and ecologically than were those regions to the north. As we have noted, the northern regions were dominated by a harsh physical environment with high seasonal concentration of some important resources but little overall faunal and cultural diversity. By contrast, southern regions had a complex and diverse physical geography that provided easy access by boat to coastal locations as well as to those on the interior by way of numerous bays and rivers. Sea ice did not restrict movement except during the brief winter season in the most northern areas. Marine fauna—especially whales, seals, walrus, and a wide variety of fish—were abundant. The coastal zone had large runs of salmon, shad, eel, alewives, and sturgeon, as well as productive shellfish beds and waterfowl. Land game was equally abundant, moose, deer, and black bear being the principal species, and beaver and other fur-bearers were plentiful. The diversity and abundance of these animals, and their complex patterns of availability and seasonality insured a wider range of economic possibilities, and permitted a far greater number of cultural adaptations than was possible in the north. Finally, the presence of many wild plant foods and an established agricultural practice south of the Saco River in southern Maine provided a margin of storable food that introduced a new and critical factor—partial freedom from subsistence pursuits—that affected the conduct of social, political, and economic relations, both among native cultures and between them and European groups.

Native peoples had responded to these more generous conditions with a variety of local adaptations to island, coastal, riverine, plateau, and upland environments. Indian population densities were far higher than in subarctic and arctic regions, and a large number of different cultures were represented, many with sharply defined linguistic and tribal boundaries. Societies ranged from small, nomadic hunting groups to complex chiefdoms and regional confederacies controlled by tribal councils and powerful sachems, sagamores, and shamans. At the time of contact native groups interacted in various ways in coastal areas and inter-tribal economic exchange systems dispersed utilitarian as well as socially valuable commodities throughout the region, many destined for prestigious individuals. Native religious beliefs were expressed in a variety of complex burial traditions, with ancient roots and elaborate grave furnishings. Reciprocity was a fundamental social value affecting all relationships between spirits, between man and spirits, between individuals, and between social groups and tribes. The concept of reciprocal social exchange, frequently expressed by ritual gift-giving at the beginning of an encounter, whether hostile or friendly, extended to relationships between native groups and Europeans. However, this custom was frequently misunderstood and often was actively exploited in European dealings with Indians.

These conditions strongly influenced contact history and the effects of European contacts on cultures of this region. The environment was more complex, more variable, and more productive; cultures were more diverse, occupied smaller territories, and were accustomed to conflict. Practicality, reciprocity, and formal (though not actual) egalitarianism prevailed.

What happened when Europeans arrived on the scene? First of all, the areas that ultimately became New England and the Maritimes were not primary targets of European interest, which was focused both north and south of the region for most of the sixteenth century. Spanish and French Basque whaling and fishing began in the mid-1500s in and north of the Gulf of St. Lawrence (Trudel 1981), though French operations rapidly spread south to Cape Cod, with Champlain's explorations beginning in 1604. To the south, the Spanish, the English, and—in the Hudson River after 1608—the Dutch established entrepreneurial ventures. Direct European involvement in this region did not begin until after 1600.

What, then, is to be said of the preceding century? Unfortunately this is a period that is very poorly known either historically and archeologically. Initial contacts began at least as early as Verrazano's voyage of 1524, and perhaps earlier (Quinn 1977; Salisbury 1982:32). By the time Gosnold visited the coast of Maine in 1602, natives were wearing large copper breastplates and European costumes including waistcoats, breeches, hose, and shoes in seafashion style (Brereton 1906, in Bourque and Whitehead 1985). Bourque and Whitehead argue that these and other materials had been made available to peoples of the Maine coast by native Souriquois (Micmac) and Etchemin (Malecite) middlemen travelling in wooden shallops from the Nova Scotia and Gulf of St. Lawrence regions, where they had obtained these goods from fishermen and traders.

Clearly this situation in the Maritimes region resembles the development of native trade noted in seventeenth- and eighteenth-century Labrador Inuit society. Obviously, widespread changes in native institutions were also occurring as individuals, groups, and tribes adjusted to the many new opportunities and dangers arising from European presence (Hoffman 1961; Salisbury 1982; Trudel 1981). Although such questions have not been explored archeologically here, future attention should be directed at uncovering evidence of similar kinds of native-based social and economic developments as have been suggested for Labrador in this stage of contact history. It seems unlikely that documentary research alone will suffice.

In its historical development, the Northeast may be seen as having undergone a period of exploration and initial exploitation similar to that of the arctic regions previously described. The Basque fishermen who rapidly deluged the Gulf of St. Lawrence after its discovery by Cabot soon began to establish shore stations for drying fish and maintaining equipment. Fishing and trading operations persisted side by side throughout the century, with different emphases in different regions. Through time, however, the numbers of vessels increased and trading, which diversified after the beaver pelting process was established in the market around mid-century, became ascendent. Thus throughout the 1500s and well into the 1600s a floating or seasonal trade predominated through the New England and Maritimes region. Direct and sustained interaction with native peoples did not begin until the mid-1600s. Thus far, there is some order in acculturation history as we proceed southward and forward in time; the patterns established for European-native contact in the arctic seem to be replicated with some degree of accuracy in the south as well.

The second set of papers presented in this volume represents a series of contact situations in this general region, specifically in southern New England and upstate New York, that carry the acculturation trajectory farther along in "developmental" time, i.e., out of the initial contact phase and into a more advanced stage of European-native interaction. The topics addressed in these papers include seventeenth-century Narragansett religious ritual, land title shifts on the central Connecticut frontier, and political developments leading toward establishment of the League of the Iroquois. While it is tempting to present these case studies in some "unilineal" or "evolutionary" framework with regard to the intensity, stage, or nature of European contact, I have resisted this impulse in favor of a geographical arrangement, coast to interior, east to west, simply because it seems evident that there is no clear (as yet) established sequence or hierarchy of acculturation processes that would do justice to the specific environments, histories, and contemporary situations pertaining to these particular cases.

However it is important to note that both the Narragansett and the Connecticut cases take place in the mid-1600s, when Indian groups of these regions were involved with the colonization phase of European involvement in New England; permanent bridgeheads had been established at Plimoth in

1620, and settlers and traders had expanded up the river valleys, penetrating the Indian lands and seeking to enlarge and expand their spheres of influence and opportunities. While the process of European expansion is not at issue here, one cannot proceed without recalling the devastation wrought upon native cultures in many of these areas by the epidemics of the early and mid-1600s. These epidemics greatly weakened (and in some cases, destroyed) the native societies that existed in these areas and permitted the void to be exploited and filled by the disease-resistant European settlers who were beginning to stream into the new lands (Dobyns 1983; Salisbury 1982). We must also note the rapid reversal of roles, from native supremacy to European subjugation, that occurred at this time, often within the space of a few years or a decade, and rarely taking more than a generation.

The first of these papers concerns the response of the Narragansett to changing conditions of this period. The authors describe a Narragansett cemetery dating to 1650–1670 that has been recently excavated and is being interpreted in collaboration with Indian descendants. This is essentially a preliminary report on one of the few archeological projects currently under-way in the Northeast that provides information on religious development in an historic-period native site. As one of the few Northeastern Indian tribes which survived the devastating impact of European diseases in southern New England and has preserved its identity intact, the Narragansett are an excellent subject for archeological, historical, and ethnographic study. This paper provides information on seventeenth-century Narragansett religion, material culture, demography, and health. As a bypassed enclave of native peoples behind the European frontier of the day, the Narragansett show the effect of reduced physical fitness from exposure to European diseases. Evidence from this cemetery and others (Simmons 1970, 1978) also documents the response of Narragansett religious institutions to the stressful times of early seventeenth-century European contact through ceremonial intensification involving burial of large quantities of valuable European commodities. When the Narragansetts were spared destruction by the epidemic of 1616–18, their belief that this sacrifice of European goods to the god Cautantowwit was responsible for their survival set the stage for the religious intensification documented in these studies. The Narragansett case, while presenting a classic opportunity to investigate this acculturation response, is not, however, unique. Cemeteries and ossuaries dating to early contact periods are known for many cultures and regions in Eastern North America. Although their excavation remains socially and ethically sensitive, these sites are the most important sources of information for reconstructing early Indian history and for studying social process and change.

The second paper presents a case vital to the understanding of culture change in cases of land tenure shift. Shifts in the use-rights and ownership of land is probably the single most important feature of culture contact in North America, and it was particularly important in the disappearance of Indian groups from the East. Thomas documents the process leading up to title shifts from Indian groups of the middle Connecticut River valley to traders and settlers in this region. Social and economic issues play a large part in this process, as do the disparate nature of the native groups, their lack of effective leadership, the multi-faceted English "entrepreneurial" approach (as contrasted with the Spanish "institutional" approach, discussed in Part IV), and the presence of competing European groups in surrounding areas. This paper clearly demonstrates the complexity of European and native interests involved in a mid-century frontier situation. Although it is questionable whether these events and processes could be identified from archeological data alone, Thomas makes a strong case for European influence on native subsistence and settlement pattern changes, and these data are eminently recognizable in the ground. The rich data sources for this area make it an excellent target for European-Indian acculturation studies (e.g. McEwan and Mitchem 1984).

The final paper in this section concerns the development of political structure among the Iroquois tribes of New York State. Englebrecht argues that tribal organization and the League of Iroquois originated from developments beginning in prehistoric times, and that these trends were consolidated during the sixteenth and seventeenth centuries under prolonged, indirect European influence. These arguments are based on ceramic collections, settlement pattern data, and oral traditions. In considering these data it is important to note that the geographic location of these Iroquois was far from centers of early European expansion, which resulted in their being insulated from the worst effects of disease and tribal disintegration that occurred in more coastal regions. This enabled many Iroquois groups to maintain their landbase, native economy, and socio-political system, and to engage in relations with other Indian groups and outsiders in a more selective fashion.

An important component in future studies of Iroquois development hopefully will include the broader role of European material culture in social and economic change observed in mortuary data available from this region. These data are particularly strong, as are the data on prehistoric cultural development. The Iroquois, therefore, present exceptionally rich materials for archeological investigations of early contact matters.

REFERENCES CITED

Axtell, James
1981 The European and the Indian. London: Oxford University Press.

Bailey, Alfred
1969 The Conflict of European and Eastern Algonkian Cultures 1504–1700: A Study in Canadian Civilization. Toronto: The University of Toronto Press.

Biggar, Henry P., ed.
1922– The Works of Samuel de Champlain. 7 Vols. Toronto: Champlain Society.
1936

Bourque, Bruce J., and Ruth H. Whitehead
1985 Tarrantines and the Introduction of European Trade Goods in the Gulf of Maine. Ethnohistory (in press).

Dobyns, Henry F.
1983 Their Number Become Thinned: Native American Population Dynamics in Eastern North America. Knoxville: University of Tennessee Press.

Innis, Harold A.
1940 The Cod Fisheries: The History of an International Economy. New Haven: Yale University Press.

Jennings, Francis
1975 The Invasion of America. Indians, Colonialism, and the Cant of Conquest. Chapel Hill: University of North Carolina Press.

Lescarbot, Marc
1907– The History of New France. Toronto: The Champlain Society.
1911

McEwan, Bonnie G. and Jeffrey M. Mitchem
1984 Indian and European Acculturation in the Eastern United States as a Result of Trade. North American Archaeologist 5(4):271–285.

Morison, Samuel Eliot
1971 The European Discovery of America: The Northern Voyages. New York: Oxford University Press.

Quinn, David Beers

1974   England and the Discovery of America, 1481–1620. New York: Alfred A. Knopf.

1977   North America from Earliest Discovery to First Settlements. New York: Harper and Row.

1979   New American World: A Documentary History of North America to 1612. Vol. 3. David B. Quinn, Alison Quinn, and Susan Hillier, eds. New York: Arno Press and Hector Bye, Inc.

Salisbury, Neal

1982   Manitou and Providence: Indians, Europeans, and the Making of New England, 1500–1643. New York: Academic Press.

Simmons, William S.

1970   Cautantowwit's House, an Indian Burial Ground on the Island of Conanicut in Narragansett Bay. Providence: Brown University Press.

1978   Narragansett. *In:* Handbook of North American Indians, 15. Bruce G. Trigger, ed. pp. 190–197. Washington, D.C.: Smithsonian Institution.

Snow, Dean R.

1980   The Archaeology of New England. New York: Academic Press.

Trigger, Bruce G.

1976   The Children of Aataentsic. Montreal: McGill-Queen's University Press.

1978   Handbook of North American Indians, 15. Bruce G. Trigger, ed. Washington, D.C.: Smithsonian Institution.

Trudel, Francois

1981   Inuit, Amerindians and Europeans: A Study of Interethnic Economic Relations on the Canadian Southeastern Seaboard (1500–1800). Ph.D. dissertation, University of Connecticut.

Winthrop, John

1853   The History of New England from 1630–1649. J. Savage, ed. Boston: Little, Brown, and Co.

Preliminary Biocultural Interpretations from a Seventeenth-Century Narragansett Indian Cemetery in Rhode Island

Paul A. Robinson, Marc A. Kelley, and Patricia E. Rubertone

A B S T R A C T

Excavations by Brown University and the Rhode Island Historical Preservation Commission at a seventeenth-century Narragansett Indian cemetery (RI-1000) in Rhode Island during 1982 and 1983 recovered the skeletal remains and grave associations of fifty-six individuals. This paper provides background on the region and the project, describes the composition of the cemetery, presents preliminary findings, and sets forth areas for future research concerning religious, economic, and social implications of the mortuary data. Although tuberculosis was widespread and the grave associations were predominantly European, the burial form and cemetery organization suggest a strong adherence to traditional mortuary practice and persistence of Narragansett Indian religious beliefs.

1. Issues and Problems

T. J. Brasser summarizes the major problem confronted by students of the contact period: "The history of the Indians is hidden behind that of the European traders and colonists, and only the main outline of what was happening can be discerned" (1978:82). With that caveat, Brasser presents a generalized model describing the effects of European contact upon Indian groups in the Northeast. Briefly stated, contact began with an initial friendly Indian reaction followed by a period of suspicion and hostility provoked by European mistreatment of the Indians. Epidemic disease and the abuse of liquor is then thought to have reduced and demoralized native populations. Remaining Indians then questioned their religious beliefs, adopted European technology, and through the fur trade became dependent upon the European market system. Economic dependence resulted in the steady deterioration of native technology and finally in poverty and malnutrition following the eventual loss of the fur trade.

This model is based upon the observations of Europeans who for the most part poorly understood native culture or simply neglected to record pertinent observations. Limitations of the written records are widely recognized (Brasser 1978; Jennings 1975; Kupperman 1982). Since 1950 ethnohistory has been hailed as an approach to embrace the written European interpretations as well as the native by using anthropological approaches to understand and interpret primary source materials. While the ethnohistoric approach offers an improved understanding of the contact period (Salisbury 1982), the strength of its conclusions remains limited by the biases inherent in European writings. In addition, archeological investigations have often been conducted without the benefit of modern techniques in artifact conservation, osteological analysis, soil floatation, palynology, and chemistry. Finally, most analyses of the contact period are conducted without involving living descendents of the native group.

The approach used at RI-1000 integrates several disciplines, involves the Narragansett Tribe, and draws upon anthropological concepts and theory, which are used to re-examine the historical and ethnohistorical interpretation of the contact period. While specific components of Brasser's model may apply to specific instances of culture contact, it is clear in our study of the Narragansett Indian tribe in the seventeenth century that some of Brasser's model is not applicable. For example, epidemic disease was not an important factor in reducing Narragansett population (Cook 1973). It is much more likely that tuberculosis and perhaps pneumonia were responsible for causing a slow but steady population reduction. Also, it is apparent that religious beliefs remained intact or perhaps were intensified. Similarly, the role of European technology, the extent to which it was adopted, and the extent to which the Narragansetts became dependent upon the world market system have not been established.

The larger implications of our work for improving the understanding of seventeenth-century culture contact will be discussed in future publications. However, one misinterpretation can be clarified at this time. In *New England Frontier: Puritans and Indians, 1620–1675,* Alden T. Vaughan notes the paucity of Narragansett conversions to Christianity, and the generally low numbers of conversions in New England as a whole. These figures are low, he indicates, partly because the "Narragansetts were so intractable," and partly because Roger Williams was preoccupied with other matters (Vaughan 1979:303). Vaughan then goes on to explain how "characteristics that were deeply rooted in Indian society and culture also helped thwart the Puritan missionaries . . . even the best Indian converts rarely expended the kind of energy essential to fulfillment of the Puritan program [or] to earn the surplus that would . . . insure them a more integral role in the white man's society" (Vaughan 1979:305–306).

While Vaughan's observation about the paucity of conversions is correct, anthropological interpretation of the archeological data at RI-1000 offers a more comprehensive understanding of Indian religious values during the seventeenth century. As a result of this research we conclude that Narragansett religious and mortuary practices persisted or perhaps intensified during the seventeenth century and that this mortuary behavior was an expression of group solidarity and cohesiveness against the cultural and biological pressures of the European invasion. We will return to this point later, but offer it here as yet one more example of the need for a basic re-examination of the processes of culture contact during the seventeenth century in New England, such as that now underway (Axtell 1981; Cronon 1983; Salisbury 1982).

2. The Setting

2.1. Before 1600

The coastal region of southern New England is characterized by river valleys that since the last glaciation have been transformed into tidal estuaries. Narragansett Bay, the focal point for Narragansett settlement and subsistence, became fully estuarine by approximately 3000 B.P. (Artemel, *et al.* 1983). The fertile sandy loam soils along the Bay and the numerous fresh water springs, small tidal estuaries, and salt ponds provided a diverse subsistence base that by 1000 A.D. included hunting, fishing, shellfish collecting, plant collecting, and agriculture (Salwen 1978; the Thomas-Sekataus 1976).

There are few archeological data on settlement patterns prior to contact with the Europeans and the written observations of individuals such as Verrazano in 1524 and Roger Williams in 1643. Williams (1936:46–47) described a seasonal pattern of coastal family farming settlements and interior winter sites. The Thomas-Sekataus (1976:9) observe that these sites were villages composed of aggregated families.

The archeological evidence does not refute the applicability of Williams's observations for the period prior to European contact. Inland sites of substantial size have been located but await further investigation. One example is a 35-acre Late Archaic inland settlement located behind the coastal moraine along the Chipuxet River (Morenon 1982). The site may be representive of the later winter settlements described by Williams and the Thomas-Sekataus.

2.2. Seventeenth-Century Narragansett Culture

The trading and exploring voyages of Adriaen Block and other Dutch explorers between 1612 and 1614 provide data on many Indian groups between Narragansett Bay and western Long Island (Salwen 1978). In addition, William Bradford, the Governor of Plimouth Colony, noted several excursions into Narragansett territory beginning in 1622. The writings of Roger Williams, however, are the most detailed primary sources on seventeenth-century Narragansett culture. Williams's study of Narragansett language and customs, published in 1643, is the first English language ethnography of an American Indian people (Simmons 1978).

In Williams's and other European accounts, the Narragansetts were distinguished from other New England Indian groups on several counts. They were the most populous remaining New England tribe in the early 1600s. Unlike many other Indian groups, the Naragansetts were not affected by the diastrous epidemic of 1617–1619, which killed thousands. According to Wampanoag observers, the Narragansetts were saved from the epidemic by a ritual that involved the burning of their material possessions. The Narragansetts are also thought to have remained outside the effects of that epidemic because of the distance they maintained from infected tribes (E. Sekatau 1984). The Narragansetts were also characterized by their ability in industry and trade; they were skilled craftsmen noted for their production of shell and metal objects (Simmons 1978).

Narragansett subsistence was based on the cultivation of corn, beans and squash, the hunting of game, and the collection of forest and marine resources (Simmons 1978; the Thomas-Sekataus 1976). They followed a restricted pattern of seasonal movements tied directly to the utilization of these resources. According to Williams (1936:46–47), the most important seasonal move was from summer fields near the sea to winter quarters in wooded valleys. Temporary camps were set up for the hunting season, which began at the time of the harvest and extended into winter. These camps were occupied by hunters and by their wives and children if the hunting range was not too far away. In general, women performed most agricultural tasks, including planting, hoeing, and preparations for the harvest.

In religious matters, the Narragansett chief practitioner was a powwow (medicine man) who was called to his role by vision experience or in a dream. The powwow presided over calendrical rituals and rites performed in the event of drought, famine, sickness, war, and other matters. These rituals were addressed to Cautantowwit, the creator, or chepi, an appearing spirit, perhaps the spirit of a deceased person with which the powwow had direct rapport. After death, the Narragansetts believed that souls returned to Cautantowwit's house in the southwest where they continued in an afterlife similar to life on earth (the Thomas-Sekataus 1976; Williams 1936:130, 137).

In political matters, the Narragansetts were ruled by a pair of lineally related sachems, one older and one younger. Sachems were responsible for protecting their followers, allocating land, providing for the poor, and administering punishment for wrongdoers (Simmons 1978:193). Although they were the strongest single Indian group in southern New England in 1675, the Narragansetts did not immediately enter King Philip's War, but attempted to maintain neutrality. The Narragansetts did, however, shelter Wampanoag from the east, whom the Sachem Canonchet refused to turn over to the English. As a result, the colonists invaded Narragansett country in December 1675. In the massacre in the Great Swamp, the Narragansetts lost many men, women, and children who were killed when their palisaded settlement was burned.

After King Philip's War ended in 1676, the remaining Narragansett Indians were dispersed: some were sold in Carribean slavery or worked locally for white families who were awarded land and Indian labor for serving in the war; some settled with the Niantics, who had remained neutral during the war; and others moved west into New York and Canada (Simmons 1978).

3. Excavation

RI-1000 is a seventeenth-century Narragansett Indian cemetery containing the remains of fifty-six individuals located in North Kingstown, Rhode Island (figure 1). Excavations at this site, conducted between June 1982 and September 1983, represent the first systematic, inter-disciplinary excavation of a New England Indian cemetery. As such, they were organized from a biocultural perspective and involved archeologists, a physical anthropologist, a palynologist, and specialists in soil science, chemistry, geology, and ento-

Figure 1. *Map of Southern New England Showing Locations of RI-1000, West Ferry, and Burr's Hill*

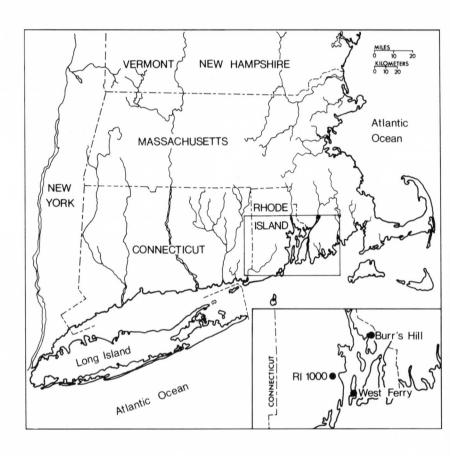

mology. In addition, planning was developed in consultation with the Narragansett Indian Chief Sachem and Tribal Council. The Chief Sachem and Council designated a tribal member to work with the project on a daily basis during fieldwork and as liaison during analysis. This systematic interdisciplinary approach and the participation of the Narragansett Chief Sachem and Tribal Council have facilitated synthesis of perspectives on seventeenth-century history and the dynamics of culture contact.

In June 1982, the Rhode Island Historical Preservation Commission was notified that Indian graves had been accidently disturbed by bulldozing on private land. The cemetery was unmarked, not recorded in the state files, and unknown to the Narragansett Tribe. Following its accidental discovery, the Historical Preservation Commission, the landowner, and representatives from the Tribal Council met to evaluate the damage and develop a strategy for protecting the remaining graves.

All parties agreed that preservation in place was preferred, but that if preservation proved impossible or unwise, archeological excavations would be undertaken. A combination of soil coring and small shovel scrapings established that much of the cemetery remained intact and that between thirty and fifty individual remains were undisturbed. While the site was being delineated, the disturbed soils were sifted, leading to the recovery of the skeletal remains of at least nine individuals and their grave items (Robinson and Gustafson 1983).

When the site was delineated and the disturbed materials were evaluated and placed in the context of the development plans, it became clear that preservation in place would be difficult and probably not wise. In the first place, a shopping center was planned for construction directly over the cemetery. Of even greater concern was the fact that the artifacts recovered from the disturbed portion were so important and valuable that any remaining portions of the site would become the target of vandalism.

Following the initial salvage efforts of 1982, the cemetery was covered with fill. Preservation alternatives were discussed with the Narragansett Chief Sachem and Tribal Council and with the landowner. Archeological recovery of the entire site was agreed upon, and a funding proposal was developed by the Rhode Island Historical Preservation Commission, Brown University, and the National Park Service. A research team was assembled before fieldwork began to assure that data suitable for an interdisciplinary approach would be collected. In particular, the needs of palynology, physical anthropology, conservation and archeology were addressed.

During fieldwork, sediment samples for pollen analysis were collected to test the differential pollen preservation potential on brass, iron, and ceramic items, and from the grave linings and textiles. Soil samples were taken to evaluate the relationship between skeletal preservation and soil pH, and for flotation. In addition, the physical anthropological studies were conducted to determine sex and age. Sex was determined with Phenice's visual technique for the *os pubus* (Kelley 1978; Phenice 1969), the sciatic notch, parturition scars, the size and ruggedness of the skull, and the overall robusticity and morphology of the post-cranial skeleton. Age was determined using epiphyseal closure, dental eruption and calcification, pubic symphysis morphology, dental wear, vertebral osteophyte formation, and cranial suture closure. Bones were measured *in situ* so that existing stature formulae could be evaluated. Finally, a professional conservator helped conserve perishable materials.

All the graves were mapped during the first two weeks of the field season, revealing a striking order within the cemetery. Rows of burials were oriented perpendicular to the general southwest orientation of the cemetery and, with one exception, the head of each grave pointed to the southwest (figure 2). Simmons (1970) noted a similar pattern in a Narragansett burial ground located several miles east of RI-1000 on Conanicut Island. The orientation is no doubt an important symbol of the Narragansett belief that Cautantowwit, the creator, resides in the southwest.

Excavation revealed individuals buried in a tightly or loosely flexed position; most lay on their right side, facing east, with the top of the cranium pointing toward the home of Cautantowwit. In general, grave items were positioned in the areas east of the individuals.

4. Preliminary Findings and Discussion

4.1. Biological Factors

In general, the biological profile suggests a population under stress. Analyses of the demographic composition of RI-1000 leave little doubt that certain individuals were excluded from interment. In particular, fetal remains and infants less than two and one-half years of age are entirely absent. Furthermore, while subsequent age categories are well represented, adult females outnumber males by approximately two to one. While this may, to some

Figure 2. *Plan of Burials at RI-1000*
Dotted line indicates probable locations of burials displaced in 1982.

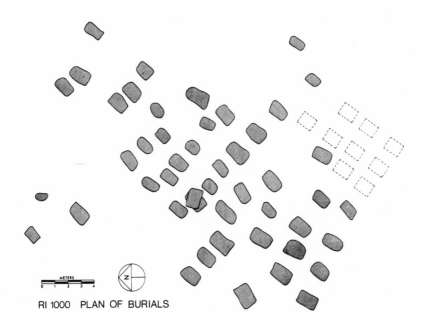

RI 1000   PLAN OF BURIALS

Table 1. *Breakdown of RI-1000 Remains by Age and Sex*

	Male	Female	Uncertain*
Fetal	0	0	0
NB–2.5	0	0	0
2.5–3.0	0	0	1
3.1–4.9	0	0	9
5.0–9.9	0	0	3
10.0–14.9	3	6	
15.0–19.9	2	6	
20.0–21.9	1	1	
25.0–29.9	1	3	
30.0–34.9	5	3	
35.0–39.9	2	2	
40.0–44.9	0	4	
45.0–49.9	1	0	
50+	0	3	
Total	15	28	13

*It has been possible to determine sex for seven of the thirteen sub-adults under age 10 using associated grave goods and pelvic morphology (Boucher 1955; Weaver 1980); six of these are females, one is male.

extent, be explained by polygynous practices (the Thomas-Sekataus 1976), it is also possible that some males died or were buried away from home.

The breakdown by age and sex is presented in table 1. After adjustment of the mortality profile to counter the effects of infant underrepresentation, it still remains clear that this group was experiencing considerable stress. Adolescents make up about 28 percent of the cemetery, in contrast to pre-contact adolescent mortality levels of between 2 and 5 percent (Kelley 1980; Saul 1972; Ubelaker 1974). As discussed below, the probable source of much of this stress was widespread tuberculosis.

The distribution of ages at death also contrasts markedly with another Narragansett cemetery in Rhode Island, the West Ferry site (Simmons 1970). Figure 3 indicates differences between the two cemeteries, the West Ferry site corresponding more closely to pre-contact frequencies. Preliminary artifact analysis suggests that RI-1000 was used primarily between 1650 and 1670, and perhaps later (Turnbaugh 1984a, 1984b). The West Ferry site may have

Figure 3. *Histogram Showing Ages at Death of Individuals at RI-1000 and West Ferry*

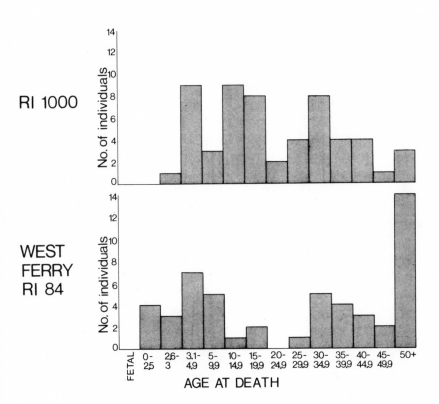

been used as much as a generation earlier, from 1620 to 1660. Thus, the ages of death at West Ferry may reflect a period prior to the sustained impact of European-introduced and aggravated disease in Narragansett country.

Pathological analysis at RI-1000 indicates the presence of the following endemic morbidities: arthritis, osteoporosis, non-specific infections, minor congenital defects, and vitamin C deficiency. Evidence of iron-deficiency anemia, major trauma, and cancer is absent. One young female had a skeletal lesion highly suggestive of treponemal infection. In view of the seventeenth-century contact period context of this cemetery, the infection was very likely venereal syphilis.

As measured by skeletal lesions, tuberculosis appears to have been extremely prevalent at RI-1000. Eight individuals displayed smooth-walled destructive lesions of the lower thoracic and lumbar vertebral bodies; in several cased only one-third of the body remained. Twelve individuals, four of whom had concomitant spinal lesions, exhibited swelling or periostitic lesions on the internal surface of the ribs. The association between rib periostitis and pulmonary tuberculosis in skeletal collections has been documented previously (Kelley and Micozzi 1984). Finally, three individuals, two of whom had concomitant spinal or rib lesions, suffered from tubercular arthritis of the hip. These lesions are oval-shaped, smooth-walled, and penetrate the cartilaginous plate between the femoral head and neck in subadults. A breakdown by age and sex reveals that two cases were in children, seven in adolescents, and eight in adults. Both sexes were equally affected. Collectively, the spine, rib and hip lesions, along with the demographic distribution, strongly favor a diagnosis of skeletal tuberculosis.

With a total of seventeen out of fifty-six persons, or 30 percent, exhibiting tubercular skeletal lesions, it seems clear that this disease was very widespread compared to pre-contact times. An analysis of over fourteen hundred pre-Columbian Indian remains from the Indian Knoll (Kentucky) and Grasshopper ruins (Arizona), for example, failed to produce a single case of skeletal tuberculosis (Kelley 1980). This is not to say that tuberculosis was absent from pre-contact American inhabitants; it did occur (see Allison et al. 1973; Buikstra 1982), but at substantially lower rates. We are currently investigating several physical and cultural factors that may have influenced the incidence of tuberculosis among the seventeenth-century Narragansett Indians. Some of the factors being considered include European contact, introduced domesticated animals (e.g., cattle), and altered dietary and subsistence patterns, with corresponding increase in local population densities and respiratory complications resulting from wood smoke inhalation. Severe dental disease also exceeds pre-contact patterns (tables 2 and 3).

Roger Williams and later Richard Smith operated a trading post near this cemetery from 1637 or 1638 to King Philip's War in 1675. The introduction of trade items such as refined sugar or molasses, and an increase in starch (especially maize and flour) in the diet are under consideration as factors in this high level of dental disease.

The skeletal analysis suggests that the Narragansetts were suffering from disease to the extent that adolescents, often characterized by low mortality rates, were dying in unusually high numbers. Given this abnormal situation and the overwhelming numbers of European (see figures 4 and 5) vs. Indian

Table 2. *Number of Individuals with Carious Teeth at RI-1000* *

Age	Number (Affected/Group Total)	Percentage Affected
Subadults (0–16 years)	12/21	57.1
Males (16+ years)	10/11	90.9
Females (16+ years)	19/21	90.5
Total	41/53	77.3

*Does not include burials 5, 8, 54.

Table 3. *Frequency of Antemortem Tooth Loss in Males and Females*

	Anterior Teeth		Posterior Teeth		Total	
Element	Number*	%	Number*	%	Number*	%
Males (N=11)						
Maxilla	4/39	7	31/100	31		
Mandible	10/66	15	20/110	18		
Total					63/335	19.4
Females (N=18)						
Maxilla	17/108	16	76/180	42		
Mandible	44/108	41	90/180	50		
Total					227/576	39.4
Overall Tooth Loss (Male and Female)					292/911	32.1

*Missing/Potential Total

Figure 4. *Artifacts Recovered from RI-1000*
The iron horseshoe and claw hammer were found with an adult male (not shown are iron scrap and wedges suggesting presence of a blacksmith's tool kit). The latten seal-and-baluster spoon (center) and the slipped-in-the-stalk spoon (right) both have tin-wash coating, a post-1650 feature, and were found associated with adolescent females. (Photo: G. Gustafson, Rhode Island Historical Preservation Commission)

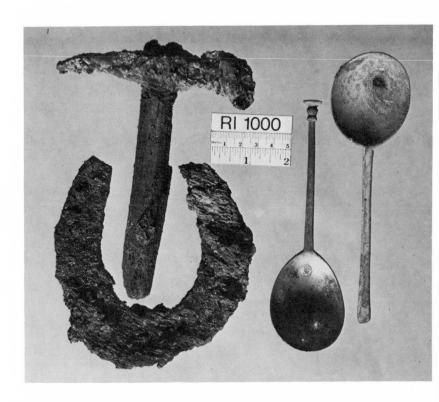

Figure 5. *Containers Recovered from RI-1000*

The European wine bottle, (left) ca. 1660–1670, was found with adult female. The German stoneware pitcher (right) was found in displaced, bulldozed soil. The seal is dated 1630 and has been preliminarily identified by J. Bradley of the Massachusetts Historical Commission as City of Amsterdam. (Photo: G. Gustafson, Rhode Island Historical Preservation Commission)

artifacts in the graves (documented in the lists below), the overall organization, orientation, and uniformity of the cemetery (see figure 2) is striking.

Artifacts discovered during the excavation, subjected to preliminary sorting based on their apparent origin, revealed a substantial emphasis on European objects among grave inclusions at RI-1000.

Objects of European
origin included:

17 latten spoons
14 wine and apothecary bottles
10 clay pipes
3 ceramic vessels
20 Jesuit and signet rings
3 iron vessels
6 brass kettles
13 bells
23 buttons
10 hoes and adzes
2 scissors
3 brass cups
36 brass hoops
15 iron hooks
11 blacksmith tool kit
ca. 6,350 glass beads
2 brass boxes
8 iron knives
nails
1 brass buckle
1 wood frame mirror
5 lead shot

1 strike-a-light
1 glass lens
2 brass finial
European textiles

Indian-produced or
-modified objects included:

4 brass hair ornaments
7 brass spoons
3 brass rings
1 brass bracelet
ca. 2,150 brass beads*
ca. 4,800 shell beads
1 bone comb
3–4 ceremic vessels
2 stone molds
5 stone pestles
1 soapstone pipe
6 graphite pieces
14 whetstones
native-woven textiles

*Some are probably European-made.

4.2. Mortuary Practices

The use of mortuary practice to affirm cultural values is well documented. Raymond Firth noted in his study of the Tikopia that religious beliefs about the fate of the soul express social continuity. "It is a reassurance that not merely the personality, but also the society, goes on. When the society is not threatened by external forces this aspect is not so significant. But if it is so threatened, then the emphasis of the eschatology upon continuity may become critical" (Firth 1955:23). Similarly, in a recent study of acculturation in Brazil, Gross et al. (1979) noted that in many instances indigenous features of religious and social life were preserved or intensified after western contact.

Our preliminary interpretations of RI-1000 suggest that Narragansett mortuary and religious practices persisted and perhaps intensified during the seventeenth century. These interpretations are supported by examining the archeological correlates of Narragansett religion at the West Ferry cemetery (1620–1660) and RI-1000 (1650–1670).

The chief religious practitioner was the medicine man, who presided over calendrical rituals and rites performed in response to drought, famine, sickness, and war (Simmons 1978). In addition, the Thomas-Sekataus (1976:4) noted that the medicine man "was called upon to start all gatherings whether it be a marriage . . . or burial of a dignitary." After death the soul was believed to return to Cautantowwit in the southwest, where it continued in an afterlife similar to life on earth (Simmons 1978). The journey of the soul to Cautantowwit's house was a passage between states of existence, as was birth. Individuals were buried in a flexed posture to symbolize this transition (Brown and Sekatau 1983, personal communication; Simmons 1970).

The burial of an individual was supervised by a respected tribal member, the mockuttàsuit or powwow (Sekatau, personal communication; Williams 1936:202). The deceased was placed on mats, wrapped in blankets, and buried with objects consistent with his or her occupation, preferences, and status. These objects accompanied the individual on the journey to Cautantowwit's house (Simmons 1970). The archeological correlates of these religious beliefs and mortuary practices occur at the levels of individual and cemetery. For individual remains, body posture and grave or body orientation are important. Within a cemetery these attributes can be evaluated in terms of their overall homogeneity or heterogeneity. If Narragansett religious beliefs and mortuary practice persisted during the seventeenth century, one would expect little variation through time in the attributes of posture and orientation. This persistence hypothesis can be tested by comparing RI-1000 with another Narragansett Indian cemetery, the West Ferry site. The West Ferry site was used between 1620–1660; RI-1000 was used between 1650 and 1670. The two cemeteries thus provide information on mortuary practice for much of the direct and sustained contact period in Rhode Island.

Both cemeteries show remarkable homogeneity. Of forty-eight individuals for which orientation was discernable at West Ferry, forty-four pointed to the southwest, and four to the south. Of the forty-seven individuals in RI-1000 whose orientation could be ascertained, forty-six pointed southwest and one pointed south. All of the individuals in both cemeteries were in a flexed posture. This similarity in orientation and posture and the importance of these attributes as symbols of Narragansett Indian religious beliefs indicate a persistence in religious beliefs during the time these cemeteries were used, approximately 1620 to at least 1670.

Of additional interest is the increased efficiency in the use of space at RI-1000. Individuals are generally placed more closely together at RI-1000, each having an average 5.8 square meters of space, in contrast to 7.7 square meters per individual at West Ferry. This increased efficiency suggests a more rigorous attention to detail and perhaps an intensification of mortuary practice, as suggested by Gross *et al.* (1979). Future analysis will examine this possibility by measuring skeletal orientations, degree of flex, and placement of artifacts.

5. Future Research

While burial sites clearly provide the archeologist with evidence concerning religious behavior and biological aspects of culture, they also provide a basis for making inferences about other aspects of sociocultural systems, including economic behavior and trade. Snow (1980), summarizing changes in mortuary practices through time in the Northeast, notes that among the Iroquois during the Late Woodland period burials tended to be flexed and without grave goods. With the arrival of trade goods, the numbers of grave inclusions increase. This apparent increase (allowing for preservation differences) in the numbers of grave offerings at the time of European contact probably reflects impacts upon the social structure and organization of Indian groups in the Northeast. Although the extent of change among the Narragansetts is not yet clear, it is likely that some change occurred and it was through mortuary expression that these new social values were incorporated and rationalized.

The effects of seventeenth-century Indian-European trade must also be re-addressed. Technological explanations which suggest that Indian groups abandoned their traditional crafts and technologies in favor of European manufactures are not supported by archeological evidence from RI-1000. Systemic explanations which view trade as serving broad social and political functions have downplayed opportunities created for economic entrepreneurship and other innovative behavior among individual Indians and Indian groups. The traditional assessment of seventeenth-century trade implies that the Indians were passive victims of European expansion and mercantilism.

Both European accounts and ethnohistorical studies have suggested that the Narragansetts played a specialized role in trade through their manufacture of shell pendants and currency (wampum) and metal items. Wampum was important to the seventeenth-century economy of New England not only as a medium of exchange among Indian groups and between Indian groups and Europeans, but also as a form of legal tender for both private and public debts within the European community (Weeden 1884). Its manufacture may have afforded the Narragansetts a rather specialized role in an evolving system of interaction and trade linked to European settlement and mercantilism. In this context, not only were there specialized roles to be assumed by Indian groups in a wider network of interactions involving other Indian groups, colonists, and the European nation-states (e.g., Ray 1978), but new opportunities were created for individuals outside of their traditional economic roles.

These new opportunities were linked directly or indirectly to the demand and supply for provisions and fur, especially beaver pelts, which yielded materials used in the production of felt for cloth and hats fashionable in Europe after the sixteenth century (Wolf 1982:159). Although there is some evidence that the Plimoth colonists acquired fur in the Narragansett Bay region in the 1620s, southern New England as an ecological habitat for beaver may not have been as productive as the areas to the far north. McManis (1975:30) suggests that this is implied by the rapidity with which the Pilgrims had to expand their fur-trading activities beyond the boundaries of their colony. If the Narragansett region could not supply fur directly, it could participate indirectly by supplying the means for this exchange—wampum. While wampum may have functionally drawn the beaver out of the interior forests (Weeden 1884), its value as trade commodity—one which could command all others—may have created incentives for economic gain among the Narragansett Indians. These entrepreneurial activities probably resulted in changes in tribal economic and political domains.

Understanding the context of this Indian-European trade and the specialized roles assumed in it, whether carried out at the tribal or at the individual level, is important to interpreting culture change in seventeenth-century New England. Moreover, it is essential to attempting any meaningful interpretation of the archeological materials recovered from RI-1000. Analyzing this material assemblage at several different scales, from that of the individual to that of the world system, should facilitate a better understanding of elements attributable to intra-cultural or inter-cultural differences.

At the individual and within-group level, material variability among individual graves in terms of kind, quantity, and placement will be examined and correlated with other measurable characteristics within the population (e.g., gender, age, nutritional status) in order to better understand mortuary customs, and social and economic roles within seventeenth century Narragansett society. At the same time, the material assemblage will be analyzed from a regional context and from that of a seventeenth-century world system. Structuring the analysis in this way should result in a better understanding of the processes of culture contact through material culture. Simple assumptions about the acculturation process are no longer tenable. Understanding Narragansett Indians and their role in the events and developments of the seventeenth century necessitates moving beyond these preconceptions and trying to understand not only the elements that changed, but also those that persisted and perhaps even intensified.

ACKNOWLEDGMENTS

The efforts of numerous individuals and institutions made this project possible. The Narragansett Chief Sachem and Tribal Council provided support throughout the project and during the 1983 field season appointed a tribal member, John B. Brown III, as Tribal Field Representative. Volunteer support was especially useful in matching paid efforts. We thank in particular Kevin McBride and Nick Bellatoni's Public Archaeology Survey Team from the University of Connecticut at Storrs; Dr. E. P. Morenon's Rhode Island College field school; The Public Archaeology Laboratory, Inc.; Mike Hebert; and Chris Campbell.

The project is funded by a National Park Service grant administered by the Rhode Island Historical Preservation Commission.

REFERENCES CITED

Allison, M. J., J. Mendoza and A. Pezzia
1973 Documentation of a Case of Tuberculosis in Pre-Columbian America. American Review Respiratory Disease 107:985

Artemel, J., et al.
1983 Providence Cove Lands: Phase III Report. Northeast Corridor Project. Washington, D.C.: U.S. Department of Transportation, Federal Railroad Administration.

Axtell, J. L.
1981 The European and the Indian. New York: Oxford University Press.

Boucher, B. J.
1955 Sex Difference in the Fetal Sciatic Notch. Journal of Forensic Medicine 2:51–54.

Brasser, T. J.
1978 Early Indian-European Contacts. *In:* Handbook of North American Indians, Northeast 15. Bruce G. Trigger, ed. pp. 78–88. Washington, D.C.: Smithsonian Institution.

Buikstra, J., ed.
1982 Prehistoric Tuberculosis in the Americas. Evanston, Illinois: Northwestern University Archaeology Program.

Cook, Sherburne F.
1973 The Significance of Disease in the Extinction of New England Indians. Human Biology 45:485–508.

Cronon, W.
1983 Changes in the Land: Indians, Colonists, and the Ecology of New England. New York: Hill and Wang.

Firth, R.W.
1955 The Fate of the Soul: an Interpretation of Some Primitive Concepts. Cambridge: Cambridge University Press.

Gross, D. R., et al.
1979 Ecology and Acculturation Among Native Peoples of Central Brazil. Science 206:1043–1050.

Jennings, F.
1975 The Invasion of America. New York: W. W. Norton.

Kelley, M. A.
1978 Phenice's Visual Sexing Technique for the Os Pubus. American Journal of Physical Anthropology 48:121–122.
1980 Disease and Environment: A Comparative Analysis of Three Early American Skeletal Collections. Ph.D. dissertation, Case Western Reserve University.

Kelley, M. A. and M. S. Micozzi
  1984   Rib Lesions in Chronic Pulmonary Tuberculosis. Paper presented at 53rd Annual Meeting of American Association of Physical Anthropology, Indianapolis.

Kupperman, K. O.
  1982   Settling with the Indians. The Bulletin of the Archaeological Society of Connecticut 15:1–12.

McManis, Douglas R.
  1975   Colonial New England, A Historical Geography. New York and London: Oxford University Press.

Morenon, E. P.
  1982   Archaeological Investigations along Ministerial Road, South Kingstown, R.I. (Rhode Island College) Occasional Paper in Anthropology and Geography 13.

Phenice, T. W.
  1969   A Newly Developed Visual Method of Sexing the Os Pubus. American Journal of Physical Anthropology 30:297–302.

Potter, Elisha R.
  1835   The Early History of Narragansett. Collections of the Rhode Island Historical Society 3.

Ray, Arthur J.
  1978   History and Archaeology of the Northern Fur Trade. American Antiquity 43:26–34.

Robinson, P. A. and G. Gustafson
  1983   A Partially Disturbed 17th Century Indian Burial Ground in Rhode Island: Recovery, Preliminary Analysis, and Protection. The Bulletin of the Archaeological Society of Connecticut 45:41–50.

Salisbury, N.
  1982   Manitou and Providence: Indians, Europeans, and the Making of New England 1500–1643. New York: Oxford University Press.

Salwen, Bert
  1978   Indians of Southern New England and Long Island: Early Period. *In:* Handbook of North American Indians, Northeast 15. Bruce G. Trigger, ed. pp. 160–176. Washington, D.C.: Smithsonian Institution.

Saul, F. P.
  1972   The Human Skeletal Remains of Altar De Sacrificios. Papers of the Peabody Museum of Archaeology and Ethnology 63(2).

Sekatau, E. S.
   1984   Comments as Viewed by the Medicineman, (Narragansett) Tribal Ethnohis-
          torian and Tribal Council Designee and Approved by Chief Sachem and
          Tribal Council on March 3, 1984.

Simmons, W. S.
   1970   Cautantowwit's House, an Indian burial Ground on the Island of Conani-
          cut in Narragansett Bay. Providence: Brown University Press.
   1978   Narragansett. *In:* Handbook of North American Indians, Northeast 15.
          Bruce G. Trigger, ed. pp. 190–197. Washington, D.C.: Smithsonian Insti-
          tution.

Snow, D. R.
   1980   The Archaeology of New England. New York: Academic Press.

Thomas-Sekatau, E. S. and E. W. Thomas-Sekatau
   1976   The Nahahiggansick Indians. *In:* Reflections of Charlestown, R.I. 1876–
          1976. The Charlestown Bicentennial Book Committee. Westerly, R.I.:
          The Utter Company.

Turnbaugh, W.
   1984a Sociocultural Significance of Grave Goods from a 17th Century Narragan-
          sett Cemetery. Paper presented at 49th Annual Meeting of Society for
          American Archaeology, Portland.
   1984b The Material Culture of RI-1000, a Mid-17th-Century Narragansett Indian
          Burial Site in North Kingstown, Rhode Island. Kingston: Department of
          Sociology and Anthropology, University of Rhode Island.

Ubelaker, D. H.
   1974   Reconstruction of Demographic Profiles from Ossuary Skeletal Samples.
          Smithsonian Contributions to Anthropology 18.

Vaughan, A. T.
   1979   New England Frontier. Puritans and Indians 1620–1675. (Revised edition,
          orig. edition published 1965.) New York: W. W. Norton.

Weaver, D. S.
   1980   Sex Differences in the Ilia of a Known Sex and Age Sample of Fetal and
          Infant Skeletons. American Journal of Physical Anthropology 52:191–195.

Weeden, William B.
   1884   Indian Money as a Factor in New England Civilization. Johns Hopkins
          University Studies in Historical and Political Science VIII–IX.

Williams, Roger
   1936   A Key into the Language of American (1643). 5th edition. Providence: The
          Rhode Island and Providence Plantations Tercentenary Commission.

Winslow, Edward
   1910   Winslow's Relation (1624). *In:* Chronicles of the Pilgrim Fathers, John Masefield, ed. pp. 267–357. New York: E. P. Dutton.

Winthrop, John
   1825–   The History of New England from 1630 to 1649. 2 vols. James Savage,
   1826   ed. Phelps and Farnham, Thomas B. Wait and Son.

Wolf, Eric R.
   1982   Europe and the People Without History. Berkeley: University of California Press.

Cultural Change on the Southern New England Frontier, 1630–1665

Peter A. Thomas

A B S T R A C T

This paper explores the Indian-colonial experience in the middle Connecticut River valley, particularly those aspects of contact that revolved around the fur trade and Indian land. The exchange of pelts for European goods by Indian traders provided not only utilitarian personal items, but also commodities which were further circulated to reinforce indigenous social and political networks. The importance of the fur trade for both societies also motivated English and Indian leaders to work to resolve inter-societal problems.

In conjunction with the jockeying for political and economic power among both colonial and Indian groups in the Northeast, the fur trade produced a number of changes in the cultural patterns of Native American communities. The substitution of Indian land for furs as trade commodity further modified social and economic patterns. A model of change is developed from historical sources; this model is partially evaluated using archeological data recovered from a Squakheag (Sokoki) village site of 1663–1664, located on the Connecticut River in southwestern New Hampshire.

1. Introduction

The Indian-European contact experience and the rate of change in indigenous cultural systems in southern New England was varied. In those areas, particularly along the coast, where English populations were large enough to challenge Indian communities directly for local resources and political authority, either through direct aggression or through their Indian allies, or where Indian communities were under the direct supervision of English missionaries, Indian-white relations proved to be quite different from those in remote areas where English settlements were small and isolated. In order to balance the historical literature which has dealt almost exclusively with Indian-English relations along New England's coastal fringe (Leach 1958; Vaughan 1965; Jennings 1975; Salisbury 1982), this paper focuses on the contact experience as it unfolded in the middle Connecticut River valley on the New England frontier. The characteristics of Indian-white relations which developed here were not unique. Slowly increasing colonial populations versus Indian populations destabilized by disease and warfare, trade between the Indian and European societies, competition for resources, the development of patron/broker-client relationships, and factionalism within Indian communities over how to deal with their alien neighbors were recurring themes as America's frontier expanded westward during the next two centuries.

Upon receiving an invitation to present this paper, my first inclination was to look to the archeological data base as a departing point for my discussion. Archeologically, however the contact situation in the entire region is virtually unexplored. Collections, mostly uncatalogued, of Indian and European trade goods from contact period sites have existed for years; but only during the past few years has there been an attempt to draw these data together. James Bradley's study of trade beads (1984), for example, records the existence of at least fifty-two Contact (1500–1620) and Plantation (1620–1675) period sites in eastern Massachusetts, Maine, New Hampshire and Rhode Island. In the published literature only seven site reports shed much light on seventeenth-century Indian cultural patterns. The Connecticut valley is archeologically unknown aside from some brief notes made during the 1897 excavation of a seventeenth-century Indian fort in Springfield, Massachusetts (Wright 1897) and from more recent excavations conducted at the Squakheag (Sokoki) site of Fort Hill in Hinsdale, southwestern New Hampshire (Thomas 1979).

Evaluations of coastal sites are more common. William Simmons, in *Cautantowwit's House* (1970), describes the human remains and trade goods from a seventeenth-century Narragansett burial ground located on an island in Narragansett Bay. More recently, an exemplary collection of short articles has appeared which deals with Burr's Hill, a seventeenth-century Wampanoag burial ground in Warren, Rhode Island (Gibson 1980). Lorraine Williams (1972) uses a model of change developed by Edward Spicer, *et. al.* (1961) to evaluate the contact situation as it is reflected archeologically at two sites, Fort Shantok in southern Connecticut and Fort Corchaug on Long Island. Burt Salwen (1966) and Ralph Solecki (1950) contributed the initial site reports. Collectively these reports on coastal sites suggest the types and rates

of material culture change among native groups, but they offer little explanation as to how such changes came about. A synthesis of the available archeological literature would therefore contribute little to the problem of European-Indian cultural interaction.

As an alternative, this paper employs an ethnohistorical approach to focus
on a number of changes in the cultural systems of Indian groups living in the
middle Connecticut River valley between the present-day city of Springfield,
Massachusetts and the town of Hinsdale, New Hampshire. Along this stretch
of New England's longest river valley, there were at least five seventeenth-
century Indian communities—Woronoco, Agawam, Norwottuck, Pocumtuck and Squakheag (figure 1). Through an ethnohistorical analysis, a proces-
sual model is developed to explain why and how such changes took place.
This model, which emphasizes the role of the Indian trade, does not explain
culture change per se, but—given a certain parallel in the prevailing environment and social conditions in other regions of North America—it may help
us to understand at least some of the mechanisms of change that existed.

Finally, as an archeologist, I am also interested in seeing how such changes
are reflected in archeological data. For this reason, several inferences generated from the ethnohistorical sources are evaluated with specific references to
the cultural remains recovered from the Fort Hill site. This fortified village
site was occupied between the fall of 1663 and the spring of 1664 by the
Squakheag community, a group of about five hundred Western Abenakis
then living in southwestern New Hampshire. This group is referred to in
French documents as the Sokokis (Day 1965).

2. The Ethnographic Setting

In 1636, Indians in the middle Connecticut River valley witnessed the
expansion of English settlements as eight men and their families took up
residence in Springfield, Massachusetts (figure 1). In the years that followed,
a number of Indians developed relationships with members of the English
community. Some individuals who lived in the villages of Agawam or
Woronoco established ties with Springfield residents almost immediately.
Members of the Norwottuck and Pocumtuck villages had less frequent contacts with English colonists until the late 1650s. Not until 1651 is a member
of the Squakheag or Sokoki community even mentioned in surviving records.
English, Dutch, and French sources which provide documentation on Indian
communities in the valley are sparse; those that have survived suggest the

Figure 1   *Indian Villages and English Towns in the Middle Connecticut River Valley*

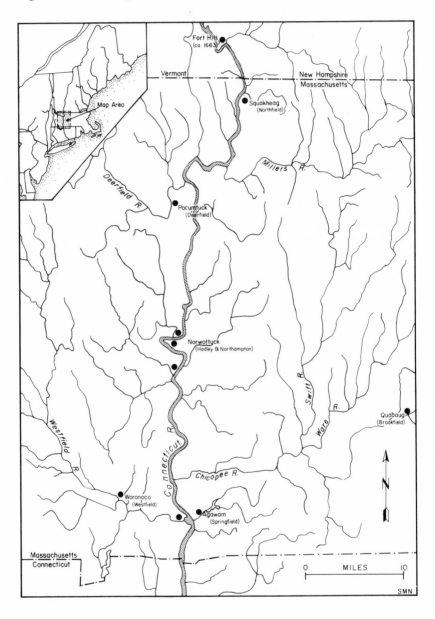

following about general settlement and subsistence patterns characteristic of the valley's native American residents.

Community units, particularly after the early epidemics of the seventeenth century, appear to have been small, with populations numbering between 150 and 500 during periods of extended residence. In the early years of the century and prior to the smallpox epidemic of 1633–34, Connecticut valley groups apparently maintained a dual settlement system in which small hamlets occupied by extended families were grouped around a centrally located village site which was the focus of political and religious activities. Village sites were spaced at approximately 25-mile intervals along the river. Hamlets, the focus of family horticultural activities, were dispersed along the fertile floodplains. For example, records of a 1636 sale of Indian land near Springfield, Massachusetts, clearly suggest that family or lineage landholdings were scattered over a number of square miles around Agawam. Several studies have shown that psychological factors may encourage such a relatively dispersed settlement pattern (Carneiro 1968:136; Lee 1972:140; Leacock 1969:14). When community aggregates exceed 400 or 500, stresses and strains frequently develop which may lead to open schisms among leading factions. Residence in small hamlets, with access to a position of defense only during crises, therefore, is an efficient method of avoiding social dissonance. An account of the Narragansett country in 1636 by John Winthrop, Jr., also suggests group dispersion as a pattern recognizable in coastal southern New England (Winthrop, Jr. 1863), as does Roger Williams's comment on the number of Narragansett "towns" (Williams 1827:28).

Within a few months after their arrival in Springfield, William Pynchon, Henry Smith, and Jehu Burr obtained a quitclaim from a number of local Indians to lands surrounding this nascent English town (Wright 1905:11–12). Unlike many of the English deeds acquired in the coastal regions, the arrangement was not made with a leading sachem, probably because no paramount leader existed, nor did the conditions of the agreement blatantly restrict the seller's use of this territory. Although one or more Indian settlements were located west of the Connecticut River, nuclear or extended families apparently held traditional claims to certain localities on both sides for planting fields or other activities. While exactly delineated tracts of garden land along the river were alienated, the boundaries of upland parcels farther from the river are vague. The lowland floodplains thus supported the major resource base. Claims for the existence of large, bounded, family-owned hunting territories, however, find no support in the seventeenth-century New England records (for an alternate situation among groups in Quebec, see Leacock 1954).

There is a general lack of archeological evidence concerning the existence of fortified villages in the sixteenth and early seventeenth centuries in New England. Bert Salwen (1975:58) maintains that they were uncommon in the Hudson watershed, although from A.D. 1100 on sites in the interior part of New York frequently were situated on defensible ground or were palisaded. The theory that internecine warfare was a factor of life by A.D. 1300, at least in neighboring New York, has considerable support, although its causes are open to debate (Ritchie 1969:281; Witthoft and Kinsey 1959:33; Salwen 1975:58; Engelbrecht, this volume).

Admittedly, New York evidence does not speak for New England, but since Mohawk raids were occurring in eastern Massachusetts in the early 1620s (Wood 1898:60–63), and perhaps before, it would appear expedient for these coastal communities to have developed some type of defense strategy. Small forts were, in fact, built along the Massachusetts Bay coast; Champlain described one located on the Saco River in southern Maine in 1605; and, according to de Laet, Adriaen Block reported a "village resembling a fort for protection against the attacks of enemies" on the lower Connecticut River in 1614 (Wood 1898:89; Champlain 1907:63; de Laet 1909:42). Additionally, an observation by William Bradford indicates that fortifications existed on the middle reaches of the Connecticut River in 1633 and that communities within the valley were not all on friendly terms. He noted: "Ther was a company of people lived in [the] country, up above in [the] river of [Connecticut], a great way from the trading house [at Windsor, Connecticut], and were enimise of those Indians which lived aboute [the English] and of who they stood in some fear. . . . About a thousand of them had inclosed themselves in a forte, which they had strong palisadoes about" (Bradford 1898:387). It is conceivable, therefore, that fortified sites commonly existed in New England and that most communities between Agawam and Squakheag had at least one defensible position within which they could find security. Still, unfortified hamlets were also probably common, as they may have been for several centuries. The relatively dispersed residence pattern persisted, but it is also true that considerable consolidation of hamlet populations within fortified villages occurred after mid-century.

Although both villages and hamlets are referenced in the English documents, little mention is made of smaller, more transient, seasonal hunting and trapping camps or of special-purpose sites such as fishing stations. Given the annual subsistence round which is outlined below, such sites must exist, but they have apparently gone unnoticed by archeologists.

In an earlier paper, I provided detailed information on the subsistence activities of Indian groups who lived in the middle Connecticut River valley (Thomas 1976). A brief summary of the annual subsistence cycle is presented here.

Beginning in March, when large spawning runs of alewives, shad, and salmon commenced, families gathered by one of the large falls along the Connecticut—Holyoke, South Hadley, Turners Falls, Vernon—or along one of the Connecticut's major tributaries. For a month or so, large quantities of fish were consumed and processed for later use. By late April and throughout May activities became more diversified. Corn fields were prepared and seeds planted. Fishing may have continued throughout this period, and some hunting of migrating waterfowl and a few mammals occurred. By summer, communities were centered in the hamlets surrounded by family planting fields where crops were tended. A more diverse variety of fish was probably exploitable throughout the summer, and fishing continued in ponds, rivers, and tributaries. During the late summer, while crops were maturing, wild plant foods, medicinal herbs, and plant fibers were gathered. By late summer, corn, beans, and squash had matured. Beginning in early fall, horticultural produce, nuts, and berries were collected, dried and stored. When these activities were completed, the fall hunting period began. Small bands of hunters or single families established hunting lodges, frequently at considerable distances from the main settlements. Many families occupied these isolated stations until late December, smoking and drying meat for late winter consumption. From December until mid-March the hamlets were again heavily populated. During these months stored foods provided the bulk of the food resources, supplemented by what could be taken by local hunting and ice fishing. With horticultural crops contributing a significant portion of the Indian diet, communities were anchored to the lands adjacent to their planting fields in both summer and winter. Village members were drawn away only by the spring fishing runs up the Connecticut River and its tributaries or by the fall hunt, in which parties ranged into the Berkshires to the west and into northern areas in present-day Vermont, southern Quebec, and New Hampshire.

As these settlement and subsistence data suggest, community size was fairly small. The social, economic, and political units which functioned to integrate these communities were even smaller. These factors have, however, been too infrequently recognized. From the time the English arrived in the New World until the twentieth century, colonial administrators as well as most subsequent writers have seen Indian "tribes" in southern New England as well-defined political units with recognizable leaders and identifiable territorial boundaries (see for example, Alden Vaughan 1965:53). Upon reviewing specific chains of historical events during the seventeenth-century, however, it becomes apparent that persistent tribal unity is a figment of everyone's imagination. As social, political, and economic entities, most seventeenth-century southern New England Indian groups fall within a type of "egalitarian" society (Service 1975:47–70) which Marshall Salhins (1968) has defined as a "segmentary tribe." As such, the primary political, social, and economic unit was the village, which was frequently organized around one or more lineages, supported by a semi-mobile contingent of kith and kin. The "tribe" as such was episodic. Generally, what defined a segmentary tribe was cooperation among communities in response to outside pressures. In retrospect, it is nearly impossible to define the "tribal" affiliations of most of New England's Indian villages.

Political leadership was community-based. In 1648 William Pynchon described the political structure of an Indian group living near present-day Brookfield, about thirty miles east of Springfield, Massachusetts (see figure 1). This community is frequently considered to form part of the Nipmuc tribe. He wrote, "There are several Small Sachims of Quabaug, and in all neer places [in the villages nearer Springfield] there are other small Sachims, no one Sachim doth Rule all. . . ." (Temple 1887:36). This characterization probably applied to nearly all of the Indian societies in the Connecticut River valley.

Leadership was generally a matter of group consent. Several characteristics in a New England sachem seem to have elicited this needed consent. Within the group, generosity, as well as the ability to reconcile differences among various factions, was critical. Where external threats existed, leadership was a far more complex quality. By the late sixteenth century, and probably before, generosity held a joint position with ingenuity, skill in controlling supernatural forces, diplomacy, and the ability to succeed in war. Although authority was based in consent, it was invariably reinforced and broadened by means of extending family relations. Since the kin group was the body to which an individual owed a primary obligation, it followed that a sachem with a large extended family could organize such a unit to meet political and economic challenges from within his community and from without.

Another type of leadership became increasingly visible as conditions became highly unstable during the seventeenth century. Various individuals gained prominence as a result of personal drive, magnetism, and the ability to manipulate resources, rather than from any ascribed right to leadership in their cultural systems. Such personalities have come to be called "big-men" in other geographical areas of the world. One quality of big-man authority stands out above the rest: personal power. Big-men frequently build their authority by bending their skills in one particular direction—to acquiring goods for redistribution to their immediate followers and to wider social units.

A big-man political system in the more classic form found in western Melanesia and in some African tribes (Sahlins 1965:201–206; Epstein 1968:53–68) hardly existed in New England, but, as Burton and Lowenthal (1974) have demonstrated, big-men did emerge, particularly when they could consolidate fragmented communities, control the wampum and fur trade, and manipulate the European colonists. As will be seen, a number of Indian men in the middle Connecticut valley built a base of authority by obtaining differential access to English goods through their dealings in the fur trade. It was such individuals who frequently acted as spokesmen for their villages with colonial authorities. When the fur trade collapsed, it was also these individuals who ceded Indian lands in order to maintain a system upon which they had come to rely.

3. The Nature and Processes of Change in the Middle Connecticut River Valley: 1630–1665

Indian leaders in New England were forced to make political and economic decisions involving regional considerations well before European colonization began. Trade networks, and even incipient political confederacies, existed in a number of sections (Morrison 1976). Until the mid-1630s, however, day-to-day contacts between Indians and Europeans took place only within the coastal areas. Native leaders in the Connecticut valley were not directly or continually faced with the need to decide how the two societies should articulate. After 1636, although they were not likely to encounter problems brought about by close social and religious interaction, Indians in the valley were repeatedly confronted with specific issues involving land, trade, and political independence as the English settlements multiplied. Increasing Indian-English contact meant that repeated accommodations had to be made in both cultural systems if open ruptures between the two societies were to be avoided. Thus, not one, but a multiplicity of determinant changes took place, each with its own logic and time frame. Small alterations in one pattern inexorably produced mutations in others. Between the mid-1630s and 1665, a number of decisions were made that produced alterations in native political, economic, and social patterns. The extent to which the choices made by Indian families maintained the integrity of their communities rested upon two different factors: 1) the long-term effectiveness of such decisions (which were frequently based on a restricted political and economic view of the North Atlantic world) and 2) the ease with which cultural variables could be altered to insure a smoothly functioning system. Direct contact between English colonists and Indians in the Connecticut valley produced a situation in which change and uncertainty were inevitable by-products.

It appears that the types of cultural responses made in a changing environment were positively correlated with the amount of information flow and complementarity between the colonial and Indian societies. Thus any means by which alien communities could insure consistent communication, as well as the transfer of desired resources, might prove mutually advantageous. Where individual Indians and Englishmen chose to deal with each other, the ethnohistorian may be able to assess some of the goals and strategies which came into play, as well as some of what Barnes (1968) has called "bridging transactions," which were available to insure that both societies could exist side by side. In the middle Connecticut River valley, a series of such bridging transactions was ultimately responsible for a number of fundamental changes in native cultural systems.

3.1. Patrons, Brokers, and Clients: Early Settlement

One variety of bridging mechanism seen in a number of geographical areas is the "patron/broker-client" relationship (Strickon and Greenfield 1972). Such relationships tend to arise in situations where state and egalitarian societies exist in close proximity, where boundaries exist between the state apparatus and less complex societies, where resources are limited, and where there exists a system of formal social, political, and economic positions which specific individuals can manipulate to achieve desired goals. In the valley, just such conditions developed. Here, English patron/brokers and Indian clients bridged the cultural gap by means of the fur trade. A number of Indians who became clients of English trading agents also employed such relationships internally to foster their families' social and political prestige.

Initially, patron-client relationships did not exist, but by the late 1640s such strategies were beginning to operate. The pivotal character in this slowly emerging system was William Pynchon, the founder of Springfield, Massachusetts. For the most part, William Pynchon functioned more as a broker than as a patron, that is, he was primarily the focal English entrepreneur through which European items were funneled to Indian recipients. On rare occasions, however, Pynchon did function in typical patron fashion by forestalling the General Court's intervention in Indian affairs and, as magistrate, by acting as judicial arbiter in local English-Indian disputes (Temple 1887:37–38). After 1652, he was succeeded by his son, John, who truly became an entrepreneur with executive and judicial power, as well as by several minor patron-traders up river who constantly dealt with a number of Indian clients and made the system a practical reality.

This factor is particularly important in view of the conditions of social and political distance that grew up between the Springfield settlers and their Indian neighbors. Within a decade after the town's settlement in 1636, interaction between the Indian and white communities around Springfield began to take on a recognizable form. Social boundaries were closely prescribed by colonial law. Interracial marriage was forbidden. Political and judicial boundaries between the two societies were prescribed in practice. Once the quitclaims to Indian lands had been acquired by William Pynchon at Springfield, the colonists set about tending to the town's business with little apparent hindrance from the area's former occupants. Where conflicts did develop, the Indian communities in the middle reaches of the valley outside of Springfield acted in an autonomous fashion (Hazard 1969:II,63). Although the British magistrates frequently assumed otherwise, their jurisdiction effectively stopped at the borders of the English towns. The only other avenue of consistent contact was therefore the Indian-European trading network—a fact that had significant ramifications.

The roots of the trading system which evolved extend into the unrecorded past. The incorporation of New World resources into the Western market system began nearly as early as the first contacts between Europeans and Indians in the North Atlantic region. French fishermen pursued sporadic bartering in the 1530s, and by 1580 vessels were sailing to the Gulf of Saint Lawrence and southward with the sole intent of acquiring American furs.

It is unlikely that this early trade of furs for European goods affected only native American coastal communities. Rather, trade items were rapidly dispersed into interior reaches of North America through native middlemen via networks which had functioned for centuries. From what is known of economic activities among segmentary tribes in other regions of the world, it is unlikely that such exchanges were haphazard. Village alliances, kin networks, and individual partnerships probably existed in New England and may have directly affected the immediate dispersal of European merchandise. There is little doubt that alterations were made to accommodate the broadly expanding foreign trade of the 1600s, but most changes came about by modifying existing cultural norms, not by the adoption of some radically new set of ideas.

A brief look at the trading system that developed in the Connecticut Valley may help to explain a number of these points. Once Springfield was established in 1636, its leading citizen, William Pynchon, found a ready market for the wampum, cloth, and other items he had transported from the coast. From its inception, barter between Indians and settlers brought the colonists two primary commodities. The first was maize. Until English grains could be grown in the valley in sufficient quantities to feed English families, a local traffic in native horticultural produce was crucial for the immigrants' survival. Corn brokerage was a major part of Pynchon's business.

The Indians' role as provisioners for the British settlers affected the local villagers in several ways. First, as long as the colonists were dependent upon their Indian neighbors for a portion of their food resources, the English could not adopt a hostile attitude or belligerent posture without significant risk to their own security. Until mid-century, therefore, residents at Agawam, Woronoco, Norwottuck, and Pocumtuck were able to exploit this bargaining position to thwart unwanted English encroachment. Second, the use of food stuff for trade meant that consistent surpluses were necessary if a favorably balanced exchange were to be maintained. On a long-term basis, therefore, an adequate land base was essential to the stability of an Indian community whose food resources, as well as a trade surplus, rested on continued availability of good horticultural land. For at least several decades after English settlement, these local dealings in food resources constituted a major reciprocal point of contact between the English and their Indian neighbors.

The second major item sought by William Pynchon and his sub-traders was beaver pelts. Although agricultural produce was derived directly from the surpluses at Woronoco, Agawam, Norwottuck, and Pocumtuck, it is unlikely that beaver pelts were taken in the immediate region in significant quantities. Sources lay in the hinterlands—in the hilly and mountainous country to the west and north. Pynchon evidently acquired furs in three ways: from local hunters, from local villagers acting as middlemen, and directly from distant areas via overland routes. A multi-faceted acquisition and distribution network was well established by the late 1630s.

Pynchon's statement concerning the timing of such trade is important. He wrote of the Indians, "It is their ordenary time in the time of snow in the beginning of Winter to trade their skinns" (Green 1888:31–32). What this habitual season of exchange suggests is that subsistence procurement practices had not been substantially modified in the valley by the late 1630s. Rather, beaver and other animals were trapped or hunted during the summer by individuals and during the extended October-December hunt in the uplands by small family groups. The extensive exploitation of fur-bearing mammals was simply viewed as adjunct to traditional hunting patterns, not as an end in itself. The fall hunt for deer could not be discontinued, nor was there apparently sufficient motivation for many to abandon the lowland villages during deep winter to tend trapping lines or to hunt in the upland regions. Such a practice was apparently more characteristic of northern bands of hunters and gatherers who lacked horticultural resources to tide them through the winter months. This situation may further indicate that during the 1640s adequate supplies of European goods could be obtained without putting any appreciable stress on indigenous cultural systems.

By the mid-seventeenth century Indian villagers throughout southern New England were faced with a number of regional and local issues that threatened their political integrity as well as their cultural norms and values. Since 1620 marginal English plantations centered in the Cape Cod and Massachusetts Bay area had mushroomed into over forty towns which were inhabited by more than 20,000 immigrants. Other Europeans, notably the French and Dutch, also began to extend their economic and political spheres of interest. Even more significantly, inter-village feuding was intense and raids were common. No individual, whether Indian or colonist, could escape the political and economic shock waves reverberating throughout the Northeast.

How were peoples with conflicting points of view and goals to settle their differences? Where was the arena of resolution? Between English colonists and neighboring Indians the points of articulation where compromise was likely were extremely limited. Trade held out the one significant hope. It was the only area where interdependency frequently existed.

Although knives, hatchets, looking glasses, clothing, wampum, pelts, maize, and other items were disseminated throughout the native communities through a network of reciprocal exchange, they functioned as more than simply consumable commodities. Trade did not act simply as a mechanism for the transfer of imported goods. The socio-cultural interactions surrounding the trafficking of such goods were as much a point of consideration as what or how many specific items were being bartered. In its simplest form, the exchange of commodities began or underscored social relationships within any Indian's family and village or between political allies. This was especially characteristic of big-men, although the practice was pervasive within all of the segmentary tribes. The dispersal of European goods, which were funneled through a small number of colonial traders to Indian villages, also performed a significant bridging function between the colonial and indigenous societies. Along with the manufactured commodities went information—a vital resource for strategy planning. To insure this flow of information a number of Indian spokesmen (clients) within the Connecticut valley established commercial connections with William Pynchon, who was not only a major merchant (broker), but a member of the Governor's Council and Chief Justice as well. This gave him at least the potential to function in patron fashion. Economic transactions kept political doors open, and as long as mutually satisfactory business ties could be maintained, there was less potential for destabilizing actions to be taken by either side. In short, the interdependency engendered by the Indian-white market provided enough incentive for individuals in both societies to reach an accord on other matters. Where the boundaries of power domains were being contested, and where relative social isolation was maintained, economic exchanges furnished a forum for discussion and a bridge to compromise.

3.2. Transition, 1650–1665

The period between 1650 and 1665 was marked by considerable uncertainly in a number of Indian villages in the middle Connecticut valley. Significant shifts occurred in the regional power domains of the segmentary tribes throughout the Northeast. At a more local level, the potential for increased Indian-English conflict intensified as the English population of Springfield expanded and as new towns sprang up to the north. Growing interest in the Westfield River valley and the establishment of Northampton (1654), Hadley (1659), and Hatfield (1661) had profound implications for inter-societal diplomacy. This growth of colonial populations and the increase of geographic proximity between English and Indian towns resulted in a number of personal confrontations among members of both societies. The native land base, and thus the ability to produce surplus horticultural produce, came under increasing stress.

As in the past, there was an obvious need to resolve situations of conflict. The fur trade and the development of a number of patron/broker-client relationships continued to be one means to compromise. However, as regional hostilities proliferated and as the source of pelts moved farther northward, the buffering effect of the fur trade came under serious strain. The Squakheag's fortified village (Fort Hill) was abandoned in the spring of 1664 after an Iroquois raid the preceding December, and Pocumtuck was destroyed by the Mohawks in February, 1665. The consequences were nearly catastrophic. Indian labor, but more particularly land, began to replace pelts as both collateral for extended credit and as a valuable replacement item for furs. This fifteen-year period proved to be one of flux, of consistent experimentation with a number of strategies, and of community disintegration.

While the fur trade provided a bridging mechanism between the English and Indian societies, continued participation for Indian traders had other consequences, not the least of which were the growing need to modify seasonal exploitation patterns in order to acquire pelts, the increasing competition in the hunting and trapping territories, and the necessity for developing ways of incorporating foreign trade goods into endemic patterns of consumption and distribution. While many old cultural patterns were being readapted to a changing world, it became increasingly difficult, due to the incessant warfare among the Indian communities themselves, to maintain the vitality of the fur trade at all. Two forces were at play. The first was a centrifugal force generated from recurring attempts to consolidate or expand native and colonial power domains, which threatened to tear the trading system apart. The second was a centripetal force generated from the recognition that trade was important for sustaining good inter-societal relations and for acquiring foreign commodities.

The amount of disruption to which the fur trade itself was subjected was not solely the function of internal changes occurring within Indian societies or of the depletion of available sources of pelts. It was also directly conditioned by the successes or failures of various segmentary tribes throughout the Northeast in maintaining or expanding their political power domains. One fact which John Pynchon's trading ledgers makes abundantly clear is that there were gross fluctuations in the number of skins which valley hunters secured each year. Annual variations ranged from 3,723 pounds of beaver pelts exported in 1654, Pynchon's most successful year, to only 191 pounds of furs in 1664. Figure 2 summarizes the volume of beaver accumulated by Pynchon over a period of nineteen years. A synthesis of the existing historical data (Thomas 1981) makes it abundantly clear that such fluctuating patterns in the volume of beaver were directly related to the political climate in the middle Connecticut valley and surrounding region. Virtually every peak recorded in figure 2 corresponds to a year of relative peace; every trough corresponds to a period of feuding among the New England tribes.

While political strife was effectively undermining the trading system, other factors worked to keep it operating. Answers to the following questions may help to explain how facets of the system were working. First, what types of goods were being consumed? Second, how were these goods incorporated into the Indian cultures? Third, how was the system maintained?

The range of European goods available at the trading houses of John Pynchon in Springfield and his agents in Northampton, Westfield, and elsewhere was extremely broad (Pynchon 1652–1701). Of the most frequently used metal hardware goods, 6,451 knives, 1,677 pairs of scissors, 4,235 awls, 12,869 fish hooks, 11,481 needles, 134,000 pins, 2,723 "tin glasses" or mirrors, and 2,147 clay tobacco pipes were traded between 1652 and 1664. The total monetary value of these goods was slightly in excess of £200. As was true during the 1640s, cloth goods continued to be the principal item of exchange in the Indian-English trade in the Connecticut valley. Roughly 5,830 yards of "trading cloth," 2,382 yards of duffel, and 7,984 yards of "shag cotton" entered the exchange network. To this volume can be added lesser quantities of other types of cloth, as well as such finished articles of European clothing as caps, coats, shirts, waistcoats, buttons, and stockings. This totals to roughly 18,850 yards of cloth valued at over £5,000. (For extended discussions of this trade see Thomas 1979:155–202, 456–475.) As the figures indicate, the consumption of cloth goods was more than twenty-five times that of all glass, iron, brass or copper items combined—at least in terms of their monetary value.

Of the items mentioned in Pynchon's trading ledgers, knives (4), scissors (2), fish hooks (5), awls (2) and clay pipes (63) were recovered during archeological excavations of the Squakheag's fortified village, which they built during the fall of 1663 and abandoned in the following spring. In addition, two jew's harps, a possible trunk latch, a hatchet blade, the socket portion of an ax or hoe, a musket lock and barrel, nine nails, a totally oxidized iron kettle, a button mold, innumerable pieces of brass kettles

Figure 2   *Yearly Acquisition and Export of Beaver Pelts by John Pynchon, 1652–1670*

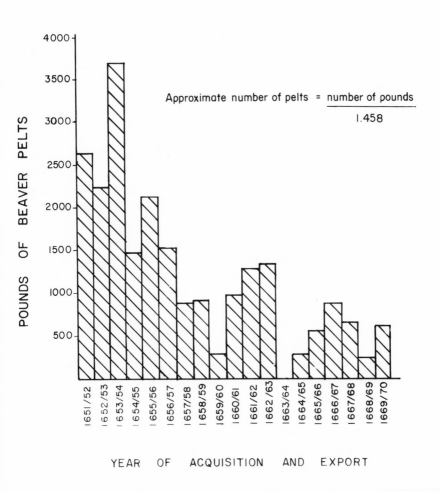

which had been reworked into projectile points, and glass beads were also retrieved (Thomas 1979:364–391, 544–546). No items of cloth were recovered even though the preservation of organic materials was generally excellent. The obvious differential rates of survival for cloth and metal items at archeological sites such as Fort Hill and the fact that archeologists rarely have someone's trading ledgers to fall back on means that considerable caution must be exercised in interpreting data derived from archeological sites of the Contact era.

What was the impact of trade on the communities between Agawam and Squakheag, whose aggregate population in 1663 is conservatively estimated to have been between 1,764 and 2,200 individuals? Some idea may be gained by reconstructing the average annual per capita consumption pattern. Disregarding the obvious annual fluctuations for a moment and assuming that each individual Indian was a consumer, then the rate would approximate: .71 to .89 yards of cloth, .25 to .31 knives, .06 to .08 scissors, .16 to .20 awls, .49 to .61 fish hooks, .44 to .54 needles, .10 to .13 tin boxes, and .08 to .10 pipes. Even if children are entirely excluded as consumers of European goods, annual consumption rates for one adult male and female are still low: 1.78 to 2.23 yards of cloth per year, less than one knife yearly, a pair of scissors every five to six years, slightly more than one fish hook per year, etc. One underlying pattern is clear. Trade with the English could provide only for minimal replacement of industrially manufactured items. Any notion that by 1660 native Americans, or at least those living in non-coastal regions, had become dependent upon European goods for utilitarian reasons and that the society at large had become bound to the colonial traders to meet their material needs must be seriously reconsidered. However, another form of dependency had developed.

The annual average consumption figures suggest that European goods were distributed unevenly in the Indian societies. With tremendous fluctuations occurring in the yearly returns from the beaver and otter hunts (figure 2), it must be concluded that there were periods in which items could simply not be replaced if they were broken or lost. Therefore, any Indian who could manipulate an English trader to acquire credit, who could control the flow of the available pelts in his own community, or who could provide an alternative resource for exchange, could achieve a considerable advantage over less enterprising individuals. It may be remembered that the manipulation of resources for redistribution to one's followers was employed to validate or reinforce any community leader's prestige and authority. It is also true that trade goods originating in Europe and wampum, which Pynchon and his sub-traders acquired from the coast, came to function as gifts between friends, as validations of social relationships, and as tokens of peace tendered to potential enemies. A limited number of Indian men and women in the valley who could manage furs or other resources and maintain community harmony became prominent figures in the Indian-English trade. Viewed from a broad standpoint, at least one segment of the Indian population had become truly dependent on multiple trading arrangements.

It was the development of a credit system that ultimately became a key facet of the fur trade, providing a number of Indians with influence, resources for distribution, and a means for maintaining Indian-white communications. Native Americans relied on two major resources for their trading endeavors—horticultural produce and pelts—both of which were highly seasonal in nature. English goods and wampum could be obtained throughout the year if one's "credit ratings" were maintained. On a short-term basis, the practice had considerable advantages. In order for such a system to work in a balanced fashion, however, at least two conditions had to be met. Consumption of trade items had to be kept at levels commensurate with resource acquisition, and for rational planning to occur, the quantities of pelts and horticultural produce had to be predictable. Given the rapidly changing political, social, and economic environment of the Northeast, it was virtually impossible to meet the latter condition. Between 1652 and 1657, the annual average returns of beaver amounted to 2,290 pounds. Between 1658 and 1663, annual returns averaged 953 pounds, a decline of 59 percent. On a long-term basis, therefore, the establishment of a credit system proved virtually catastrophic for a large number of Indian families. Indian leaders who relied on the fur trade for many reasons found themselves faced with a monumental predicament. They needed an alternative resource to pelts and horticultural produce. Increasingly, land seemed to provide the answer, if only for a short time and not without the prospect of considerable stress arising.

3.3. How to Pay the Piper: Furs or Land

Assuming that there was differential access to trade goods by Indians in the valley, along with stratified levels of consumption, then the introduction of land into the English-Indian market accentuated an existing trend. Those individuals who wished to interact with the colonists had to be able to manipulate resources which their English contacts wanted—initially pelts and food stuffs. In time, land became significant. Those who chose a more conservative approach either became tolerant of their neighbor's dealings, became antagonistic, or moved to other areas. Such a trend is but one example of a pattern which repeated itself in Indian communities during the next three hundred years. Even as late as the 1950s, such factionalism was visible within the Menominee and other tribes during termination proceedings. Individuals who regularly interacted with the white community or who had obtained a favored status in the bureaucracy of the Bureau of Indian Affairs pursued a course of action which was radically different from that propounded by the segment of the tribe which had had less than favorable dealings with the federal government (Ames and Fisher 1959; Edgerton 1962). Whether in the seventeenth or twentieth century, individuals, depending upon their individual histories, developed alternative strategies for resolving social stress.

Data concerning Indian subsistence strategies and settlement patterns make it possible to make a number of inferences about other probable changes. English documentation suggests that the settlement pattern during the 1630s was characterized by dispersed hamlets clustered around a central fortified village. During the 1640s, populations began to coalesce into centralized areas. Increased social tension and intensified use of land in the immediate vicinity of the larger villages were two of the probable outcomes of this apparent fusion. Furthermore, if the population estimates of 1,750 to 2,200 for the middle portion of the valley are accurate, then the Indian community of Agawam-Woronoco required the active commitment of eighty acres of planting fields per year. Those at Norwottuck, Pocumtuck and Squakheag, would have needed 75 to 115, 100 to 150, and 100 acres of fields, respectively. If normal horticultural practices were maintained, at least double this amount would have been utilized over the next twenty years. Therefore, the loss of native land reserves could have a considerable impact on their ability to plant and harvest staple crops of corn, beans and squash, and particularly on the production of surpluses for trade with neighboring colonists. Balanced against these factors was the gross drop in returns which could be expected from the fur trade. By the late 1650s, therefore, a number of factors were operating to limit resource exploitation.

By 1660, land and the fur trade were inexorably tied together. The connecting link between them was the English traders' use of credit. Land became the demanded collateral for goods which were received on the promise that pelts would be forthcoming the following season. This shift is significant because it marks the transition from a period when Indian hunters could act independently—trapping for beaver and otter at their own volition—to a period when Pynchon and his sub-traders placed increasing demands on a hunter's time. Given the unsettled political conditions, however, these new obligations could not be met. As may be surmised from a review of figure 3, within less than fifteen years the loss of the Indians' land base in the middle Connecticut valley was nearly complete.

By the early 1660s a number of factors had combined to produce a situation of crisis for the communities at Agawam, Woronoco, and Norwottuck, and to a lesser extent, for those at Pocumtuck. Tremendous English expansion had occurred in the valley. From eight families in 1636, Springfield's population had grown to ninety-one families with over 450 members. Northampton had been founded in 1654. By 1660, fifty-seven men had received homelots for themselves and about two hundred and fifty members of their families. Hadley had been established in 1659, and five years later, 211 were in residence (Burt 1898, 1:40–45; Trumbull 1898, 1:88). Thus, by 1664, approximately nine hundred immigrants had staked out their claims in the valley where they were probably employing over twelve thousand acres of land, divided among agricultural fields, houselots, woodlots and open pastures.

Concurrently, the Indian populations had rebounded after the ravages of the smallpox epidemic in 1633/34. By 1664, the population of the villages between Agawam and Norwottuck was nearly identical to that in the English towns (about 764 to 951). However, the land base had become grossly restricted (figure 3). Although many of the transfer deeds to Indian lands contained specific clauses which allowed the Indians to hunt, fish, gather wild plants, collect wood, and build their wigwams on the town commons (Wright 1905), prime horticultural land was scarce. Agawam families were probably restricted to fewer than twenty acres. Fields at Pojasick on the Westfield River had not as yet been mortgaged, but stress may have been felt as former Agawam residents joined their kinsmen upriver. At Norwottuck, the village on the Hadley side still used between twelve and twenty acres of adjacent corn fields, but this could hardly have been sufficient to support its inhabitants. Residents on the western side of the Connecticut River were faced with worse conditions.

Not only were subsistence resources extremely taxed, but the potential for harvesting surplus crops for exchange in the English towns had been virtually

Figure 3 *English Deeds to Indian Lands Noted by Year of Transfer*

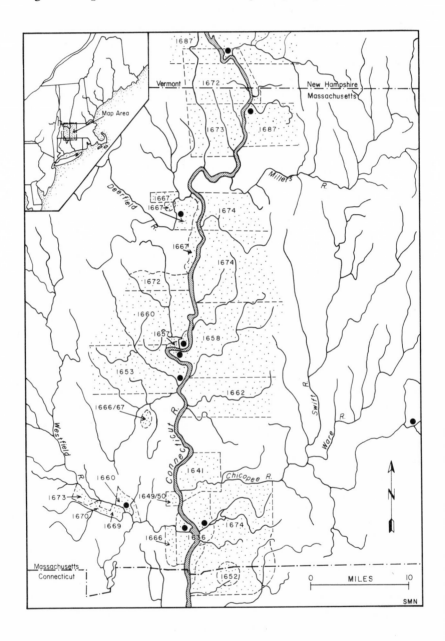

eliminated. If the erosion of one resource base were not bad enough, Mohawk raids into northern New England, the uncertain truce which existed among the segmentary tribes in southern New England, and the resultant depression in the fur trade compounded matters. Indian spokesmen who now relied on the Indian-English exchange network to meet a number of needs were faced with the prospect that the system might collapse entirely. "Free-will" sales of what was probably excess land in the late 1650s, the mortgaging of territorial reserves beginning in 1659, and the slight rebound in the fur trade that occurred between 1661 and 1663 kept hopes alive.

Archeological data recovered from the Squakheag site of Fort Hill support the conclusion that stress was occurring. This site is particularly informative due to its short period of occupation and the fairly large area of the site which was sampled. It is known from English documents that this fortified village of about five hundred residents was built in the fall of 1663, attacked by a large Iroquois war party in December, and abandoned during the early months of 1664. Archeologically, a single six-month period of occupation is represented. About 7 percent, or 3,700 square feet, of the site has been excavated; an additional 14 percent, or 7,300 square feet, has been tested to determine the location of such features as hearths and pits used for storage and/or refuse disposal. A large inventory of artifacts has been recovered and food remains have been analyzed from ninety-seven features (Thomas 1979:334–392, 486–552). Because the nearest colonial town was over forty miles away, the land base around the Squakheag village was still intact and English encroachment into the community's hunting territory had not occurred. Thus, the patterns seen here may have been even more pronounced in the Indian villages closer to the English settlements of Northampton, Hadley, and Springfield.

At Fort Hill, within ninety-seven features—mostly hearths and emptied storage pits—208 lenses which contained cultural refuse were identified. The faunal and floral remains represent constituent parts of an August-February diet. Faunal analysis is based on a sample of 13,785 whole or fragmented bones, of which 1,731 could be identified as to species. The most common items within the 208 refuse units by frequency are: a species of berry or nut which matures between August and October (present in 56 percent of the refuse units) sumac (37 percent), raspberry or blackberry (37 percent), and elderberry (28 percent) had the highest frequencies; deer (41 percent); some species of fish (32 percent), including salmon, alewife, sucker, carp, perch, sunfish, catfish, bass and dace, with shad being the most common (12 percent); freshwater mussel (31 percent); beans (29 percent); bear (28 percent); turtle (19 percent); dog (16 percent); game bird (9 percent); squirrel (7 percent) and moose (6 percent). Other fauna represented include shrew, mouse, chipmunk, raccoon, woodchuck, skunk, muskrat, beaver, fox, bobcat, rabbit and porcupine. Although it is known from historical records that there were large stores of maize at Fort Hill, charred kernels were recovered in only eight lenses—a fact which has considerable implications for archeological interpretations of subsistence patterns at Late Woodland period sites.

From an analysis of the fall-winter food remains, what one sees as the central trend in the Squakheag's subsistence pattern is an intensification of local exploitation. Species which were traditionally taken during this fall and early winter period were pursued, but the evidence of village-site butchering of entire deer and bear carcasses leads to the conclusion that small family or band units did not leave the village in order to carry out hunting and trapping activities at distant camps as they once had done. Such a shift in deer hunting strategies apparently meant that the prime protein base had to be supplemented by small game, turtle, and particularly fish and dog. Such species occur in from 7 to 32 percent of all refuse units analyzed. Furthermore, a calendar recorded by John Pynchon from Indians living near Springfield indicates that there was a traditional pause between the fall harvest and the regular consumption of maize (Pynchon 1645–1650:iii). While the low incidence of preserved corn at the Fort Hill site makes confirmation impossible, the large number of storage pits which had been emptied by late fall implies that the consumption of maize began immediately after harvest. Again, both these characteristics appear at variance with the subsistence model presented earlier.

What may be strongly inferred from these trends is that the core strategies were maintained, while the basic subsistence pattern was undergoing considerable stress. The intensification of warfare, which was generated in part from competition in the fur trade, greatly increased the need to maintain a defensive posture. In response, Squakheag families could not spend any appreciable time isolated in the uplands during the fall. If such practices were carried on repeatedly, an eventual over-exploitation of the local deer and bear populations could be expected, as well as an increased reliance on fish and smaller mammals taken at non-optimal periods. The excessive time spent in subsistence procurement, the concomitant decline in the time spent trapping for pelts, and the need to increase trading contacts to insure the flow of goods and information during periods of heightened conflict placed heavy constraints on Squakheag's residents.

The artifactual data recovered at Fort Hill suggest that the Squakheags were attempting to deal with two world views—a traditional one in which their culture provided an integrated pattern of strategies for action and an alien one which held both advantages and disadvantages, but which was not always understood. The blending of cultural ideas is evidenced by the continuation of traditional work in ceramics, bone, and shell. Ceramic vessels are of a particularly high quality. At the same time European goods of metal, glass, and ceramics were incorporated into daily life; some commodities, particularly brass kettles, were reworked into items which took on traditional forms; Jesuit rings handed out after catechism classes during Squakheag visits to Montreal were juxtaposed with brass, shell, and mudstone items which expressed an indigenous symbolism.

4. Conclusions

With the abandonment of the Squakheag village in the early spring of 1664 and the destruction of Pocumtuck in February 1665, refugees began to flow steadily into Norwottuck and villages to the south. In particular, a number of former Pocumtucks found sanctuary at Norwottuck. With their resources already severely strained, the future must have looked exceedingly bleak. Hotly contested court cases to resolve land claims, the frequent purchase of corn and beans by Indians from John Pynchon, and native petitions to the County and General Court of Massachusetts for relief followed.

By 1670, the fur trade in the Connecticut valley was nearly dead. Thus, a period of about thirty years—a single generation—saw the establishment, expansion, and virtual collapse of a trading system which facilitated the exchange of native American products, particularly pelts and horticultural crops, for industrially manufactured goods brought by English immigrants. More significantly, the network of exchange had a far broader function than the mere dissemination of utilitarian trade items. Trading posts became the points through which both societies could resolve differences. In the early days, the resultant amicability was a positive feature of the Indian-English trade. The export of beaver and otter pelts was a vital part of the Massachusetts Bay Colony's economy, and the supplies of corn and beans from native villages proved critical for the survival of newly established English towns. As long as the supplies of pelts were forthcoming, colonial entrepreneurs—particularly the Pynchons, who monopolized economic and political power in the middle Connecticut valley—were fairly consistent in serving Indian interests. For their part, leaders within the valley's segmentary tribes were split in their attitudes concerning the most useful economic and political strategies. Nonetheless, that segment of the community that advantageously employed contacts with the English was able to obtain foreign-made goods for consumption and for the development of prestige; secure commodities, particularly wampum, to be used to build native alliances; and participate in exchanges critical for gaining information about a markedly alien society and for discussing crucial issues which arose between themselves and their foreign neighbors. By the late 1650s, both societies had become dependent upon the trading system for a number of reasons.

Within a decade, the smooth functioning of the system was threatened. The growth of both the indigenous and immigrant populations produced a high degree of stress. Competition for land increased. When the fur trade became depressed and internecine warfare among Indian communities intensified, a number of settlers began to question the policy of having native villages within close proximity to their homes. At this point, the lack of flexibility in either economy and the decreasing amount of reciprocity between the two systems produced a crisis. The strategies which had once been central to Indian-English relations grew increasingly unproductive. Too much was impinging on the system. It would take only another ten years and the ravages of King Philip's War to complete the rift which had begun to develop.

Rather than end with what amounts to a traditional historian's scenario of the Indians' demise, I will return briefly to the notion of segmentation with which this paper began. As I have noted, no political unit larger than the village consistently acted together in the Connecticut valley. The Squakheag, Pocumtuck, Norwottuck, Woronoco and Agawam "tribes" were simply village polities. Moreover, factionalism developed within the villages themselves. Families controlled resources, whether the commodity was corn, furs or land. At Norwottuck, Woronoco, and Agawam some families who consistently found it to their advantage to deal with the English traders for pelts, and ultimately for land, followed goals that were at cross-purposes with those of other members of their own towns. To speak of Pocumtuck motivations or Norwottuck strategies as if all community members were in agreement, one must consciously bend reality. To speak of Indian tribal politics without recognizing such fragmentation, factionalism, and shifting family and village alliances may lead to the misinterpretation of the Contact period in southern New England.

These factors are significant, because in trying to understand the processes of Indian-white interaction, an awareness of the roles played by individuals or extended kin groups within the Indian communities is essential. Without this recognition, many writers have viewed Indian tribes as simply acting or reacting to changing English policy without any motivation except that of self-preservation from colonial encroachment (Jennings 1975:145, 227, 255, 287, 315). I suggest that some Indian leaders were no less guilty than some English of pursuing self-aggrandizement at the ultimate expense of other members of their own society. Individual motives on both sides molded the processes of change. Human action is the stuff from which history is made and the means by which societies and cultures are transformed. Native Americans on the southern New England frontier were not passive witnesses to their own demise. Rather, for better or worse, and with varying degrees of success, many were active participants in shaping their own destiny.

REFERENCES CITED

Ames, David W., and Burton R. Fisher
  1959   The Menomines Termination Crisis. Human Organization 18(3):101–111.

Barnes, J.A.
  1968   Networks and Political Process. *In:* Local-Level Politics: Social and Cultural Perspectives. Marc J. Swartz, ed. Chicago: Aldine.

Bradford, William
  1898   Bradford's History 'of Plimoth Plantation.' Boston: Wright and Potter Printing Co., State Printers.

Bradley, James W.
  1984   Blue Crystals and Other Trinkets: Glass Beads from 16th and Early 17th Century New England. *In:* Research Records #16. Proceedings of the 1982 Glass Trade Bead Conference. Charles Hayes, gen. ed. Rochester, N.Y.: Rochester Museum of Science Center.

Burt, Henry M.
  1898   The First Century of the History of Springfield; The Official Records from 1636 to 1736, with an Historical Review and Biographical Mention of the Founders. Vol. 1. Springfield, Massachusetts: H. M. Burt.

Burton, William and Richard Lowenthal
  1974   The First of the Mohegans. American Ethnologist 1:589–599.

Carneiro, Robert I.
   1968   Slash-and-Burn Cultivation Among the Kiukuru and Its Implications for Cultural Development in the Amazon Basin. *In:* Man in Adaptation: The Cultural Present. Y. Cohen, ed. Chicago: Aldine.

Champlain, Samuel de
   1907   Voyages of Samuel de Champlain, 1604–1618. (Original narratives of Early American History.) W. L. Grant, ed. New York: C. Scribner's Sons.

Day, Gordon M.
   1965   The Identity of the Sokokis. Ethnohistory 12:237–249.

Edgerton, Robert B.
   1962   Menomines Termination: Observations on the End of a Tribe. Human Organization 21(1):10–16.

Epstein, A. L.
   1968   Power, Politics, and Leadership: Some Central African and Melanesian Contrasts. *In:* Local-Level Politics: Social and Cultural Perspectives. Marc J. Swartz, ed. Chicago: Aldine.

Gibson, Susan G., ed.
   1980   Burr's Hill: A 17th Century Wampanoag Burial Ground in Warren, Rhode Island. Studies in Anthropology and Material Culture. Vol. 2. The Haffenreffer Museum of Anthropology, Brown University.

Green, Mason A.
   1888   Springfield, 1636–1886: History of Town and City. Boston: C. A. Nichols and Co.

Hampden County
   n.d.   Liber A and B. Manuscript compilation. Hampden (Massachusetts) County Registry of Deeds.

Hazard, Ebenezer, ed.
   1969   Records of the United Colonies of New England. *In:* Historical Collections, consisting of State Papers, and other authentic documents, intended for materials for America. Vol. 2. [Reprinted] Freeport, New York: The Books for Libraries Press.

Jennings, Francis
   1975   The Invasion of America: Indians, Colonialism, and the Cant of Conquest. Chapel Hill: University of North Carolina Press.

Laet, Johan de
   1909   Extracts from his "New World" [1625]. *In:* Narratives of New Nether-

land, 1609–1664. (Original Narratives of Early American History.) J. Franklin Jameson, ed. New York: C. Scribner's Sons.

Leach, Douglas E.
1958 Flintlock and Tomahawk: New England in King Philip's War. New York: Macmillan.

Leacock, Eleanor
1954 The Montagnais "Hunting Territory" and the Fur Trade. American Anthropologist 56(5), Part 2. Memoir No. 78.
1969 The Montagnais-Naskapi Band. *In:* Contributions to Anthropology: Band Societies. D. Damas, ed. National Museum of Canada Bulletin 228:1–13.

Lee, Richard B.
1972 !Kung Spatial Organization: An Ecological and Historical Perspective. Human Ecology 1(2):125–147.

Morrison, Alvin H.
1976 Dawnland Directors: Status and Role of 17th Century Wabanaki Saga-mores. Papers of the Seventh Algonquian Conference, 1975. Ottawa: Carleton University Press.

Pynchon, John
1652– [Account books kept in Şpringfield, Massachusetts, containing accounts
1701   with Valley settlers and local Indians.] 6 vols. Manuscripts on file at the Connecticut Valley Historical Museum, Springfield, Massachusetts.

Pynchon, William
1645– [Record of Accounts with Early Settlers and Indians. Carried forward from
1650   previous book, around September, 1645 and to a new book around March, 1650 [51]. Probably transcribed by John Pynchon.] Manuscript on file at the Forbes Library, Northampton, Massachusetts.

Ritchie, William
1969 The Archaeology of New York State. Rev. ed. Garden City: The Natural History Press.

Sahlins, Marshall
1965 On the Sociology of Primitive Exchange. *In:* The Relevance of Models for Social Anthropology. Michael Banton, ed. A.S.A. monographs 1. New York: Praeger Pub.
1968 Tribesmen. Englewood Cliffs, New Jersey: Prentice-Hall.

Salisbury, Neal
1982 Manitou and Providence: Indians, Europeans and the Making of New England, 1500–1643. New York: Oxford University Press.

Salwen, Bert
1966 European Trade Goods and the Chronology of the Fort Shan Site. Bulletin of the Archaeological Society of Connecticut 34:5–38.
1975 Post-Glacial Environments and Cultural Change in the Hudson River Basin. Man in the Northeast 10:43–70.

Service, Elman R.
1975 Origins of the State and Civilization: The Process of Cultural Evolution. New York: Norton.

Simmons, William S.
1970 Cautantowwit's House: An Indian Burial Ground on the Island of Conanicut in Narragansett Bay. Providence: Brown University Press.

Solecki, Ralph
1950 The Archaeological Position of Historic Fort Corchaug, Long Island and Its Relation to Contemporary Forts. Bulletin of the Archeological Society of Connecticut 24:5–35.

Spicer, Edward H., ed.
1961 Perspectives in American Indian Culture Change. Chicago: University of Chicago Press.

Strickon, Arnold and S.M. Greenfield, eds.
1972 Structure and Process in Latin America: Patronage, Clientage and Power Systems. Albuquerque: University of New Mexico Press.

Temple, Josiah H.
1887 History of North Brookfield, Massachusetts. Boston: Published by the town.

Thomas, Peter A.
1976 Contrastive Subsistence Strategies and Land Use as Factors for Understanding Indian-White Relations in New England. Ethnohistory 23(1):1–18.
1979 In the Maelstrom of Change: The Indian Trade and Culture Process in the Middle Connecticut River Valley:1635–1665. Ph.D. dissertation, Department of Anthropology, University of Massachusetts.
1981 The Fur Trade, Indian Land and the Need to Define Adequate "Environmental" Parameters. Ethnohistory 28(4):359–379.

Trumbull, James H.
1898 History of Northampton, from Its Settlement in 1654. Vol. 1. Northampton: Press of Gazette Printing Co.

Vaughan, Alden T.
1965 New England Frontier: Puritans and Indians 1620–1675. Boston: Little, Brown and Co.

Williams, Lorraine E.
  1972 Fort Shantok and Fort Corchaug: A Comparative Study of Seventeenth-Century Culture Contact in the Long Island Sound Area. Ph.D. dissertation, Department of Anthropology, New York University.

Williams, Roger
  1827 A Key into the language of America, or a help to the language of the natives in that part of America called New England [1643]. Rhode Island Historical Society (collections 1:17–61).

Winthrop, John, Jr.
  1863 Letter to John Winthrop, Sr., dated April 7, 1636. Massachusetts Historical Society Collections, 4th ser. 6:531–532.

Witthoft, John, and Fred W. Kinsey, eds.
  1959 Susquehannock Miscellany. Harrisburg: Pennsylvania Historical Museum Commission.

Wood, William
  1898 New England's Prospect. Boston: E. M. Boynton.

Wright, Harry A.
  1897 Discovery of Aboriginal Remains near Springfield, Massachusetts. Scientific American 76(11):170.
  1905 Indian Deeds of Hampden County [Massachusetts]. Springfield, Massachusetts: Private printing.

New York Iroquois Political Development

William Engelbrecht

A B S T R A C T

This paper argues that both New York Iroquois tribes and the League of the
Iroquois had their origins in prehistoric times. The advent of Europeans ultimately
resulted in the further consolidation of these organizations during the Protohistoric and
Historic periods. The isolation of the New York Iroquois from direct contact with
Europeans during the sixteenth and early seventeenth centuries gave Iroquois institutions time to develop without direct European interference. Support for this view is
sought both from archaeological data and from oral tradition.

1. Introduction

Nearly 150 years elapsed between the European discovery of North America
and the beginning of first-hand documentation of the New York Iroquois.
What effect, if any, did Europeans have on Iroquois political development
during this period? This paper argues that both New York Iroquois tribes
and the League of the Iroquois developed gradually, the process beginning in
prehistoric times and continuing into the historic period. During the Protohistoric period in New York (the sixteenth and early seventeenth centuries),
Europeans indirectly contributed to the consolidation of Iroquois tribes and
the League.

During the sixteenth and early seventeenth centuries, European trade
goods were reaching New York Iroquois villages with increasing frequency,
although there is little evidence of direct European contact with these groups.
It is therefore difficult to identify changes which may have occurred in
Iroquois society as a result of the European presence in North America. In

order to assess Iroquois political development during this period, two sepa-rate lines of evidence will be used: archeology and oral tradition.

To paraphrase Sears (1961), archeologists cannot dig up political systems. The data that archeologists deal with generally constitute only an imperfect reflection of the actual past behavior the archeologist is seeking to infer. If patterns of past behavior can be successfully inferred, the problem of relating this behavior to social or political institutions remains. An additional problem is that the archeological data base for the New York Iroquois is generally inadequate for inferring most aspects of socio-political organization. Despite over a century of archeological investigation in New York State, there are numerous gaps in our knowledge of the Iroquoian occupation of the state. Many Iroquoian sites are poorly known, and some have been largely destroyed. There are few Iroquoian villages that approach total excavation, so we know little about the internal structure or population of most villages. My hope is that one benefit of this paper will be to focus attention on the need for new data as well as the need to look at old data in new ways.

Using oral tradition to trace Iroquois political development also has limita-tions. Sometimes different or conflicting versions describing a particular event exist. Also, oral traditions are often rich in allegory and therefore cannot be interpreted in the same way as an historical narrative. Despite these problems, oral tradition, like archeological data, does contain information about the past. The strategy employed in this paper is to seek possible areas of congruence between archeology and oral tradition as they apply to Protohis-toric Iroquois political development.

2. Tribal Development

The early seventeenth-century Seneca, Cayuga, Onondaga, Oneida, and Mohawk are commonly referred to as tribes, though modern Iroquois prefer the term "nations." While the Oneida may have had a single village at this time, the other Iroquois groups consisted of two or more. It is assumed that these villages were not functionally differentiated. Since communities shifted their location a few miles every ten to twenty years due to the depletion of soil and firewood in their immediate vicinity, over time a single community is represented by a number of sites in an area. Sequences of village movement have been worked out for a number of areas, including the Niagara Frontier, where a tribe of the Erie may have lived. With the exception of the Onon-daga and Oneida, who were geographically close to one another, the tribes were separated by an average distance of approximately fifty-five miles. Figure 1 illustrates the areas in which sixteenth- and early seventeenth-century village sites are clustered.

The development of these population clusters remains to be worked out for all areas. Though the data are incomplete, there appears to be a trend toward increasing site size from the Owasco to the Iroquois period (Ritchie and Funk, 1973:364), implying the development of larger communities. In most cases, it is not clear whether these larger communities are the result of population increase or the merger of two or more smaller communities. In either case, defense was probably a major factor in encouraging the mainte-nance of larger communities. Many prehistoric sites are both palisaded and situated with reference to defensible terrain, suggesting that hostile external relationships were a fact of life during the Late Prehistoric and Protohistoric periods in New York.

These larger communities may have had organizational features character-istic of historic Iroquois tribes, but determining this from the archeological record is difficult. Typically, historic Iroquois tribes were composed of two or more villages located not more than about ten miles apart. Trigger suggests:

> . . .the need for defense produced larger settlements, until these reached the limits at which Iroquois slash and burn horticulture could operate efficiently. Once these limits had been reached, these same forces led to the development of defensive alliances in which friendly villages settled in close proximity. (1976:158–159)

Such alliances between villages would have formed the basis for the devel-opment of tribal identity encompassing two or more communities.

Two alternative processes of tribal development which might be reflected archeologically are 1) the fusion of smaller communities to form larger communities, and 2) alliances between communities. Ideally the fusion of smaller communities into larger ones might be revealed through ceramic analysis, while alliances could be reflected archeologically by the existence of contemporaneous village sites not more than about ten miles apart. While a tribe may consist of a single village, closely spaced contemporaneous Iroquois village sites are taken to indicate the existence of a tribe for the purposes of this paper. Used in this manner, the term "tribe" could refer either to a loose alliance between communities or to a more integrated political organization.

The identification of tribes by the distribution of communities enables one to infer the minimum time depth of specific tribes. Similar site distributions

Figure 1 Sixteenth- and Seventeenth-Century Seneca (a) and Onandaga (b) Sites

Onandaga villages: 1, Rochester Junction; 2, Dann; 3, Kirkwood; 4, Powerhouse; 5, Lima; 6, Dutch Hollow; 7, Bosely Mills; 8, Feugle; 9, Cameron; 10, Adams; 11, Tram; 12, Warren; 13, Factory Hollow; 14, Conn; 15, Taft; 16, Belcher; 17, Richmond Hills; 18, Fort Hill; 19, Boughton Hill; 20, Bunce; 21, Beale; 22, Steele; 23, March; 24, Wheeler Station. Seneca villages: 25, Schoff; 26, Coye (Toyadasso) and Coye II; 27, Keough; 28, Bloody Hill; 29, Christopher; 30, Burke; 31, Carley; 32, Indian Castle; 33, Indian Hill; 34, Cemetery; 35, Nursery; 36, Barnes; 37, McNab; 38, Temperance House; 39, Atwell; 40, Quirk; 41, Pompey Center; 42, Sheldon; 43, Chase; 44, Dwyer

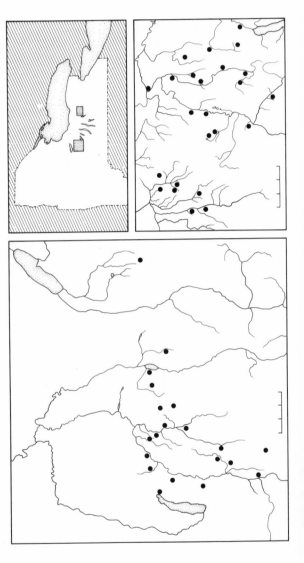

in earlier times imply the existence of the same political unit. The initial appearance of the known tribal pattern (figure 2) suggests that the particular tribe is at least that old. This gives only a minimum estimate, however, since some variant form of tribal organization may have been in existence in the area earlier.

2.1. Onondaga and Seneca Archeology

Rather than reviewing information for all historically known tribal areas, this paper focuses on two of the best known: the Onondaga and Seneca. Tuck (1971) noted changes in the Onondaga area in the fifteenth century which suggested to him the formation of the Onondaga tribe. These changes included the shift from small dispersed communities to two closely spaced communities, the large one probably being formed by the merger of two smaller communities. The close geographical proximity of the two communities suggests an alliance or non-aggression pact. It is this pattern of a large and a small community which persists into protohistoric times in the Onondaga area. Bradley (1979:346) argues that there is further consolidation during the historic period, when the Onondaga lived in a single large village. The Onondaga data therefore suggest a continuing process of population nucleation or fusion, with a distribution resembling that of the early seventeenth-century Onondaga tribe appearing in prehistoric times.

Data from the Seneca area present a different picture. Wray (1973) has traced the historically observed pattern of two larger communities, each with an associated smaller community, back in time to about the mid-sixteenth century. While there are earlier Iroquoian sites in the area, their relationship to these later sites is not clear. The writer recently examined ceramics from two of these earlier sites, Footer and Farrell. Neither collection exhibited much ceramic similarity with collections from later Seneca sites (see table 1).

While the locations of Footer and Farrell suggest that the populations of these sites were ancestral to the sixteenth-century Seneca, ceramic analysis does not demonstrate a strong continuity. Other communities with different ceramic traditions probably merged with the descendants of the Footer and Farrell populations to form the large sixteenth-century Seneca communities.

To see if the fusion model developed from Tuck's Onondaga data could be applied to the Seneca, ceramics from the Adams site were examined. Adams is the earliest large western village in the Seneca sequence. If this village were the product of fusion of two or more separate communities, then ceramics

Figure 2 *Model of Iroquois Political Development and Population Distribution*

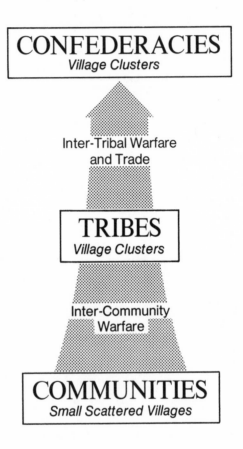

from this site should be relatively heterogeneous, reflecting different ceramic traditions developed in different communities. Coefficients of homogeneity were calculated for Adams and six later Seneca sites, as well as for Farrell and Footer (see table 2). The ceramics from Adams proved to be the most heterogeneous (figures 3 and 4), lending support to a fusion model for Seneca development. More information on early sites in the Seneca area and environs are needed to test this model further.

Site / Site/Date (A.D.)	Farrell	Footer	Belcher	Richmond Mills	Adams	Cameron	Factory Hollow	Dutch Hollow	Cornish	Warren	Powerhouse
Farrell 1300–1350		161	158	150	146	138	137	138	135	139	131
Footer 1350–1400			148	145	142	133	129	135	128	134	128
Belcher 1450–1550				173	151	145	137	143	133	142	134
Richmond Mills 1450–1550					159	165	155	160	147	159	152
Adams 1550–1575						148	141	149	137	155	140
Cameron 1575–1590							175	181	167	172	168
Factory Hollow 1580–1610								178	185	175	176
Dutch Hollow 1590–1616									173	177	177
Cornish 1600–1620										173	179
Warren 1615–1630											177
Powerhouse 1630–1650											

Table 1. *Coefficents of Agreement as Measured by Ceramic Similarity among Seneca Sites*

According to Tuck, in the Onondaga area the Christopher site represents the fusion of two earlier communities, one at Bloody Hill and one occupying the Keough site. Tuck was not able to examine a large sample from Christopher. Since material is available, it should be studied to see if it is also more heterogeneous than that of later sites. Ramsden (1978:108) notes evidence of artifact heterogeneity on the Parsons and Draper sites, two large Huron sites

Table 2. *Coefficients of Homogeneity for Seneca Sites. The higher the coefficient, the more homogeneous the ceramic assemblage. Adams is the most heterogenous.*

Site	Date (A.D.)	Coefficient
Farrell	1300–1350	.71
Footer	1350–1400	.74
Adams	1550–1575	.65
Cameron	1575–1590	.70
Factory Hollow	1580–1610	.74
Dutch Hollow	1590–1616	.72
Cornish	1600–1620	.76
Warren	1615–1630	.71
Powerhouse	1630–1650	.75

probably dating to the early sixteenth century which, he believes, reflect the fusion of separate communities. Similar analyses of the first large fifteenth- and sixteenth-century sites in other areas should be undertaken to see if the ceramics are heterogeneous. If so, this would lend further support to the fusion model of Iroquois tribal development.

Oral tradition commonly states that there were two separate groups of Senecas at the time of the formation of the League (Parker 1916:87). This agrees with the Protohistoric and early Historic Seneca settlement pattern of two major villages, each with smaller settlements nearby. Different versions of the Seneca origin myth have been recorded by Morgan, Schoolcraft, Cusick, and others. As Niemcyzcki (1983:25–26) has noted, these different versions may reflect different populations which merged to form the Seneca. In Seaver's (1824) account, a giant snake threatens the people but is eventually slain. Beauchamp (1892) believed that this allegory preserved the memory of an early conflict which helped to unify the Seneca. This interpretation is compatible with George Hamell's equation of the serpent or fire dragon of Iroquois myth with forces of disharmony or disorganization (George Hamell, personal communication).

Conflict and population merger or fusion can therefore be inferred from both oral tradition and archeology. During the Late Prehistoric period, blood feuds, religious motivation, and the desire to acquire prestige on the warpath led to escalating conflict between Iroquoian communities (Trigger 1969:52). With the advent of Europeans, competition for access to furs or to European trade goods further intensified Iroquois warfare. This warfare created widely

Figure 3 *Ceramic Vessels from the Adams Site (Seneca, c. 1565–1575 A.D.)*
These objects' diverse decoration illustrates the heterogeneity of this site assemblage. (RMSC cat. nos., clockwise from upper left: 614/94, 383/94, 269/94, 264/94; photographs courtesy of Rochester Museum and Science Center)

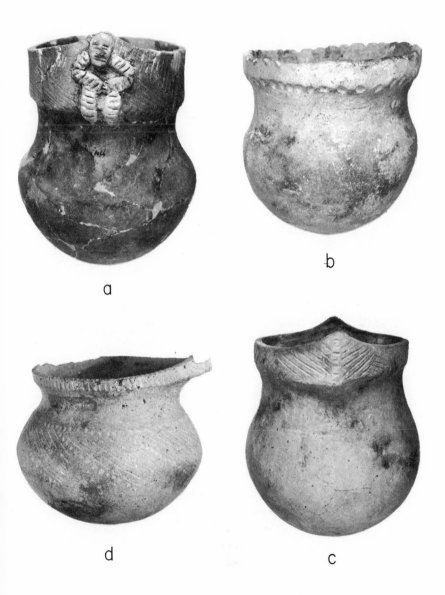

a

b

d

c

Figure 4 *Ceramic Vessels from the Adams Site (Seneca, c. 1565–1575 A.D.) These objects' diversity illustrates the heterogeneity of this site assemblage. (RMSC cat. nos., clockwise from upper left: 609/94, 610/94, 268/94, 409/ 94; photographs courtesy of Rochester Museum and Science Center)*

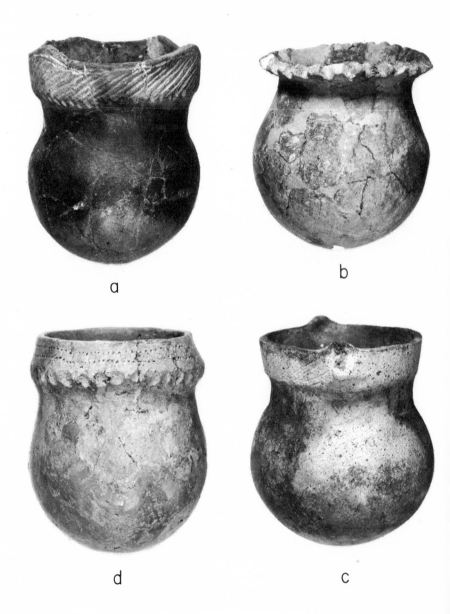

a

b

d

c

spaced population clusters which provided the basis for tribal development. Sahlins (1961:326) has noted that the degree of political consolidation within a tribe is dependent on external circumstances. Continued warfare would have operated to transform closely spaced allied villages into a single cohesive political unit.

2.2. Clans

The emergence of larger population units or tribes encouraged new forms of social integration. Service (1962:141) and others have stressed the role of pan-tribal sodalities in tribal organization, and Tuck (1971) postulated growth in organizations like the False Face Society during the process of Iroquois tribal formation. Clan affiliation became an important integrative mechanism as well. Clans were an important component of Iroquois political organization in historic times and clan affiliation remains important to New York Iroquois today. In historic times, members of the same clan were found in different communities or even in different tribes. Early European visitors to Iroquois villages noted clan symbols above longhouse doors which could be identified by travelling Iroquois seeking shelter among fellow clan members.

If we assume that Iroquois longhouses were generally occupied by members of a matrilineage and their spouses, then a study of the number and size of houses on different sites over time would reflect the number and size of lineages on these sites. While these data are incomplete, the general temporal trend seems to be that of: 1) increasing number of structures, and 2) decreasing size of structures. At one extreme is a site like Bates, dating to around A.D. 1200 and consisting of a single longhouse which may have housed around fifty people (Ritchie and Funk, 1973:251). At the other extreme are historically observed Iroquois villages consisting of many small houses, most of which must have housed nuclear families.

In the Onondaga area, the longest houses were found during the fifteenth century, and Tuck (1978:328) noted a trend of decreasing longhouse size from the Prehistoric to the Protohistoric periods, even though sites continued to increase in size and the number of longhouses per site also increased.

Tuck suggests that this trend is related to tribal formation, perhaps from a relaxation of matrilocal residence rules as a result of greater freedom of movement between villages of the same tribe. Warrick (1982) cites a similar trend in Ontario and suggests that longhouses began to decrease in size once alliances between communities were established. Such alliances could have given individuals or families greater residential flexibility, especially if the same clans were found in both communities.

The European presence in North America may also have contributed to decreasing longhouse size by increasing mortality rates. European-introduced diseases took a heavy toll on North American Indian populations, and the discovery of multiple primary burials on the Seneca sites of Adams, Tram, Steel, and Powerhouse suggests that the Protohistoric and Early Historic Seneca were no exception. Clans, being relatively large units, would have provided more stability and continuity during this demographically unstable period.

While the decreasing size of longhouses suggests that lineages as residential units were increasingly composed of fewer individuals, the increasing number of houses suggests that more lineages were appearing on sites. The increase in the number of houses could be explained by the fission of single lineages or the incorporation of small groups or lineages from other populations. In historic times, the Iroquois adopted both individuals and groups, thus helping to maintain their population. With many smaller lineages present, clan segments probably took over many of the earlier functions of lineages within a community. In addition, shared clan affiliations provided a mechanism for fostering intercommunity or intertribal cooperation.

It is possible that the orientation of structures on Iroquois sites could reflect clans. Trigger (1981:35) notes the possibility that the tripartite arrangement of longhouses on the Mohawk site of Garoga could be interpreted as reflecting the three Mohawk clans of Bear, Wolf, and Turtle. However Ritchie and Funk (1973:331) find that this arrangement best fits the shape of the hilltop on which Garoga is situated. In addition, the historic Mohawk Caughnawaga site (1666–93) shows a dual, rather than tripartite division which might reflect moiety organization. If the internal structures of more sites were known, hypotheses relating these arrangements to features of social organization could be tested.

Cemetery data can also be used to infer the presence of clans. There are often multiple cemeteries associated with Protohistoric Seneca village sites. The existence of these multiple cemeteries suggests the presence of social divisions, and it has been suggested that these represent clan or moiety cemeteries (Wary and Schoft 1953:55). If such social divisions were not as important earlier, then earlier sites should be characterized by single, rather than multiple cemeteries. With the exception of the twelfth-century Sackett site, this appears to be the case, though more data are needed.

In *Iroquois Cosmology,* J. N. B. Hewitt (1928) relates a tradition of the formation of Iroquois clans. An individual states:

> . . .the time has now come when we should form clans which should exist. The reason that we should thus do, is that now, verily we have become numerous. . . .

and again:

> . . .there exists an unadjusted matter, we are separating one from another, continually, here upon earth (Hewitt, 1928:597).

The tradition further states that mortality rates were unusually high at this time. People camped in groups on either side of a stream and were assigned their clan affiliation. This account suggests that clans arose in response to social need resulting from larger communities, disorganization, and increased mortality. The reference to a high death rate suggests the Protohistoric period.

Clans in some form may actually have great antiquity in the Northeast, as their widespread distribution suggests (Tooker:1971). The argument presented here is that they became increasingly important during the fifteenth through seventeenth centuries as Iroquois tribal organization developed. Larger communities and alliances between communities would have fostered the growth of integrative institutions such as clans. Such integrative mechanisms were well developed by the mid-seventeenth century, for Iroquois tribes successfully absorbed people from diverse groups at this time.

While the longhouse remains an important symbol of Iroquois life, the trend of decreasing longhouse size and increasing number of longhouses argues for the decreased importance of lineages as integrative features of social organization. In place of lineages, clans and clan segments assumed an increased role, contributing to the cohesiveness of Iroquois tribes and later to the League of the Iroquois.

3. Confederacy

In early historic times the Iroquois Confederacy or League of the Iroquois was composed of the Seneca, Cayuga, Onondaga, Oneida, and Mohawk. Just as these Iroquois tribes were formed by alliances between villages, so the League may have started out as a series of alliances between tribes. Trigger (1976:163) suggests that the formation of a confederacy was an extension of the same forces which had already created tribal structures. As in the case of tribes, defense against a common enemy and a desire for peace between communities would seem likely reasons leading to such alliances. During the Protohistoric period, the increasing quantity of European goods on Iroquois sites suggests an increasing concern with non-local relationships.

3.1. Oral Traditions

The foremost student of the League of the Iroquois was L. H. Morgan. Even today, over a century after his death and 130 years after the publication of *The League,* his description of the structure and functioning of the League continues to influence our thinking. Morgan received much of his information on the League from Ely S. Parker, a knowledgeable Tonawanda Seneca. However, the League as Parker described it to Morgan did not necessarily function in the same way in the seventeenth century. Though seventeenth-century accounts tell us little about the League, they do indicate that each Iroquois tribe had considerable autonomy. In fact, a number of writers have suggested that in the early seventeenth century the League was basically a non-aggression pact between constituent members, allowing each tribe to undertake enemy raids without fear of attack from neighboring allies. During the eighteenth century, Iroquois tribes often pursued independent diplomatic policies. This gave the Iroquois flexibility in maintaining the balance of power between the British and French (Tooker 1981). Thus, the available information suggests that the picture of unified action described by Morgan cannot be projected far back in time.

The question of when this alliance or League was initially formed remains to be answered. At present, it is not clear if it is a prehistoric or a protohistoric phenomenon and hence whether the European presence in North America had anything to do with its inception.

There are many oral traditions surrounding the formation of the League and they do not agree as to the time of formation. In one version, the Seneca join the League after a total eclipse of the sun during a time when the corn was ripe. A check of astronomical tables points to A.D. 1451 as the likely date for this eclipse in central New York (Tooker 1978:420). Other traditions place the formation of the League sometime during the Protohistoric period: the length of a man's life before white men came to the country. Because of these contradictions, oral tradition has generally been dismissed as being of little use in determining the date for the founding of the League.

Deganawidah, who is credited with founding the League, is said (in some versions) to have been a Huron. The Huron also formed a confederacy, and for the early seventeenth century, their confederacy is better documented. Unlike the New York Iroquois, the separate groups composing the Huron confederacy were found together when the French first visited Huronia. Archeological research as well as accounts recorded by the French suggest that the formation of the Huron confederacy was a gradual process, the confederacy first being made up of two groups, the Attignawantan and the Attigneenongnahac (Trigger 1976:163). The Huron claimed that the alliance between these two groups went back to around A.D. 1440. On the other hand, the Tahontaenrat probably did not join the Huron confederacy until about 1610 (Trigger 1976:157). While the distribution of population in Huronia was more clustered than that of the New York Iroquois (perhaps ultimately to the Huron's disadvantage), it seems logical that the formation of the League of the Iroquois might also have been a gradual process, the final alliance being but the last of a series of earlier alliances between some but not necessarily all of the five groups.

If the formation of the League of the Iroquois is best described as a series of alliances, then the conflicting oral traditions relating to its origins could be seen as referring to the formation of different alliances. For example, there may have been a prehistoric alliance or agreement between some or all of the tribes shortly after the eclipse of 1451 and then another between all of the Five Nations during the Protohistoric period. Some traditions say that the Mohawks were the first to join the League, whereas the Senecas were the last. These traditions support the idea that the League took shape over a period of time. Also, some traditions suggest that the names of the last two Seneca chiefs on the roll call of chiefs were added some time after the original council of the League (Tooker 1981:7). This, coupled with the fact that the Senecas have the fewest League chiefs, may reflect their status as late joiners of the alliance.

3.2. Ceramics and the League

In 1971, the author attempted to infer the formation of the League of the Iroquois from an examination of Iroquois ceramics. It was assumed that with the formation of the League, there would have been increased communication and movement of women between tribes of the League, and that this movement would be reflected ceramically. Pots from sixteenth- and early seventeenth-century Iroquois sites were examined, as were pots from the Niagara Frontier, an area originally to the west of the League. It was anticipated that with the formation of the League ceramic similarity between constituent members would increase, whereas pottery from the Niagara Frontier would not show this pattern. A primary assumption behind this hypothesis was that the formation of the League of the Iroquois was a relatively rapid and unique event. The results of that study did not support the original expectation. No clear difference in ceramic patterning between League sites and non-League sites was observed.

Though there was a general trend of increasing ceramic similarity between all areas through time, the amount of this increase varied. From this one could infer that intertribal female contact and movement between some tribal areas was greater than between others. The writer has gathered additional data since the 1971 study, so that now computer-coded ceramic information is available on some eight thousand Iroquois pots from forty-two village sites across New York State. These data reinforce the original inference that rates of intertribal female movement for any period are variable. Though ceramic patterning does not demonstrate that the formation of the League was a gradual process, these data can be interpreted in this light.

For example, ceramic analysis suggests little intertribal movement or inter- action on the part of women in the Niagara Frontier and Seneca areas (Engelbrecht 1974, 1978). While later Niagara Frontier sites show some Seneca-style pottery, in general ceramics from the two areas are distinctive. Sites in the Niagara Frontier cluster with one another on the basis of ceramic style and are ceramically homogeneous. Seneca sites show a similar pattern, being only slightly less homogeneous and slightly less similar to one another than are Niagara Frontier sites.

Historically, the population in the Niagara Frontier did not have an alliance with other New York Iroquois populations and this lack may be reflected in the area's ceramic distinctiveness. Seneca ceramics suggest that Seneca women were only slightly less isolated, a factor which may relate to the oral tradition that the Seneca were the last to join the League.

The Onondaga, Oneida, and Mohawk areas show a different pattern. In general, Onondaga and Oneida sites cluster with one another on the basis of ceramic style and show increased similarity with Mohawk sites through time (Engelbrecht 1974, 1978). This suggests increasing female movement between the Onondaga, Oneida, and Mohawk areas during the Protohistoric period. Iroquois woman regularly carried provisions for men on journeys

Table 3. *Coefficients of Homogeneity for Oneida Sites. The higher the coefficients, the more homogeneous the ceramic assemblage. There is a clear trend of increasing heterogeneity through time.*

Site	Date (A.D.)	Coefficient
Nichols Pond	1450–1500	.71
Buyea	1500–1550	.64
Bach	1540–1555	.63
Diable	1550–1570	.65
Wayland Smith	1570–1595	.60
Thurston	1625–1637	.58

(Thwaites 1899(38):255) and women could have traveled between tribes on their own. The Mohawk had easiest access to Dutch goods and in 1634 Van den Bogaert saw Oneida women who had come to a Mohawk village to trade. Tribal exogamy may also be reflected in these ceramic patterns. While matrilocality for the Iroquois is generally assumed, there may have been exceptions. As the smallest New York Iroquois tribe, tribal exogamy may have been more common for the Oneida, who in the sixteenth and early seventeenth century apparently consisted of a single medium-sized village. Sites in the Oneida area show a clear trend of increasing ceramic heterogeneity through time, possibly reflecting the movement of women into the Oneida tribe (see table 3).

Recently Andrefsky (1980) has argued that sites of the League Iroquois tend to have more trade material than do contemporaneous non-League sites in New York. This suggests a link between trade-related activities and League functioning. Trading between allied tribes could have increased tribal interdependence while intertribal cooperation in raiding allowed the formation of larger war parties.

4. Summary

In this paper, the terms "tribe" and "confederacy" have been used to refer to a range of organizational forms, from loose alliances to more tightly organized polities. However, power was never so centralized in historic Iroquois tribes as to preclude a measure of individual or kin group independence. Likewise, tribes appear to have preserved a measure of autonomy within the

League of the Iroquois. Within both tribes and the confederacy, the degree of political consolidation probably increased over time.

During the Prehistoric period, warfare led to larger communities and to alliances between communities (tribes). Tribal development was facilitated by the development of tribal sodalities and an increased role for clans. Continuing warfare encouraged alliances between tribes (confederacies). During the Protohistoric period, the European fur trade resulted in increased conflict, thereby accelerating trends already operating prehistorically.

The Iroquois Confederacy eventually defeated surrounding tribes and confederacies, adopting many people in the process. These large-scale adoptions helped the Iroquois to counter the increased mortality resulting from European introduced pathogens. Since the Iroquois were geographically separated from areas of European settlement until the eighteenth century, they had more time than did more easterly groups to develop politically without direct European disruption.

In the seventeenth century surrounding native American groups were no longer a threat to the Iroquois, but the major European powers continued to pose an external threat and we may assume that the League of the Iroquois continued to evolve as a political institution in response to this threat. Witness, for example, the incorporation of the Tuscarora in the early eighteenth century, when the Five Nations became the Six Nations. This incorporation can be viewed as a continuation of the process of alliance building begun by the Iroquois in prehistoric times.

The European discovery, exploration, and eventual colonization of the New World resulted in major changes in the way of life of the native peoples of North America. Many groups ceased to exist while others were fragmented and displaced. Occasionally, as in the case of the New York Iroquois, populations successfully maintained themselves in their traditional homeland during the colonial period. Though Europeans were the cause of increased warfare and mortality rates for the protohistoric Iroquois, their socio-political institutions evolved to meet these challenges.

ACKNOWLEDGMENTS

I am pleased to thank William Fitzhugh of the Smithsonian Institution, who asked me to present a talk to the Anthropological Society of Washington on the effect of early European contact on Iroquois institutions, thereby providing the focus of this paper. This study was in part made possible by an Arthur C. Parker Research Fellowship from the Rochester Museum and Science Center. The staff of the Rochester Museum, including Charles Hayes III, Charles Wray, and George Hamell (now with the State Museum in Albany), and Tricia Miller, who provided the photographs, was most helpful. Charles Vandrei and Mary Ann Niemczycki, both of the State University of New York at Buffalo, made helpful comments on an early draft of this paper. Finally, I would like to thank Elaine Henzler, secretary of the Anthropology Department at Buffalo State College, for her assistance in typing this paper.

REFERENCES CITED

Andrefsky, William
  1980 Implications of the Contextual/Structural Approach for Archaeology: An Iroquois Illustration. Masters thesis, State University of New York at Binghamton.

Beauchamp, William
  1892 The Iroquois Trail. Fayetteville, N.Y.

Bradley, James Wesley
  1979 The Onondaga Iroquois: 1500–1655. A Study in Acculturation Change and Its Consequences. Ph.D. dissertation, Syracuse University.

Engelbrecht, William
  1971 A Stylistic Analysis of New York Iroquois Pottery. Ph.D. dissertation, University of Michigan.
  1974 Cluster Analysis: A Method for the Study of Iroquois Prehistory. Man in the Northeast (7):57–70.
  1978 Ceramic Patterning between New York Iroquois Sites. *In:* The Spatial Organization of Culture. Ian Hodder, ed. Great Britain: Duckworth.

Hewitt, J. N. B.
  1928 Iroquois Cosmology: Second Part with Introduction and Notes. 43rd Annual Report of the Bureau of American Ethnology 1925–1926. Washington, D.C.: Smithsonian Institution.

Morgan, Lewis H.
  1851 League of the Ho-De'-No-Sau-Nee, Iroquois. Rochester, N.Y.

Niemcyzcki, Mary Ann
  1983 The Origin and Development of the Seneca and Cayuga Tribes of New York State. Ph.D. dissertation, State University of New York at Buffalo.

Parker, Arthur C.
1916 The Constitution of the Five Nations or the Iroquois Book of The Great Law. New York State Museum Bulletin 184.

Ramsden, Peter G.
1978 An Hypothesis Concerning the Effects of Early European Trade Among Some Ontario Iroquois. Canadian Journal of Archaeology (2):101–106.

Ritchie, William R. and Robert E. Funk
1973 Aboriginal Settlement Patterns in the Northeast. New York State Museum and Science Service, Memoir 20.

Sahlins, Marshall D.
1961 The Segmentary Lineage: An Organization of Predatory Expansion. American Anthropologist 63:322–343.

Sears, William H.
1961 The Study of Social and Religious Systems in North American Archaeology. Current Anthropology 2(3):223–231.

Seaver, James E.
1824 A Narrative of the Life of Mrs. Mary Jemison. Canandaiqua, N.Y.: J. D. Bemis and Company.

Service, Elman A.
1962 Primitive Social Organization: An Evolutionary Perspective. New York: Random House.

Thwaites, R.G., ed.
1899 The Jesuit Relations and Allied Documents. 73 vols. Cleveland: Burrows.

Tooker, Elisabeth
1971 Clans and Moieties in North America. Current Anthropology 12(3):357–376.
1978 The League of the Iroquois: Its History, Politics, and Ritual. Handbook of North American Indians, Northeast 15. Bruce G. Trigger, ed. pp. 418–441. Washington, D.C.: Smithsonian Institution.
1981 Eighteenth Century Political Affairs and the Iroquois League. The Iroquois in the American Revolution: 1976 Conference Proceedings. Charles F. Hayes, III, ed. Research Records No. 14, Rochester Museum and Science Center.

Trigger, Bruce
1969 The Huron: Farmers of the North. New York: Holt, Rinehart, and Winston.
1976 The Children of Aataentsic: A History of the Huron People to 1660. Montreal and London: McGill-Queen's University Press.

1981 Prehistoric Social and Political Organization: An Iroquoian Case Study. Foundations of Northeast Archaeology. Dean Snow, ed. New York: Academic Press.

Tuck, James
1971 Onondaga Iroquois Prehistory: A Study in Settlement Archaeology. Syracuse: Syracuse University Press.
1978 Northern Iroquois Prehistory. Handbook of North American Indians, Northeast, 15. Bruce G. Trigger, ed. pp. 322–333. Washington, D.C.: Smithsonian Institution.

Warrick, Gary
1982 The Long and the Short of Late Ontario Iroquoian House Size. Paper presented at the 1982 Canadian Archaeological Association Meetings, Hamilton, Ontario.

Wray, Charles F.
1973 Manual for Seneca Iroquois Archaeology. Honeoye Falls, N.Y.: Cultures Primitive, Inc.

Wray, Charles and Harry Schoff
1953 A Preliminary Report on the Seneca Sequence in Western New York, 1550–1687. The Pennsylvania Archaeologist 23(2).

PART III:

The Chesapeake: Two Views–

Anthropology and History

Commentary on Part III

William W. Fitzhugh

In previous sections of this work we have moved from north to south, from simpler, less productive environments to more complex environments with greater resource diversity and a capacity to sustain larger populations and higher levels of cultural complexity. The key factor has been the increasing human control over production capacity which, in the Iroquois case, reached the point that major amounts of cultural energy could be invested in non-subsistence activities such as intertribal warfare and the formation and maintenance of regional alliances, leading to confederation of tribes across a wide geographic area. Although political control over actions of the League of the Iroquois was not rigidly imposed and was formulated through leadership councils rather than by single individuals, many aspects of Iroquois life as well as that of neighboring tribes were directly or indirectly affected by collective decisions reached by the League or its constituent members. Among these were matters of economy (trade), political policy (warfare), regional alliances, and internal governance.

Ever since the days of Lewis Henry Morgan, anthropologists, historians, and political scientists have been curious about the League as a quasi-democratic, council-based political institution operating in a relatively simple native society. Archeologists have sought—and believe they have found—the roots of this intersocietal institution in prehistoric and early historic period subsistence, demographic, and settlement trends (Engelbrecht, this volume). European influence as a factor in the development of this institution in the historic period is thought to be only secondarily important. And yet, given the isolation of central New York Iroquois groups from direct European contact, the concomitant absence of detailed historic documentation until the eighteenth century, and the large amount of European trade goods that reached this region in the late sixteenth and seventeenth centuries (Pendergast 1985; Wray and Schoff 1953), one has to be concerned with the possibility that Iroquois political developments were not strictly native-stimulated. As we have seen, even sporadic indirect contact had a significant impact on Labrador Eskimo socio-economic developments, and a similar pattern is suggested for parts of the Northeast coast as a result of European-stimulated intertribal trade.

In moving into the mid-Atlantic coastal region we find ourselves confronted with a well-documented early seventeenth-century society known as the Powhatan chiefdom. For many years the Powhatans have been recognized as the largest and the most complex tribal society that existed east of the Appalachians at the time of the arrival of Europeans. For anthropologists and historians, the Powhatans have been of special interest because they are one of a few examples of ethnographically known "complex chiefdoms" in the eastern United States, and their origins and development are critical to understanding processes that may have been important in the origins of the more complex Mississippian societies that had become extinct in eastern North America several hundred years earlier. Fortunately, there is also a body of excellent historical documentation describing Powhatan society and the English attitudes towards it in the early seventeenth century.

In 1607, at the time of the founding of Jamestown, the Powhatans may have numbered some thirteen thousand individuals from thirty-one territorial districts, each controlled by a district chief or leader who was, in turn, presided over by a number of sub-chiefs, and ultimately by Powhatan himself. As Turner points out in his essay, the Powhatans had many attributes of a complex chiefdom: political control vested in a single political leader; high-ranking religious specialists; incipient hereditary class ranking; special mortuary rites and privileges; power of taxation and tributary rights, including manpower mobilization; and others (see also Binford 1964; Boyce 1978; Feest 1978a, b, c; Potter 1982; Strachey 1953; Turner 1976). The Powhatan chiefdom, therefore, clearly represents a more complex, higher-order political development than found in Iroquois country. For this reason, and because of the detailed historical documentation available, understanding the organization and historical development of the Powhatan chiefdom has assumed an important place in scholarly studies in eastern North America. This is all the more important in view of claims that the chiefdom began with the inheritance by Powhatan of from six to nine districts in the James and York River region in the late 1500s, grew to its maximum extent by 1607, and collapsed in 1646.

The rapid rise and fall of the Powhatan chiefdom has raised a number of important anthropological issues, among them a debate as to whether this development was an indigenous one or was stimulated by European contact. Although it is not the central theme of the two papers presented in this section, this question is critical in that it has not yet been resolved and probably cannot be resolved without archeological research. There is no doubt as to why the Powhatan chiefdom fell: English intervention, especially military intervention. The question remains: is Feest (1978a), basing his conclusions on ethnohistoric and historical data, correct in suggesting a European stimulus; or are its roots and impetus autochthonous, stemming from regional settlement and demographic shifts resulting from population growth, strains on agricultural production, pressure from surrounding Iroquoian and Siouan populations, and other trends noted in Late Woodland and sixteenth-century societies in this region, as claimed by archeologists who have considered this question (Binford 1964; Potter 1982; Turner 1976)?

This debate is not to be resolved in these pages, for it is one that cannot, in my opinion, be settled without more evidence than is now available. At present, the issue is divided on theoretical grounds between systemicists—in this case the archeologists—who are impressed with functional arguments and long-term developmental trends, and social and economic theorists who place emphasis on the capabilities of individuals and institutions to respond rapidly to changing conditions and opportunities.

Contact history is obviously squarely in the middle of this controversy (Quinn 1977, 1979). The Powhatans, whose core tribal region lies in the tidewater and coastal plain of central Virginia, probably were in contact with Europeans for the first time when the Spanish established the ill-fated Ajacan Mission in 1561. At that time an Indian leader, later named Don Luis, was captured and was taken to Spain. When he returned nine years later he described his lands as "chastised" by six years of famine and death. Does this imply virgin-soil epidemics? Later, in 1571, Don Luis led the fatal attack on the Jesuit mission outpost. This was followed, in 1572, by the slaughter of Indians by a Spanish retaliatory force. As noted by Fausz (this volume) these contacts, and others that had occurred between Indians and natives in Virginia and along the North Carolina coast, must have been known to the Powhatans, who would have been made wary of European strangers, were already concerned with military defense, and probably had been willing recipients of European goods as spoils of war or trade on a sporadic basis.

But unlike the Northeastern Indian contact situation, these contacts resulted from institutionalized efforts by Spanish mercantile, government, and religious groups. The same pattern continued in the founding of the Roanoke and Jamestown colonies by the English. These efforts were not entrepreneurial, as were the majority of contacts in northern regions. Spanish and English goals south of the Delaware were essentially ideological, social, and political in nature. They wanted to control the land, its peoples, and its resources, and their methods were military subjugation, not economic interaction. This difference in European policy had an enormous effect on the conduct of inter-cultural relations here. Ironically, though, the end result eventually was the same.

These two essays therefore present somewhat different case studies and concluding interpretations of primarily the same set of historical data relating to the Powhatan chiefdom. Turner takes a broad anthropological view, describing the features of Powhatan society as they can be reconstructed from ethnohistorical documents. In this account we see the functioning of a large and complex native political system appear in full-blown state within a generation of the first European visitations. While the influence of European involvement in this rapid political integration cannot yet be fully comprehended from historical or archeological data, its decline is clearly caused by European intervention after 1607.

Fausz, taking the historian's vantage point, brings a particularistic view to social relations between the English colonists and their Indian neighbors. Here we see the role of European national, social and political policy as it is played out at the level of individuals seeking to survive and manage their affairs while acting, for the most part, as pawns in a larger drama of culture contact. It was not until the Powhatan chiefdom was near its end—ravaged by disease, internal strife, and military defeat—that a new, more pragmatic English policy to European-Indian contact evolved with the establishment of mutually beneficial fur trading and other types of economic interaction in Maryland and the northern reaches of Chesapeake Bay. In presenting an alternative case study in European contact, Fausz demonstrates how the handling of documentary evidence can illuminate the intricacies of contact history, adding the "fine grain" that anthropologists so desperately need but so rarely have at hand. It goes almost without saying that if this type of detailed research were to be extended into the realm of economic structures and material remains here and in other regions, archeological approaches to early European contact studies would be greatly facilitated.

R E F E R E N C E S   C I T E D

Binford, Louis R.
  1964   Archaeological and Ethnohistorical Investigation of Cultural Diversity and Progressive Development Among Aboriginal Cultures of Coastal Virginia and North Carolina. Ph.D. dissertation, Department of Anthropology, University of Michigan.

Boyce, Douglas W.
  1978   Iroquoian Tribes of the Virginia-North Carolina Coastal Plain. *In:* Handbook of North American Indians, Northeast 15. Bruce G. Trigger, ed. pp. 282–289. Washington, D.C.: Smithsonian Institution.

Feest, Christian A.
  1978a Virginia Algonquians. *In:* Handbook of North American Indians, Northeast 15. Bruce G. Trigger, ed. pp. 253–270. Washington, D.C.: Smithsonian Institution.
  1978b North Carolina Algonquians. *In:* Handbook of North American Indians, Northeast 15. Bruce G. Trigger, ed. pp. 271–281. Washington, D.C.: Smithsonian Institution.
  1978c Nanticoke and Neighboring Tribes. *In:* Handbook of North American Indians, Northeast 15. Bruce G. Trigger, ed. pp. 240–253. Washington, D.C.: Smithsonian Institution.

Pendergast, James
  1985   Were the French on Lake Ontarion in the Sixteenth Century? Man in the Northeast 29:71–85.

Potter, Steven R.
  1982   An Analysis of Chicacoan Settlement Patterns. Ph.D. dissertation, Department of Anthropology, University of North Carolina.

Quinn, David Beers
  1977   North America from Earliest Discovery to First Settlements. New York: Harper and Row.
  1979   New American World: A Documentary History of North America to 1612. Vols. 2, 3, 4. David Beers Quinn, Alison B. Quinn, and Susan Hillier, eds. New York: Arno Press and Hector Bye, Inc.

Strachey, William
  1953   The Historie of Travell into Virginia Britania. Hakluyt Society, 2nd Series, no. 103. Louis B. Wright and Virginia Freund, eds. London: Cambridge University Press.

Turner, E. Randolph
  1976 An Archaeology and Ethnohistorical Study on the Evolution of Rank Societies in the Virginia Coastal Plain. Ph.D. dissertation, Department of Anthropology, Pennsylvania State University.

Wray, Charles F., and H. L. Schoff
  1953 A Preliminary Report on the Seneca Sequence in Western New York, 1550–1687. Pennsylvania Archeologist 23(2):53–63.

Socio-Political Organization within the Powhatan Chiefdom and the Effects of European Contact, A.D. 1607–1646

E. Randolph Turner

A B S T R A C T

English accounts describe in detail Powhatan society at the time of the establishment of the settlement of Jamestown in A.D. 1607. Examination of this information indicates that the Powhatan represented a well-developed chiefdom encompassing most of the Virginia coastal plain. Such data are reviewed in detail, especially as they relate to Powhatan socio-political organization. The effects of European contact, particularly from 1607 to 1646, then are discussed to document the collapse of the Powhatan chiefdom by the mid-seventeenth century as a viable integrated socio-political entity.

1. Introduction

In the spring of 1607 slightly over a hundred English settlers arrived in the Virginia coastal plain, beginning the first permanent English settlement in the New World. At that time, the region was occupied by the Powhatan Indians, under the leadership of a paramount chief of the same name. Powhatan society consisted of perhaps over thirteen thousand persons inhabiting slightly less than 16,500 square kilometers of the Virginia coastal plain, an average population density of at least 79 persons per hundred square kilometers (Feest 1973; Turner 1976, 1982). Territory occupied by the Powhatans stretched from the Potomac River to the divide between the James River and the Albermarle Sound and extended inland as far as the falls of the major rivers around Fredericksburg and Richmond (figure 1). Within this area, the Powhatans were divided into approximately thirty-one territorial units or districts. Of these, only six to nine, all within the James and York River drainages, had been inherited by the paramount chief Powhatan, the remainder having been gained through warfare or threat of warfare between the late 1500s and early 1600s.

The Powhatan socio-cultural institutions of 1607 reflected a remarkably complex society, particularly in comparison to other groups in the region. However, by 1646, only thirty-nine years later, the Powhatans were in a state of collapse, no longer existing as a viable, integrated entity. This rapid demise was the direct result of Powhatan interactions with English settlers between 1607 through 1646. The remainder of this paper is devoted to an examination of Powhatan socio-political organization as representative of a chiefdom society during this time period and the specific effects of English contact.

2. The Chiefdom or Rank Society: General Considerations

Identification and explanation of observed variations in socio-cultural complexity is one of the major goals of anthropological research. In recent years this interest has resulted in the formulation of developmental stages of social organization beginning with the simplest, basic level of egalitarian bands and proceeding through tribal societies to the most complex forms of stratified state societies (cf. Service 1962; Fried 1967). This paper is concerned with an intermediate stage in this sequence, the chiefdom or rank society.

Both band and tribal societies are kin-oriented and typically egalitarian except for certain inequalities expressed in age, sex, or specific personal characteristics. As noted by Fried (1967:33), egalitarian societies are characterized by as many positions of prestige in any given age-sex grade as there are persons capable of filling them, i.e., there are no means of fixing or limiting the number of persons capable of exerting power. Thus, leadership is personal and charismatic, with a noted absence of formal political hierarchies. Similarly, religious specialists (shamans) exist, but they are not organized into professional groups like priesthoods. Economic relations tend to be reciprocal in nature. Service (1962), in noting the kin-oriented and egalitarian nature of both band and tribal societies, emphasizes that in neither one have structural differentiations reached the point of formal centralization of economic, socio-political, or religious organization.

Compared with band and tribal societies, chiefdoms or rank societies have larger populations and are more complex, as evidenced by the presence of centers which coordinate economic, socio-political, and religious activities (Service 1962:143). Further, positions of valued status are limited, so that not all those individuals of sufficient talent to occupy such statuses actually achieve them (Fried 1967:109). One notes the appearance of ascribed positions in contrast to the achieved ones typical of egalitarian bands and tribes.

Economic organization is typically characterized by a redistribution network through which goods flow into and out from a specific center (Service 1962:144; Fried 1967:117; but see also Peebles and Kus 1977). Being under the control of a chief, such a system has not merely an economic role but also serves functions that are social, political, and religious. Other characteristics of economic organization frequently include incipient craft specialization and decreased participation of high-ranking individuals in subsistence activities.

As the position of chief becomes a permanent office in a society, social inequality becomes a basic characteristic, followed by inequality in consumption (Service 1962:148–149). Individuals of high socio-political rank also frequently occupy high religious standing. The charismatic, ephemeral leadership of egalitarian bands and tribes is replaced, upon the creation and perpetuation of the position of chief, with regulations that separate the chief from all others, sanctify or otherwise legitimatize him, codify his rights, privileges, and duties, and prescribe the form of succession (Service 1982: 155).

Likewise, religion in chiefdoms is noticeably different from that of egalitarian societies (Service 1962:170–171). Although shamanistic practices and related local life-cycle rituals are retained, ceremonies and rituals serving wider social purposes become more common. Supernatural beings now include ancestors of ranked individuals, and these, in turn, reflect the social order. Finally, religious specialization is characterized by the appearance of a priesthood which occupies a permanent position within the society.

Due to increases in population size, the maintenance of a stratified state demands power beyond the ties of kinship which are adequate for socio-cultural integration in egalitarian and rank societies (Fried 1967:186). Further, although chiefdoms have centralized direction, there is no true government to back up decisions by legalized force (Service 1962:159). Such a monopoly of force to back up authority is characteristic only of a stratified state and is to be contrasted to the kin-based use of force found in chiefdoms. Similarly, rank in chiefdoms is social in origin and is not a result of economic or political class differentiation.

The degree of social distinction is fostered by sumptuary rules; certain items of dress, ornamentation, perhaps kinds of foods, are reserved for one stratum and tabooed to the other. Sumptuary rules continue in primitive states but the classes become an aspect of full bureaucratic as well as social differentiation. Thus, in states the "aristocracy" are the civil bureaucrats, the military leaders, and the upper priesthood. Other people "work." Full-time professionalization in arts and crafts and sometimes in commerce develops also, and people who follow these professions can be regarded as still another class (Service 1962:172).

Thus, chiefdoms can be considered kin-oriented societies characterized by ranked positions as well as centers which coordinate economic, socio-political, and religious activities. However, true economic or political class differentiations are absent, being limited by definition solely to stratified state societies.

3. The Powhatan as a Chiefdom

For the early 1600s, when the Powhatans were at their height in terms of internal centralization and external expansion, a wide range of historical documents are available on numerous aspects of Powhatan society. As noted by Binford (1964) and Turner (1976), these documents clearly show that the Powhatan represent a well developed chiefdom. As a point of comparison, many of the Powhatan chiefdom's characteristic features have been shown elsewhere (Turner 1983) to be similar to ones in some of the more complex African and Polynesian chiefdoms discussed in studies by Taylor (1975) and Sahlins (1958). Other earlier, less accurate terms used in describing the Powhatans include a series of tribes, confederation or confederacy, empire, primitive state, centralized monarchy, and incipient conquest state (cf. Turner 1976:94–95).

3.1. Socio-political Organization

In portraying the socio-political organization of the Powhatan chiefdom, Smith (1910b:70) wrote:

> The forme of their Common wealth is a monarchicall government. One as Emperour ruleth over many kings or governours. Their chiefe ruler is called Powhatan. . . . Some countries he hath, which have been his ancestors and came unto him by inheritance. . . . All the rest of his Territories . . . they report have beene his severall conquests.

Of the approximately thirty-one territorial units under the control of Powhatan in 1607 all except one, the Chickahominy, had district chiefs. Although the Chickahominy paid tribute to Powhatan and would aid him in war in exchange for copper, they refused to acknowledge or accept a district chief until 1616, when Opechancanough assumed such a title (Beverley 1947:45; Dale 1615:57; Hamor 1615:11–12; Smith 1910b:51, 1910c:347, 514–515, 528; Strachey 1953:59, 69).

The position of chief among the Powhatans was inherited through the female line. Smith (1910b:81) documented the ascribed status of chiefs by writing concerning the successors of Powhatan:

> His kingdome descendeth not to his sonnes nor children: but first to his brethren, where of he hath 3. namely Opitchapan, Opechancanough, and Catataugh; and after their decease to his sisters. First to the eldest sister, then to the rest: and after them to the heires male and female of the eldest sister; but never to the heires of the males.

Similar observations are made by Beverley (1947:193), Simmond (1910:135), and Strachey (1953:77).

Unfortunately, the Powhatan chiefdom was in a state of collapse in 1646, primarily due to a policy of mass extermination pursued by the English during the conflicts of 1622 and 1644, and thus we have only limited data concerning the transfer of authority from one generation to another. This is particularly true of those areas conquered by Powhatan during his lifetime, and such information would have been of special importance for understanding the stabilization and unification of this rapidly expanding chiefdom. Nevertheless, several points can be deduced from the data that are available.

The historical records mention only six individuals as district chiefs or sub-chiefs related to Powhatan, although the number undoubtedly was higher. Powhatan's brothers (Opitchapan, Opechancanough, and Catataugh) all appear to have resided in the district of Pamunkey, located within the core area of the chiefdom. Opechancanough was evidently the district chief, while Opitchapan and Catataugh seem to have held lesser titles, perhaps as sub-chiefs within the district (see Hamor 1615:10; Smith 1910a:8, 17, 20–30; Strachey 1953:69). In addition, three "sons" of Powhatan (Parahunt, Pochins, and Tatahcoops) are mentioned, although these quite conceivably could have been children of one of Powhatan's relatives, dependent, of course, upon the kinship terminology used by the Powhatans. Of these three district chiefs, two held chieftainships in provinces not inherited by Powhatan; by granting them territory he had acquired through warfare or potential threat of warfare, Powhatan extended his kin ties into such areas (Strachey 1953:63–65, 67–68, 1964:80).

3.1.1. Succession

Upon his death in 1618 Powhatan was succeeded by his brother Itopatin (earlier referred to as Opitchapan), who was soon replaced for unknown reasons by Opechancanough (Beverley 1947:45; Smith 1910c:539). Smith (1910c:569–570) records a somewhat similar situation in the transfer of the position of chief between two brothers on the Virginia Eastern Shore. Although the position of chief was an ascribed one, there was evidently enough flexibility in the rules of inheritance so that the most capable close relative of the former chief could attain the position.

Limited data are available on two successors (Necotowance and Totopotamoy) to Opechancanough, who died in 1646. Unfortunately, information on their relationship to Opechancanough is unclear, although the wife of one (Totopotamoy) was said to be descended from Opechancanough (Anonymous 1836:14, 1838:13).

Additional evidence shows that the position of district chief was inherited even if no known kin ties existed with Powhatan. Besides the earlier noted Eastern Shore example, cases also are known for districts on the James, Appomattox, York, and Potomac rivers (Argoll 1906:91–93; Sacchini 1953:222; Strachey 1953:64–65; White 1846:20).

3.1.2. Marriage Practices

Aiding in the unification of the chiefdom, and by itself indicative of a rank society, was the practice of restricted polygyny. Polygyny was practiced primarily among the chiefs and their close relatives, the only group that could afford it. According to Smith (1910a:22), ". . . the Kings have as many weomen as they will, his Subjects two and most but one" (see also Smith 1910b:70; Spelman 1910:cvii; Strachey 1953:112, 116). This practice was first noted by the Spanish in 1570 along the York River (Carrera 1953:134).

Newport (1907:378) and Archer (1969a:104) specifically noted that Powhatan possessed the most wives. Strachey (1953:61) placed their number at over a hundred, dispersed among his various residences. Of these Strachey named twelve ". . . in whose company he takes more delight then in the rest, being for the most parte very young women, and these Commonly remove with him from howse to howse, either in his tyme of hunting, or visitation of his severall howses. . . .'' According to Smith (1910b:80), as Powhatan grew tired of his wives they were given as gifts to those "that best deserve them at his hands." Spelman (1910:cvii) stated that when the chief wanted new wives he informed his "cheefe men," who were sent out to the various settlements to look for the "fayrest and cumliest maids." Powhatan then chose those whom he liked, giving to their parents as presents "what he pleaseth." Spelman (1910:cvii) continued by noting:

> If any of ye Kings wives have once a child by him, he (never lieth with hir more) keeps hir no longer but puts hir from him giving hir sufficient Copper and beads to maytayne hir and the child while it is younge and then it is taken from hir and maytayned by ye King, it now beinge lawfull for hir beinge thus put away to marry with any other, The King Poetan having many wives when he goeth a Huntinge or to visitt another Kinge under him (for he goeth not out of his owne country) He leaveth them with tow ould men who have the charge on them till his returne.

Although information concerning the strengthening of alliances through the extension of kin ties is quite limited, the intermarriage of Powhatan's relatives with the families of other district chiefs was undoubtedly important in stabilizing and unifying the expanding chiefdom. Hamor (1615:41) cited a case in which Powhatan's youngest daughter was given to a chief three days' journey away for a bride price of two bushels of Roanoke beads. In addition, Beverley (1947:38) wrote that "Intermarriage had been indeed the Method proposed very often by the Indians in the Beginning, urging it frequently as a certaine Rule, that the English were not their Friends, if they refused it." The marriage of Pocahontas, one of Powhatan's daughters, to John Rolfe, an English settler, in 1613 is perhaps the classic example of attempts to establish an alliance. Earlier examples were noted by Zuniga in 1612 (Neill 1968:85). In the pre-contact situation such an extension of kin ties could have resulted over a period of time in a ramage structure similar to those first described by Kirchoff (1955) and shown by Sahlins (1958), among others, to be characteristic of many chiefdoms.

3.1.3. Status Hierarchy

Perhaps the most obvious evidence of the status hierarchy present in Powhatan society was variation in dress and the degree of respect received by the chiefs while in the presence of others. One of the best descriptions of Powhatan is presented by Smith (1910a:18–19):

> Arriving at Weramocomoco, their Emperour proudly lying uppon a Bed-stead a foote high, upon tenne or twelve Mattes, richly hung with manie Chaynes of great Pearles about his necke, and covered with a great Cover-ing of Rahaughcums [raccoons]. At his heade sat a woman, at his feete another; on each side sitting uppon a Matte uppon the ground, were raunged his chiefe men on each side the fire, tenne in a ranke, and behinde them as many yong woman, each with a great Chaine of white Beades over their shoulders, their heades painted in redde: and Powhatan with such a grave and Majesticall contenance, as drave me into admiration to see such a state in a naked Salvage.

For this particular meeting at Powhatan's principal residence, Simmond (1910:102) added, Powhatan sat on a pillow made of leather and covered with pearls and white beads and had twenty of his wives on each side of the lodge. Further details are provided by Smith (1910c:400) in a later publica-tion:

> On either side did sit a young wench of 16 or 18 yeares, and along on each side the house, two rowes of men, and behind them as many women, with all their heads and shoulders painted red: many of their heads bedecked with the white downe of Birds; but every one with something: and a great chayne of white beads about their necks.

A similar arrangement was noted by Hamor (1615:39) when he met Powha-tan several years later.

Smith (1910c:400) continued by stating that the "Queene" of Appomat-toc was appointed to bring Powhatan water to wash his hands, while another dried them with feathers. This practice had been noted earlier by Smith (1910b:80):

> When he dineth or suppeth, one of his women, before and after meat, bringeth him water in a wooden platter to wash his hands. Another waiteth with a bunch of feathers to wipe them instead of a Towell, and the feathers when he hath wiped are dryed againe.

Other documents likewise note the presence of attendants and servants as well as "ancient" orators around chiefs (Smith 1910a:24, 26, 1910b:73, 1910c:454; Strachey 1953:65; Wingfield 1969:216). Several district chiefs are similarly described (Archer 1969b:84, 92–93; Cope 1969:110; Newport 1907:377; Percy 1967:13–14, 16, 1969:147; Strachey 1953:65). Status differentiation is clearly shown in clothing and ornaments as seen in the use of furs, feathers, flowers, dyes, deer antlers, white coral, beads, pearls, copper, and other items. The use of servants is documented, and statements note that individuals stood in the presence of a district chief.

3.1.4. Wealth, Tribute, and Authority

Differences in dress as an indication of rank were to a large extent maintained by limiting access to items such as those mentioned above. Such variations in access prompted Smith (1910b:66) to note that ". . . the common sort have scarce to cover their nakedness but with grasse, the leaves of trees, or such like." The basis of these distinctions and their relation to Powhatan sociopolitical organization are best seen in descriptions of tribute and redistribution.

The most extensive accounts of the collection of tribute by Powhatan are presented by Strachey, who notes specific variations in rank.

The great king Powhatan hath devided his Country into many provinces, or Shiers (as yt were) and over every one placed a severall absolute Commaunder, or Weroance to him contributory, to governe the people there to inhabite, and his petty Weroances in all, may be in number, about three or fower and thirty, all which have their precincts, and bowndes, proper, and Commodiously appointed out, that no one intrude upon the other, of severall forces, and for the grownd wherein each one soweth his corne, plants his Apoke [tobacco], and gardeyn fruicts, he tythes to the great king of all the Commodityes growing in the same, or of what ells his shiere brings forth apperteyning to the Land or Rivers, Corne, beasts, pearle, Fowle, Fish, Hides, Furrs, Copper, beads, by what means soever obteyned, a peremptory rate sett down . . . . (Strachey 1953:87).

Every Weroance knowes his owne Meeres and lymitts to fish fowle or hunt in . . . but they hold all of their great Weroance Powhatan, unto whome they paie 8. parts of 10. tribute of all the commodities which their Countrey yeildeth, as of wheat, peaze, beanes, 8. measures of 10. (and these measured out in little Cades or Basketts which the great king appoints) of the dying roots 8. measures of ten; of all sorts of skyns and furrs 8. of tenne, and so he robbes the poore in effect of all they have even to the deares Skyn wherewith they cover them from Could, in so much as they dare not dresse yt and put yt on untill he hath seene yt and refused yt; for what he Commandeth they dare not disobey in the least thing (Strachey 1953:87).

Tribute often was collected during Powhatan's personal visits to nearby districts (Spelman 1910:cxiii), while he sent for it in those districts more distant (Smith 1910a:20). Evidently, some form of incipient specialization was present in the Powhatan chiefdom, for Smith (1910a:26) notes that Powhatan, while displaying his canoes, ". . . described unto me how he sent them over the Baye [the Eastern Shore] for tribute Beades: and also what Countries paide him Beades, Copper or Skins." In addition, Smith (1910c:406, 569) and Strachey (1953:107) specifically noted that Powhatan, and later Opechancanough, attempted to maintain monopolies over copper and other goods brought into Virginia by the English. Likewise, chiefs often laid claims on items stolen from the English (Smith 1910a:33). Such goods were placed in storehouses under the jurisdiction of various chiefs found within the larger villages, the most important of which was located near the fall line one mile from Orapaks, a village to which Powhatan moved from Werowocomoco shortly after the English arrived at Jamestown because he felt Werowocomoco was too close to the English settlement.

Another form of tribute involved human labor. Spelman (1910:cvii), in describing the planting and harvesting of the paramount chief's fields, stated that on an appointed day ". . . great part of ye country people meete who with such diligence worketh as for the most part all ye Kinges corne is set on a day." As a reward, beads were tossed by the chief in a prescribed fashion to those who had participated. The chief had those who carried the beads call over specific people whom he particularly favored, ". . . unto whom he giveth beads into their hande and this is the greatest curtesy he doth his people." As soon as his fields were ready for harvesting, the people were once again gathered, and the crops were promptly made ready for storage in "howses apoynted for that purpose."

Information concerning the redistribution of goods collected through tribute is limited to a few quite brief statements. Smith (1910b:68) noted that surplus subsistence goods collected by the chiefs were stored "till scarce times." Copper, beads, and perhaps pearls and other luxury items were sent by chiefs to those districts from which they wished aid, either in warfare or in the performance of a specific deed (Smith 1910c:591; Strachey 1953:68,

107). The redistribution of luxury items to persons for such services as in helping to plant and harvest Powhatan's fields has been noted. Spelman (1910:cx) observed that when certain individuals died, beads were tossed to the assembled "poorer people." Strachey (1953:114) noted the distribution of copper, pearls, and beads to those who had displayed bravery, courage, or outstanding use of strategy in warfare. Such accumulated goods could also be used to support communal feasts, religious activities, and the entertainment of visiting individuals of high rank lodged in the chief's village, all of which have been historically documented.

Specific references to special foods reserved for chiefs are noticeably scarce. The clearest information comes from Smith (1910b:58), who described a broth and bread made from chestnuts and chinquapins which was evidently eaten primarily by chiefs and served at their greatest feasts. Spelman (1910:cxiii) also stated that food left over from a meal occasionally was given to "ye porer sort."

A chief's rank was also indicated by his full-time protection by body-guards, as documented for Powhatan and Opechancanough (Hamor 1615:39; Simmond 1910:141; Smith 1910a:16, 18, 1910b:80, 1910c:378, 458, 518). Estimates on the number of guards vary from twenty to two hundred. Smith (1910b:80) specifically described them as ". . . of the tallest men his Country doth afford." At least in the case of Powhatan, they surrounded him both while he was traveling and during his stays at his various residences.

Failure by the guards to perform assigned duties resulted in severe punishment. Authority for such punishment, as well as others, resided with the chief. According to Smith (1910b:81), Powhatan possessed absolute power within the chiefdom, and ". . . at his feet they present whatsoever he commandeth, and at the least irowne of his browe, their great spirits will tremble with feare: an no marvell, for he is very terrible and tyrannous in punishing such as offend him." Such respect evidently arose not only because Powhatan was a chief but also because of the god-like status accorded the position (see Smith 1910b:78,81). Similar powers were held by the district chiefs, although they were still considered to be under Powhatan's jurisdiction (Smith 1910b:81). Additional information on punishment and the role of a chief is presented by Archer (1969b:90), Beverley (1947:225–226), Smith (1910b:81–82, 1910c:378), Spelman (1910:cx–cxi), Strachey (1953:62), and Whitaker (1613:26), among others.

The primary limitations placed upon Powhatan and the district chiefs seem to have been in the declaration of war and related matters, decisions in which the priests and counsellors played a major role (Argoll 1906:92; Hamor 1615:6; Strachey 1953:58, 90, 91, 104). No data exist on whether or not the position of counsellor was inherited, although it is likely that such positions were based upon age and experience (cf. Binford 1964:92). Smith (1910c:454) does mention an "ancient" orator as representing Powhatan. It is likely that the position of priest was inherited or at least restricted to individuals from wealthier and more highly ranked families (cf. Anonymous 1959:234–236; Beverley 1947:205–209, 214; Smith 1910b:77–78, Strachey 1953:98–99; White 1969:147–149; Turner 1976:119–120).

3.2. Settlement and Community Patterns

Because of centralization of socio-political organization within a chiefdom or rank society, one would expect hierarchical arrangement of settlements. This pattern is clearly indicated on Smith's (1910c:384) 1612 map of the region (for detailed discussions, see Binford 1964; Mouer 1981; Turner 1976). Most districts are represented not only by hamlets and minor villages but also by district "capitals" which Smith labeled "kings howses." The center for the chiefdom appears to have been located at the confluence of the Pamunkey and Mattaponi rivers in the Pamunkey district, where four such "kings howses" are indicated on Smith's map, the only instance of a nucleation of several of this residence type in a restricted area. A particularly high population density has been noted for this district (Turner 1976, 1982). Further, this is the specific area where Strachey (1953:69) stated that Powhatan's three brothers resided. Smith (1910b:75) also noted that the primary temples for the chiefdom were located here. Powhatan's major storehouses were situated further west near Orapaks. Smith (1910b:51) stated that Powhatan resided at Werowocomoco but soon moved to Orapaks because Werowocomoco was too near the English settlement of Jamestown on the James River. Werowocomoco, located on the York River to the east of the confluence of the Pamunkey and Mattaponi Rivers, probably was not one of the original territories inherited by Powhatan, and he initially may have taken up residence here to further unify his rapidly expanding chiefdom.

In terms of community organization within a settlement, three types of structures warrant particular attention. These include chief's houses, storehouses, and temples.

Strachey (1953:78) stated: "As for their howses, who knoweth one of them knoweth them all, even the Chief Kings house, yt self, for they be all alike builded one to another. . . ." Actually, distinctions did exist, but these were primarily based on size. According to Spelman (1910:cvi), houses for chiefs "are both broader and longer than ye rest having many dark windinges and turnings before they cum where the Kinge is" (see also Beverley 1947:176). Smith (1910b:70) noted Powhatan had dwellings thirty to forty yards long in each of his inherited territories. Such structures were also used for ceremonial purposes as well as for general entertainment. According to Strachey (1953:18), Opechancanough had four or five houses, each eighty to one hundred feet long, at Menapacute in the Pamunkey district, his principal residence. Information on average house size for lesser ranked individuals is not available.

Storehouses, under the control of a chief, also were located in or near some of the more important villages. Spelman (1910:civ) noted storehouses for maize, while Magnel (1969:153) mentioned "kings houses" full of furs. Likewise the Council of Virginia (1844:13) wrote of one "wardroabe" of Powhatan which contained some four thousand skins. Powhatan's principal storehouse was located near the fall line one mile from Orapaks in a thicket of woods (Smith 1910b:80; Strachey 1953:62). The structure, frequented only by priests, was fifty to sixty yards in length and had a carved post at each of its four corners. According to Smith, these images acted as sentinels. Items stored within this structure included skins, copper, puccoon (a red dye), pearls, beads, and bows and arrows. ". . . which he storeth up against the time of his death and burial" (Smith 1910b:80). To the above list might be added maize, as noted by Spelman (1910:cv): ". . . at Oropikes in a house . . . are sett all the kings goods and presents that are sent him, as ye Cornne."

3.3. Temples, Burials and Priesthoods

In every chief's district there was at least one temple under the jurisdiction of from one to seven priests (Smith 1910b:75–76). Such structures appear to have been located away from the villages within the woods. Smith (1910b:75–76) noted for the three principal Powhatan temples at Uttamussack in the Pamunkey district near the confluence of the Pamunkey and Mattaponi Rivers:

> This place they count so holy as that none but the priests and kings dare come unto them: nor the Salvages dare not go up the river in boats by it,

but that they solemnly cast some peece of copper, white beads, or Pocones into the river, for feare their Oke [a god] should be offended and revenged of them.

Clarke (1670:13) and Whitaker (1613:26) specifically noted that the priests lived alone in the woods in houses separated from "common" men.

Temples were as large as twenty by one hundred feet (Beverley 1947:196; Smith 1910b:75; Strachey 1953:88). Their organization, as well as decorated images and various status-denoting items associated with them, have been extensively described (Beverley 1947:197, 213, 215–216; Percy 1922:263; Smith 1910b:75, 1910c:393; Spelman 1910:cv; Strachey 1953:88–89, 94; Whitaker 1613:24).

The bodies of deceased chiefs were kept within specific back rooms, or chancels, of the temples. Smith (1910b:75) gives us the following details of the chiefs' interment:

Their bodies are first bowelled, then dryed upon hurdles till they be verie dry, and so about the most of their jointes and necke they hang bracelets or chaines of copper, pearle, and such like, as they use to weare: their inwards they stuife with copper beads and cover with a skin, hatchets, and such trash. Then lappe they them very carefully in white skins, and so rowle them in mats for their winding sheetes. And in the Tombe, which is an arch made of mats, they lay them orderly. What remaineth of this kinde of wealth their kings have, they set at their feet in baskets. These Temples and bodies are kept by their Priests.

Strachey's (1953:94) description of these practices is quite similar to Smith's, although he adds that the flesh scraped off the bones and the removed internal organs were dried and placed in small vessels (see also Beverley 1947:116).

In contrast, Smith (1910b:75) noted that for the "ordinary burials" they ". . . digge a deep hole in the earth with sharpe stakes; and the corpses being lapped in skins and mats with their jewels, they lay them upon sticks in the ground, and so cover them with earth." Jones (1956:85) described in 1724 very similar burial practices for some Indians to the west in the Piedmont region. An even greater range of variation in burial practices was indicated by Spelman (1910:cx), who wrote of a being wrapped in a mat and later placed upon a scaffold three to four yards above the ground. During the period of mourning which followed relatives of the deceased flung beads to the "poorer people" gathered, "makinge them to scramble for them, so that many times divers do breake the armes and legges being pressed by the cumpany. . . ." The rest of the day was spent in feasting, dancing, and singing. Later, when the body had decomposed, the bones were removed from the scaffold, placed in a new mat, and hung inside of the lodge of a relative of the dead individual, where they remained until the structure collapsed (see also Glover 1676:633). Although Spelman's description of these burial practices makes it clear that the body so treated was that of someone of higher status than some other members of the community, it is not clear whether that status was achieved or ascribed. In any case, the description does not match those for burials of chiefs.

As earlier noted, the priests were in charge of the temples and lived alone in the woods, separated from other individuals in Powhatan society. They, along with the chiefs, were viewed as godlike (Smith 1910b:78). According to Whitaker (1613:26), no one was allowed to approach the priests' dwellings or to speak to them without their permission, and everything they needed for subsistence, including water, was brought by unspecified individuals to a certain spot near their dwellings (see also Beverley 1947:226). Nevertheless, like the chiefs, the priests did on occasion participate in hunting, fowling, fishing, and other subsistence-related activities (Beverley 1947:213; Smith 1910c:400). Priests and lesser ranked shamans were characterized by specific variations in dress and appearance (Beverley 1947:164–166, 212; Smith 1910b:76; Spelman 1910:cxiii; Strachey 1953:95). More detailed discussions of their various duties are found in the writings of Beverley (1947:198, 218), Clayton (1965:21–23), Smith (1910a:22, 1910b:65, 71, 77), Strachey (1953:94–95), and Whitaker (1613:26).

Smith (1910b:78–79) and Strachey (1953:100, 102–103) stated that only chiefs and priests, because of their god-like status, were able to participate in an after-life, another indication of variations in rank. However, later accounts describe no such distinctions, but rather a dichotomy quite similar to the Christian concept of heaven and hell, with one's final "resting place" being dependent on one's actions and deeds in this life (Anonymous 1959:236; Beverley 1947:202; Michel 1916:131).

3.4. Chiefdom Summary

To summarize Powhatan socio-political organization during the early 1600s, there were three major status levels—paramount chief, district chief, and non-chief. The non-chief level was further divided into priests and shamans, counsellors and distinguished warriors, and finally commoners. The position of chief, and possibly that of priest, was inherited. The paramount chief and principal priests, at least, did not participate in subsistence production. A complex redistributive hierarchy was in operation, and chiefs were able to confiscate specific goods. Insignia of rank were observed through a significant range in clothes and ornaments, and chiefs had their own attendants, bodyguards, and orators. The practice of polygyny was largely restricted to chiefs. Control of socio-regulatory processes by chiefs with clear ability to inflict secular punishments has also been noted. Further evidence of a complex system of ranking was the restricted access to temples and storehouses under the control of a chief, since normally only chiefs and priests could visit these structures. Marked variations existed in burial practices, with placement in temples being limited to chiefs, whose bodies were associated with numerous items of limited distribution. Finally, both Powhatan settlement patterns and community organization are consistent with what would be expected in a chiefdom.

One may conclude that the Powhatan chiefdom was a kin-oriented society in which the chief's perogatives were primarily protected and sanctioned through the supernatural status of his ancestors. The presence of ascribed statuses and organizational hierarchies are clearly documented. Still, the degree of socio-cultural complexity had not reached that of a stratified state society, since actual economic and political class differentiations were absent.

4. Powhatan Interactions at European Contact

4.1. Early Contacts

Although European exploration of the Chesapeake Bay region may have begun as early as the first quarter of the sixteenth century (Lewis and Loomie 1953), available data indicate that Powhatan contacts with Europeans were minimal. However, maps dating back to the early to mid-1500s indicate that the region was at least known by Europeans if not actually visited. The possibility of some slave raiding and incipient trade exists (Feest 1978:254).

In 1570 a small Spanish party established the Ajacan Mission, believed to have been on the York River. They brought with them a member of a local chief's family who had been captured by the Spanish, given the name Don Luis, and transported to Spain. With Don Luis's aid, the Indians quickly wiped out the Ajacan Mission. A retaliatory expedition by the Spanish in

1572 resulted in the deaths of several Indians (Lewis and Loomie 1953). In the 1580s, Sir Walter Raleigh's settlements to the south along the North Carolina coast were known to the Powhatan. Although limited contacts were made with the Chesapeake Indians in the Virginia Beach area (Quinn 1955), this colony never became self-sufficient or expanded beyond its original locus. By 1590 the colonization attempts by the English within the region were temporarily abandoned. Other minor contacts preceding 1607 by Europeans in the Chesapeake Bay are documented by Feest (1978:254) and Potter (1976:9–10).

4.2. Development of the Powhattan Chiefdom

Feest (1978:254) has suggested that the European contacts noted above may have encouraged the rise of large political entities which culminated in the Powhatan chiefdom. Available ethnohistorical data, however, do not support this position. The origin of the Powhatan chiefdom can be traced back to sometime before the mid to late 1500s, at which time Powhatan inherited from his ancestors six to nine districts within the James and York River drainages. English accounts describe a series of small, independent chiefdoms (each containing from one to eighteen towns) along the North Carolina coast attempting to expand their range of jurisdiction through alliances and warfare during the 1580s (Lorant 1965; Quinn 1955). This is the situation Powhatan encountered when he attained control of his inherited territories. Incipient chiefdoms were already present in coastal North Carolina by the time of English contact in the 1580s, and in the Virginia coastal plain as early as 1570, when the short-lived Ajacan Mission was established. Although accounts for the Ajacan Mission (Lewis and Loomie 1953) are limited, they suggest inherited positions of leadership and restricted polygyny as well as a high population density among local Indians, particularly in comparison to other nearby areas with which the Spanish were familiar.

Nowhere in the available historical accounts is there any indication that early European contact significantly influenced changing socio-cultural organization, resulting in the formation of chiefdoms in the Virginia coastal plain. Powhatan society had developed into a relatively complex chiefdom by 1607, and European contacts before that year simply appear to have been too limited to have played an important role in this developmental process. Rather, it has been argued in recent studies combining both ethnohistorical and archaeological data (Binford 1964; Potter 1982; Turner 1976, 1983) that changes in socio-cultural complexity in Powhatan society before 1607 are best viewed as adaptations to specific stresses found in the local physical, biological, and cultural environments. These stresses have been shown likely to be related to population increase and the expansion of tribally organized socio-cultural units during the Late Woodland period which had progressed sufficiently so that intergroup competition favored the evolution of a more complex form of socio-cultural integration, culminating in the Powhatan chiefdom.

Binford (1964) was the first not only to take such a position but also to recognize that the Powhatan represented a chiefdom. In comparing the Powhatan to other nearby societies, he further established a series of correlations between the complexity of a society as measured by internal differentiation of roles and (a) number of resource zones present in a territory, (b) fishing efficiency, (c) population density, (d) complexity of settlement system, and (e) complexity of form of settlement.

Subsequently, Turner (1976:236-254) documented through archeological research changes in population distribution within the Virginia coastal plain from Early Archaic through Late Woodland times (ca. 8000 B.C. to A.D. 1600). By the Late Woodland period, available data indicate a major rise and shift in population toward that locale which historical accounts note as the center or core area of the Powhatan chiefdom, principally along the Pamunkey and Mattaponi Rivers and adjacent locales. The documented changes in population distribution seem to conform to variations in resource distribution and changes in subsistence strategies over time in the region. Further, it was shown that by the end of the Late Woodland period (if not earlier) severe population pressure on key agricultural soils was being experienced in at least the core area from which the chiefdom evolved; this stress was a likely cause of historically documented cases of warfare associated with substantial deaths and large-scale resettlement efforts in conquered areas outside this core area (Turner 1976:188–198). Thus population growth, accompanied by increasing population pressure on key agricultural soils, is viewed as resulting over time in the development of new means of socio-cultural integration, culminating in the Powhatan chiefdom. While other factors (such as the strategic position of the core area in controlling both intraregional and interregional trade networks) obviously were important, the evolution of the Powhatan chiefdom still is regarded as the result of factors indigenous to the local region.

Most recently, Potter (1982) has completed an analysis of settlement patterns from ca. A.D. 200 to 1650 for one portion of the Virginia coastal plain adjacent to the Potomac River. He views the development of small chiefdoms there (subsequently included as an out-lying area in the Powhatan chiefdom) as resulting from local factors, not European contact. His survey data also indicate that by ca. A.D. 1300 to 1500 local settlement patterns were similar to those of ca. A.D. 1500 to 1650 and consistent with those described in early seventeenth-century English accounts.

Although there are many limitations in the available archeological data for this region on the development of low-level chiefdoms and subsequently on the Powhatan chiefdom (see Turner 1983 for an extensive discussion of this problem), the above examples are consistent with ethnohistorical data indicating that European contact did not play a significant role in this evolutionary process. Such is not the case, however, for the period from 1607 to 1646. By the latter date, English interactions with the Powhatans had pronounced effects on Powhatan society.

4.3. Events Subsequent to 1607: Disintegration and Demise

The first years following English settlement in coastal Virginia were characterized by frequent conflicts with the Powhatans (cf. Washburn 1978:95–96). Numerous skirmishes are recorded as resulting from the gradual English expansion outward from their principal settlement at Jamestown as well as their attempts to trade for or seize by force from the Powhatans desperately needed subsistence supplies.

This situation prompted His Majesty's Council of Virginia (1836:10) to state that by 1609 ". . . the poore Indians by wrongs and injuries were made our enemies. . . ." Although casualties were suffered on both sides, and the Powhatan lost considerable portions of territory along the James River, neither side launched a full-scale attack against the other. The English were too weak, both physically and numerically, to undertake such a strategy. Lurie (1959:44) noting that Powhatan was still engaged in strengthening his chiefdom and perhaps could not risk extensive Indian defections to the side of the English, suggested that his primary motivation may have been the desire to control and use the English for his own purposes (for example, to establish a monopoly over their seemingly unlimited supply of copper) rather than to annihilate them, which would have been a plausible strategy during the early years of the English settlement. As earlier noted, Powhatan and later Opechancanough tried to maintain monopolies over copper and other goods brought into Virginia by the English. Similarly, chiefs frequently laid claim to items stolen from the English. Restricting access to these items would have helped consolidate the centralization of power already developing in the Powhatan chiefdom.

A short-lived period of relative peace was begun in 1614 when Pocahontas, a daughter of Powhatan, was married to John Rolfe, an English settler. She died while visiting in England, however, and her death was followed by that of Powhatan in 1618. Rapid English expansion soon precipitated hostilities on an unprecedented scale. By 1619 there were are least nine hundred settlers in Virginia distributed in twenty-three plantations on the James River and two on the Eastern Shore; by 1622 there were an additional twenty-three plantations, including three more on the Eastern Shore (Bean 1938:10). By 1621 plans were even being made for settlements as far north as the Potomac River (Beverley 1947:50).

Surprisingly, there is little information in historical documents describing early Powhatan depopulation due to contact with European diseases. This contrasts sharply with accounts from coastal North Carolina (Quinn 1955:378), where European diseases had an immediate and pronounced effect on indigenous populations. Quiros and Segura (1953:88) talk of depopulation in coastal Virginia in 1570 resulting from a six-year "famine." Whether this was in any way caused by early European contacts is unknown. As noted by Feest (1973:66), Powhatan's statement (Simmond 1910:135) that he had seen the death of "all my people" three times and was the sole survivor of his generation has been interpreted by some as indicating depopulation in the region prior to 1607. Isolated epidemics were recorded on the Eastern Shore in 1608 and in the James and perhaps York River areas in 1617 and 1619 (Feest 1973:74). Had there been substantial Powhatan depopulation resulting from European diseases, it is likely that the English would have noted it; the effects on socio-cultural organization within the Powhatan chiefdom and on interactions with the English would have been too pronounced to go undetected. In 1622 the Powhatans did begin to experience massive depopulation, but from another cause: full-scale warfare with the English.

In response to rapid English expansion after the death of Powhatan and an increasing number of hostile incidents between Indians and settlers, the Powhatan chiefdom, under the leadership of Opechancanough, attacked numerous English settlements in March 1622. On the first day of fighting just under 350 English settlers, out of a total population slightly exceeding a thousand, were killed (Waterhouse 1933:551). The massacre had been directly prompted by the death of Nemattanow, a war captain who had been killed by the English (Smith 1910c:572).

Retaliation by the English was immediate; the London Company ordered extermination of the Indians, forbidding commanders to make peace upon any terms whatsoever. Repeated expeditions sent out by the English destroyed Indian crops, fish weirs, and settlements and killed numerous Indians of both sexes and all ages. In 1623 the Council in Virginia (1935:10) claimed: "By Computatione and Confessione of the Indians themselves we have slayne more of them this yeere, then hath been slayne before since the beginninge of ye colonie." Justification of English policy is best seen in a statement written by Waterhouse (1933:5644) in 1622:

> . . . this Massacre must rather be beneficiall to the plantation then impaire it, let all men take courage, and put it to their helping hands, since now the time is most seasonable and advantagious for the reaping of those benefits which the plantation hath long promised: and for their owne good let them doe it speedily, that so by taking the prioritie of time, they may have also the prioritie of place, in choosing the best Seats of the Country, which now by vanquishing of the Indians, is like to offer a more ample and faire choice of fruitfull habitations, then hitherto our gentleness and faire comportement to the Savages could attaine unto.

Attacks on Indian settlements gradually diminished during the 1630s, by which time the English population exceeded five thousand.

By the 1630s the Powhatan polity as a viable, integrated entity encompassing much of the Virginia coastal plain was nearing a state of collapse. The strategy of killing the Powhatan through armed conflicts and starving them by disrupting subsistence activities, inaugurated by the English in 1622, undoubtedly had a pronounced effect. Unfortunately, the English accounts, which prior to 1622 provided remarkably detailed descriptions of Powhatan lifeways, no longer contained such a wealth of information. The limited data available are largely restricted to one component of Powhatan socio-political organization, the control by the paramount chief of out-lying districts within the chiefdom.

In 1607 the core area of the Powhatan chiefdom had been located along the James and York Rivers and their branches. Available evidence (Turner 1976, 1982) indicates that the boundaries extended as far north as the Potomac River and as far east as portions of the Virginia Eastern Shore (figure 1). Fragmentary evidence suggests that groups in these areas at least on occasion

Figure 1 *The Powhatan Chiefdom, ca. A.D. 1607*
Boundaries and districts as presented here are in Turner 1976, 1982.

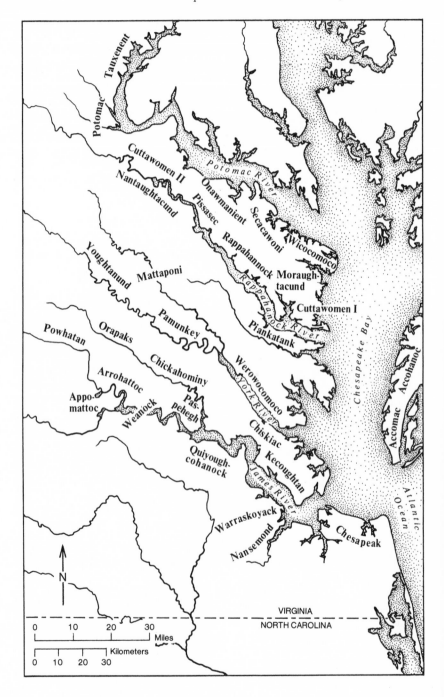

obeyed the orders of and/or paid tribute to the paramount chief. It is quite unlikely that these groups had been fully consolidated into the Powhatan chiefdom, however, for the rapid expansion of the chiefdom was a rather recent phenomenon still taking place when the English established the settlement of Jamestown in 1607. Indeed, it appears quite clear that after English contact in the Virginia coastal plain, the authority of the paramount chief was greatly diminished in the out-lying areas. Evidently, promises of protection by the English in these areas overrode the threat of punitive actions by Powhatan or Opechancanough.

The major cases of the paramount chief's orders being ignored or districts acting independently are restricted to the south bank of the Potomac River and the Virginia Eastern Shore (Potter 1976:25–29; Turner 1976:127–135, 1982:47–49). As early as 1613 the Potomac aided the English in kidnapping Pocahontas, a daughter of Powhatan, who was visiting friends and trading some of her father's commodities in the area of the Potomac district (Hamor 1615:4). The Potomac were initially afraid to participate in the plot, but did so after being offered protection against Powhatan (Argoll 1906:91–93). According to Hamor, the Potomac sided with the English against Opechancanough in the warfare which began in 1622 (Robinson 1889:13). Martin (1933a:705) also indicates that the Potomac were enemies of Opechancanough by this time, although elsewhere he (1933b:707) included the southern side of the Potomac River within the boundaries of the Powhatan chiefdom. Smith (1910c:591, 596–598) generally agrees with Hamor, but hints that the Potomac may have been secretly attempting to set up an ambush against the English. He also noted that the Secacawoni warned the English of Opechancanough's plans (Smith 1910c:586). Indians on the Virginia Eastern Shore alerted the English to Opechancanough's planned 1622 uprising and did not participate with Opechancanough against the English in this war (Neill 1968:366; Beverley 1947:51). Because of their distance from the center of the Powhatan chiefdom, they seem to have occupied a position in the chiefdom similar to that of groups on the south bank of the Potomac River. These areas were undoubtedly among the last to be affiliated with or consolidated into the chiefdom through either warfare or threat of warfare. The arrival and subsequent growth of the English by 1622 appear to have interrupted the process of more fully integrating them into the Powhatan chiefdom, resulting in an erosion of the authority of the paramount chief in these areas.

By April 1644, the English population of the Virginia coastal plain had increased to over eight thousand persons, and large-scale hostilities once again broke out. Opechancanough led an attack in which between three hundred and five hundred settlers were killed. The English retaliated as swiftly and severely as they had in 1622, burning the Powhatans' settlements and disrupting their subsistence activities. Opechancanough was captured during these reprisals and killed in 1646. A formal peace treaty was concluded that same year between the Powhatans, now under the leadership of Necotowance, and the English. Necotowance acknowledged ". . . to hold his kingdome from the King's Ma'tie of England, and that his successors be appointed or confirmed by the King's Governours from time to time. . . ." (Hening 1823:323). The Powhatans also were to vacate all land below the falls of the James and south bank of the Pamunkey/York Rivers. Movement of Indians in this area was to be strictly controlled. As acknowledgement for promised English protection, Necotowance and his successors were to provide yearly tribute to the colony's governor.

In the year of the peace treaty, the Assembly of Virginia summarized the conditions of the Powhatans as ". . . so routed and dispersed that they are no longer a nation, and we now suffer only from robbery by a few starved outlaws" (McCary 1957:80). The Powhatan chiefdom had reached a state of total collapse. Powhatan population had been greatly reduced, and sociopolitical organization in the chiefdom, which had formerly covered the Virginia coastal plain in thirty-one districts under the control of a paramount chief, had disintegrated. Attempting to curb English expansion with armed conflict was no longer feasible for the Powhatans. Rather, as documented by McCartney (1981), the year 1646 marked the point where continued survival of the Powhatan in coastal Virginia depended upon English protection.

5. Summary and Conclusions

In a document dating to 1656, only ten years after the end of English/Powhatan hostilities, Hammond (1844:20) stated: "The Indians are in absolute subjection to the English, so that they both pay tribute to them and receive all their severall Kings from them, and as one dies they repair to the English for a successor. . . ." In 1669 the first census of the Powhatans since the peace treaty found only slightly more than two thousand individuals still surviving (Feest 1973:75–77), whereas the English population of the area had reached forty thousand by 1666 (Craven 1944:76). This is in sharp contrast to the situation in 1607, when the Powhatan chiefdom, with a population perhaps exceeding thirteen thousand persons, represented one of the most complex societies then existing in eastern North America.

The rapid collapse of the Powhatan chiefdom was a direct result of large-scale warfare with the English. One cannot, however, overlook problems internal to Powhatan society that were compounded by English interactions between 1607 and 1646. As earlier noted, territorial boundaries of the Powhatan chiefdom had been substantially enlarged just prior to 1607. Historical accounts clearly indicate that this expansion was largely a result of warfare, and it is unlikely that full socio-political control had been attained over outlying districts by 1607. This situation certainly was to the advantage of the English and undoubtedly shortened the time period needed to subjugate the Powhatan.

Vestiges of ranked statuses in Powhatan society continued to be observed during the latter half of the seventeenth century and first half of the eighteenth. These remnants, involving features of socio-political organization and related religious activities, are noted in the writings of Beverley. (1947), Bullock (1649), Clayton (1965), Glover (1676), Jones (1956), Michel (1916), and several unidentified authors (Anonymous 1838, 1959), among others, as well as in various local court records. Inheritance of positions of leadership, variations in dress and respect based on rank, and interment of restricted individuals upon death in temples still occurred sporadically among the Powhatans, although invariably at the local level. The Powhatan chiefdom, as a viable, integrated society encompassing much of the Virginia coastal plain, had ceased to exist by 1646.

REFERENCES   CITED

Anonymous
  1836 The Beginning, Progress, and Conclusion of Bacon's Rebellion in the Years
        1675 and 1676. *In:* Tracts and Other Papers, Relating Principally to the
        Origin, Settlement, and Progress of the Colonies in North America, From
        the Discovery of the Country to the Year 1776. Vol. 1. Peter Force, ed.
        Washington, D.C.: Peter Force.
  1838 A perfect Description of Virginia. *In:* Tracts and Other Papers, Relating
        Principally to the Origin, Settlement, and Progress of the Colonies in
        North America, From the Discovery of the Country to the Year 1776. Vol.
        2. Peter Force, ed. Washington, D.C.: Peter Force.

1959   An Account of the Indians in Virginia. William and Mary Quarterly, 3rd series. Stanley Pargellis, ed. 16:228–243.

Archer, Gabriel
1969a   A Brief Description of the People. *In:* The Jamestown Voyages Under the First Charter 1606–1609. Philip L. Barbour, ed. pp. 102–104. London: Cambridge University Press.
1969b   A Relatyon of the Discovery of our River, from James Forte into the Maine. *In:* The Jamestown Voyages Under the First Charter 1606–1609. Philip L. Barbour, ed. pp. 80–98. London: Cambridge University Press.

Argoll, Samuell
1906   A Letter of Samuell Argoll Touching his Voyage to Virginia, and Actions There: Written to Master Nicholas Hawes, June 1613. *In:* Hakluytus Posthumus or Purchas, His pilgrimes. Samuel Purchase, ed. 9:90–95. Glasgow: James MacLehose and Sons.

Bean, R. Bennett
1938   The Peopling of Virginia. Boston: Chapman and Grimes, Inc.

Beverley, Robert
1947   The History and Present State of Virginia. Chapel Hill: University of North Carolina Press.

Binford, Lewis R.
1964   Archaeological and Ethnohistorical Investigation of Cultural Diversity and Progressive Development Among Aboriginal Cultures of Coastal Virginia and North Carolina. Ph.D. Dissertation, Department of Anthropology, University of Michigan.

Bullock, William
1649   Virginia Impartially Examined. London: John Hammond.

Carrera, Juan de la
1953   Relation of Juan de la Carrera, 1 March 1600. *In:* The Spanish Mission in Virginia 1570–1572. Clifford M. Lewis and Albert J. Loomie, eds. pp. 123–142. Chapel Hill: University of North Carolina Press.

Clarke, Samuel
1670   A True and Faithful Account of the Four Chiefest Plantations of the English in America. Of Virginia, New England, Bermudas, Barbados. London.

Clayton, John
1965   The Reverend John Clayton: His Scientific Writings and Other Related Papers. Edmund Berkeley and Dorothy Smith Berkeley, eds. Charlottesville: University Press of Virginia.

Cope, Walter
  1969 Letter to Lord Salisbury, 12 August 1607. *In:* The Jamestown Voyages Under the First Charter 1606–1609. Philip L. Barbour, ed. pp. 108–110. London: Cambridge University Press.

Council of Virginia
  1836 The New Life of Virginia: Declaring the Former Successe and Present Estate of that Plantation, Being the Second Part of Nova Britannia. *In:* Tracts and Other Papers Relating Principally to the Origin, Settlement, and Progress of the Colonies in North America From the Discovery of the Country to the Year 1776. Vol. 1. Peter Force, ed. Washington, D.C.: Peter Force.
  1844 A True Declaration of the Estate of the Colonie in Virginia. *In:* Tracts and Other Papers, Relating Principally to the Origin Settlement, and Progress of the Colonies in North America, From the Discovery of the Country to the Year 1776. Vol. 3. Peter Force, ed. Washington, D.C.: Peter Force.
  1935 A Letter to the Virginia Company of London, 20 January 1623. *In:* The Records of the Virginia Company of London. Susan Myra Kingsbury, ed. 4:9–16. Washington, D.C.: Government Printing Office.

Craven, Wesley Frank
  1944 Indian Policy in Early Virginia. William and Mary Quarterly, 3rd Series, 1:65–82.

Dale, Thomas
  1615 Letter to the R. and most esteemed friend Mr. D. M. at his house at F. Ch. in London, 18 June 1614. *In:* A True Discourse of the Present Estate of Virginia, and the Successe of the Affairs There till the 18th of June 1614, By Raphe Hamor. Pp. 51–59. London: John Beale.

Feest, Christian F.
  1973 Seventeenth Century Virginia Algonquian Population Estimates. Quarterly Bulletin of the Archaeological Society of Virginia 28:66–79.
  1978 Virginia Algonquians. *In:* Handbook of North American Indians, 15:253–270. Washington, D.C.: U. S. Government Printing Office.

Fried, Morton H.
  1967 The Evolution of Political Society, New York: Random House.

Glover, Thomas
  1676 An Account of Virginia. Philosophical Transactions of the Royal Society of London 11(126):623–636.

Hammond, John
  1844 Leah and Rachel, or the Two Fruitfull Sisters Virginia and Maryland: Their Present Condition, Impartially Stated and Related. *In:* Tracts and Other

Papers, Relating Principally to the Origin, Settlement, and Progress of the Colonies in North America, From the Discovery of the Country to the Year 1776. Vol. 3. Peter Force, ed. Washington, D.C.: Peter Force.

Hamor, Raphe
  1615 A True Discourse of the Present Estate of Virginia, and the Successe of the Affaires there till the 18th of June, 1614. London: John Beale.

Hening, William W., editor
  1823 The Statuses at Large; Being a Collection of all the Laws of Virginia, from the First Session of the Legislature, in the Year 1619. Vol. 1. Richmond: Samuel Pleasants.

Jones, Hugh
  1956 The Present State of Virginia. Chapel Hill: University of North Carolina Press.

Kirchoff, Paul
  1955 The Principles of Clanship in Human Society. Davidson Journal of Anthropology 1:1–10.

Lewis, Clifford M. and Albert J. Loomie, editors
  1953 The Spanish Jesuit Mission in Virginia, 1570–1572. Chapel Hill: University of North Carolina Press.

Lorant, Stefan
  1965 The New World: The First Pictures of America. New York: Duell, Sloan, and Pearce.

Lurie, Nancy Oestreicn
  1959 Indian Cultural Adjustment to European Civilization. In: Seventeenth-Century America: Essays in Colonial History. James Morton Smith, ed. pp. 33–60. Chapel Hill: University of North Carolina Press.

Magnel, Francis
  1969 Relation of what Francis Magnel, an Irishman, learned in the land of Virginia during the eight months he was there, 1 July 1610. In: The Jamestown Voyages Under the First Charter 1606–1609. Philip L. Barbour, ed. pp. 151–157. London: Cambridge University Press.

Martin, John
  1933a The Manner Howe to Bring the Indians into Subjection. In: The Records of the Virginia Company of London. Vol. 3. Susan Myra Kingsbury, ed. pp. 704–707. Washington, D.C.: U. S. Government Printing Office.
  1933b The Manner Howe Virginia . . . May be Made a Royall Plantation. In: The Records of the Virginia Company of London. Vol. 3. Susan Myra Kings-

bury, ed. pp. 707–710. Washington, D.C.: U. S. Government Printing Office.

McCartney, Martha W.
  1981 The Pamunkey Indians, From Contact Period to the Twentieth Century. Manuscript on file at the Virginia Research Center for Archaeology, Yorktown.

McCary, Ben C.
  1957 Indians in Seventeenth Century Virginia. Jamestown 350th Anniversary Historical Booklet Number 18. Charlottesville: University Press of Virginia.

Michel, Francis Louis
  1916 Report of the Journey of Francis Louis Michel from Berne, Switzerland to Virginia, October 2, 1701–December 1, 1702. Virginia Magazine of History and Biography 24:1–43, 113–141, 275–303.

Mouer, Daniel L.
  1981 Powhatan and Monacan Regional Settlement Hierarchies: A Model of Relationship Between Social and Environmental Structure. Quarterly Bulletin of the Archaeological Society of Virginia 36:1–21.

Newport, Christopher
  1907 A Description of the James River, the Country on its Banks, and the Aboriginal Inhabitants, 21 June 1607. Virginia Magazine of History and Biography 14:373–378.

Neill, Edward D.
  1968 History of the Virginia Company of London with Letters to and from the First Colony Never Before Printed. New York: Burt Franklin.

Peebles, Christopher S. and Susan M. Kus
  1977 Some Archaeological Correlates of Ranked Societies. American Antiquity 42:421–448.

Percy, George
  1922 "A Trewe Relacyon" of Virginia from 1609 to 1612. Tyler's Quarterly Magazine 3:259–282.
  1967 Observations Gathered out of a Discourse of the Plantation of the Southern Colony in Virginia by the English, 1606. David B. Quinn, ed. Charlottesville: University Press of Virginia.
  1969 Fragments Published in 1614. *In:* The Jamestown Voyages Under the First Charter 1606–1609. Philip L. Barbour, ed. pp. 146–147. London: Cambridge University Press.

Potter, Stephen R.
  1976   An Ethnohistorical Examination of Indian Groups in Northumberland
         County, Virginia: 1608–1719. M.A. thesis, Department of Anthropology,
         University of North Carolina.
  1982   An Analysis of Chicacoan Settlement Patterns. Ph.D. dissertation, Depart-
         ment of Anthropology, University of North Carolina.

Quinn, David Beers
  1955   The Roanoke Voyages, 1584–1590. Hakluyt Society, 2nd Series, Nos. 104–
         105. London: Cambridge University Press.

Quiros, Luis de, and Juan Baptista de Segura
  1953   Letter of Luis de Quiros and Juan Baptista de Segura to Juan de Hinistrosa,
         12 September 1570. *In:* The Spanish Jesuit Mission in Virginia 1570–1572.
         Clifford M. Lewis and Albert J. Loomie, eds. pp. 85–94. Chapel Hill:
         University of North Carolina.

Robinson, Conway
  1889   Abstract of the Proceedings of the Virginia Company of London 1619–
         1624, Prepared from the Records in the Library of Congress. Collections of
         the Virginia Historical Society, New Series, Vol. 8.

Sacchini, Francisco
  1953   Borgia, The Third Part of the History of the Society of Jesus. *In:* The
         Spanish Jesuit Mission in Virginia 1570–1572. Clifford M. Lewis and
         Albert J. Loomie, eds. pp. 215–227. Chapel Hill: University of North
         Carolina Press.

Sahlins, Marshall D.
  1958   Social Stratification in Polynesia. Seattle: University of Washington Press.

Service, Elman R.
  1962   Primitive Social Organization. New York: Random House.

Simmond, William
  1910   The Proceedings of the English Colonie in Virginia since their first begin-
         ning from England in the yeare of our Lord 1606, till this present 1612. *In:*
         Travels and Works of Captain John Smith. Edward Arber, ed. pp. 85–174.
         Edinburgh: John Grant.

Smith, John
  1910a A True Relation of Occurrences and Accidents in Virginia, 1608. *In:*
         Travels and Works of Captain John Smith. Edward Arber, ed. pp. 1–40.
         Edinburgh: John Grant.
  1910b A Map of Virginia With A Description of Its Commodities, People,
         Government, and Religion, 1612. *In:* Travels and Works of Captain John
         Smith. Edward Arber, ed. pp. 41–84. Edinburgh: John Grant.

1910c The Generall Historie of Virginia, New England, and the Summer Isles, 1624. *In:* Travels and Works of Captain John Smith. Edward Arber, ed. pp. 273–784. Edinburgh: John Grant.

Spelman, Henry
1910 Relation of Virginia. *In:* Travels and Works of Captain John Smith. Edward Arber, ed. pp. ci–cxxi. Edinburgh: John Grant.

Strachey, William
1953 The Historie of Travell into Virginia Britania. Hakluyt Society, 2nd Series, No. 103. Louis B. Wright and Virginia Freund, eds. London: Cambridge University Press.
1964 A True Reportory of the Wreck and Redemption of Sir Thomas Gates, July 15, 1610. *In:* A Voyage to Virginia in 1609. Louis B. Wright, ed. pp. 1–101. Charlottesville: University Press of Virginia.

Taylor, Donna
1975 Some Locational Aspects of Middle-Range Hierarchical Societies. Ph.D. dissertation, Department of Anthropology, City University of New York.

Turner, E. Randolph
1976 An Archeological and Ethnohistorical Study on the Evolution of Rank Societies in the Virginia Coastal Plain. Ph.D. dissertation, Department of Anthropology, Pennsylvania State University.
1982 A Reexamination of Powhatan Territorial Boundaries and Population, ca. A.D. 1607. Archeological Society of Virginia Quarterly Bulletin 37:45–64.
1983 Problems in the Archaeological Identification of Chiefdoms: An Example from the Virginia Coastal Plain. Paper presented at 1983 Middle Atlantic Archaeological Conference Annual Meeting. Copy on file at Virginia Research Center for Archaeology, Yorktown.

Washburn, Wilcomb E.
1978 Seventeenth-Century Indian Wars. *In:* Handbook of North American Indians 15:89–100. Washington, D.C.: U. S. Government Printing Office.

Waterhouse, Edward
1933 A Declaration of the State of the Colony and Affaires in Virginia, 1622. *In:* Records of the Virginia Company of London. Vol. 3. Susan Myra Kingsbury, ed. pp. 541–571. Washington, D.C.: U. S. Government Printing Office.

Whitaker, Alexander
1613 Good News from Virginia. London: Felix Kyngston.

White, Andrew
1846 A Relation of the Colony of Lord Baron of Baltimore, in Maryland, Near Virginia; A Narrative of the Voyage to Maryland; and Sundry Reports. *In:*

Tracts and Other Papers, Relating Principally to the Origin, Settlement, and Progress of the Colonies in North America, From the Discovery of the Country to the Year 1776. Vol. 4. Peter Force, ed. Washington, D.C.: Peter Force.

White, William
  1969 Fragments published in 1614. *In:* The Jamestown Voyages Under the First Charter 1606–1609. Philip L. Barbour, ed. pp. 147–150. London: Cambridge University Press.

Wingfield, Edward Maria
  1969 A Discourse of Virginia. *In:* The Jamestown Voyages Under the First Charter 1606–1609. Philip L. Barbour, ed. pp. 213–234. London: Cambridge University Press.

Patterns of Anglo-Indian Aggression and Accommodation along the Mid-Atlantic Coast, 1584–1634

J. Frederick Fausz

ABSTRACT

Distinct and variable patterns of Anglo-Indian aggression and accommodation emerge when contact experiences are analyzed from a regional perspective (the mid-Atlantic coast) in a discrete chronological framework (1584–1634). The hospitality or hostility that derived from these intercultural contacts was founded in the potential for self-interest and self-preservation that the various indigenous and intruding groups perceived in each other. From the colonization of Roanoke in 1585 through the early decades at Jamestown (1607–1625), Englishmen discovered that the proximity of colonial settlements to villages of area Indians promoted violence and hostility, and that their only native allies were located some distance away. However, decades of conflict in the Chesapeake altered this pattern of interaction, and with the founding of Maryland in 1634, the closest Anglo-Indian neighbors along the north bank of the Potomac River developed harmonious and stable alliances for mutual profit and protection.

Sir Thomas Dale our religious and valiant Governour, hath . . . by warre upon our enemies, and kinde usage of our friends, . . . brought them to seeke for peace of us, which . . . they dare not breake.

—The Rev. Alexander Whitaker, Virginia, 1614

1. Introduction

On 30 March 1634, after some three weeks of exploring the Potomac River, Lord Baltimore's Maryland colonists established their capital city, in peace and with the permission of the native population, opposite the village of

Yoacomaco, in the land of the Piscataways ([Lewger and Hawley] 1910:74). "Is not this miraculous," wrote Father Andrew White, one of the Jesuits with the expedition, "that a nation . . . should like lambes yeeld themselves, [and be] glad of our company, giveing us houses, land, and liveings for a trifle?" (White 1910:42). Less than a month later, Captain Cyprian Thorowgood sailed north from St. Mary's City to the mouth of the Susquehanna River, where he encountered Captain William Claiborne's Virginia beaver traders doing a brisk business with the Susquehannocks. "So soone as they see us a comeing," he reported, "Claborn'es men persuaded the Indians to take part with them against us . . . but the Indians refused, saying the English had never harmed them, neither would they fight soe neare home" (Thorowgood 1634:[1]).

These brief glimpses into the status of human relations in the Chesapeake world of 1634 came at the end of a half-century of Anglo-Indian contacts along the mid-Atlantic coast. They reveal behavior on the part of Englishmen and Indians alike that had been shaped and molded by contact experiences in those previous fifty years and thus represented a new, more mature, innovative, and pragmatic era of intercultural relations.

The search for self-interest and self-preservation was consistent and compelling among all ethnic groups, and the reluctance of the Susquehannocks to engage in combat without provocation, and especially "soe neare home," paralleled the decision of the Yoacomacoes to offer "liveings" to the Maryland English in order to save themselves from the ravages of the Susquehannocks. Never before had coastal Algonquians of the Chesapeake proven to be quite so amicable and accommodating to English colonists or had Englishmen demonstrated such hate and hostility to their own countrymen as in 1634. By that date, the rigid ethnocentric and ideological boundaries that had divided Englishmen from Indians and contributed to five decades of confrontation and conflict had been replaced by pragmatic inter-ethnic interest group alliances for mutal advantage. These accommodationist policies cut *across* racial and cultural lines and tended to alienate Englishmen from Englishmen and Indians from Indians in a new era of competition for resources and territory, for self-interest and self-preservation (see Trigger 1976:I, 24–5; Fausz 1982).

To comprehend fully the evolution of Anglo-Indian relations—from initial fascination and hospitality, to later fear and hostility, and ultimately to the adoption of cooperative alliances for mutual benefit—it is necessary to analyze cultural adaptation within a strictly defined geographical area, in a limited span of time, and by similar intruding and similar indigenous groups. In the mid-Atlantic laboratory of cultural relations, the chronology of contact and the evolution of Algonquian responses neatly coincide with the geography of the region, following a south-to-north, earliest-to-latest sequence between 1584 and 1634. Relations in one area easily spilled over to affect relations in another in this region of fluid boundaries and mobile populations. Contact at Roanoke Island produced initial hospitality that quickly turned to hostility between 1584 and 1587; this legacy of mutual aggression contributed to the eruption of massive intercultural violence in Virginia in the 1609–1614 and 1622–1632 periods; and finally, these traumatic disruptions sent ripples throughout the Chesapeake, encouraging native populations north of the Potomac River to adopt long-term policies of accommodation and alliance with selected English groups after 1632.

The Algonquians of the mid-Atlantic coastal plain (see figure 1; appendix 1)—in particular the Roanoacs of North Carolina, the Powhatans of Virginia, and the Piscataways of Maryland—shared several important cultural attributes in the pre-contact era. Each usually practiced an extensive maize-beans-squash-tobacco horticulture within a temperate tidewater climate and supplemented their slash-and-burn crop production with seasonal communal migrations to hunt large game, catch vast quantities of marine products, and forage for nuts, berries, and roots. These "sedentary commuters" or "seasonal nomads" maintained relatively dense populations in semi-permanent villages of multi-family, loaf-shaped bark or reed lodges located along major water systems. They all worshipped primary deities of terror and vengeance (Kiwasa, Okee) within a complex polytheistic religious structure and organized regional alliances on the basis of cultural loyalties and common needs for defense against hostile Siouan or Iroquoian peoples on their borders (Fausz 1977, chps. 2,4; Feest 1978a, 1978b, 1978c; Merrell 1979; Quinn 1955). The Powhatan chiefdom known as Tsenacommacah was the largest, most complex, and best-organized and -administered of all the mid-Atlantic Algonquian polities (Fausz 1977: chp. 1; Turner 1982; Feest 1978b; appendix II), but the Roanoacs and Piscataways also created hierarchical, socially stratified societies featuring polygyny, trade monopoly, matrilineal descent of chieftains, and rank-differentiated functions, attire, and burial rituals (Feest 1978a, 1978b; White 1910:41–45; [Lewger and Hawley] 1910:83–88; Harriot 1955).

These Algonquians of the mid-Atlantic coastal plain at contact found themselves restricted to tidewater zones by strong, hostile, and culturally-alien peoples west of the fall line, and their cultural identity and territorial

Figure 1   *Tribal Areas of the South Atlantic Slope, ca. 1600*

Key: 1, Nanticoke (Alg.); 2, Piscataway (Alg.); 3, Powhatan (Alg.); 4, Chicahominy (Alg.); 5, Accomak/Accohannoc (Alg.); 6, Chesapeak (possibly extinct by 1607); 7, Nansamund (Alg.); 8, Chawanoac (Alg.); 9, Weapemeoc (Alg.); 10, Roanoac/Secotan (Alg.); 11, Pamlico (Alg.); 12, Neuse (Iro.); 13, Tuscarora (Iro.); 14, Meherrin (Iro.); 15, Nottoway (Iro.); 16, Monacan (Siouan); 17, Manahoac (Siouan); 18, Susquehannock (Iro.)

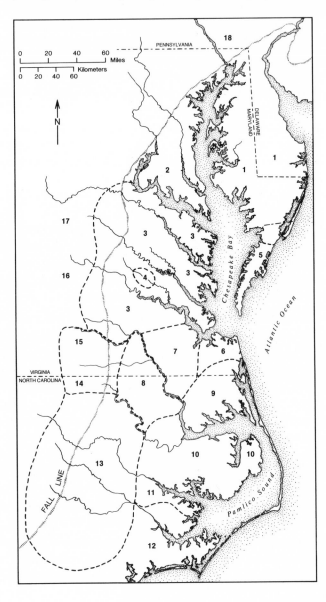

integrity had been shaped by decades of endemic aboriginal warfare (Fausz 1977: chps. 2, 3; Feest 1978a, 1978b, 1978c; see appendices I, Ia, IIa). Both initial, short-term accommodation and hospitality and subsequent long-term hostility with English intruders between 1584 and 1622 derived from the inelastic boundaries of the coastal Algonquians and their need to pursue self-interest and to ensure self-preservation vis-a-vis their Siouan and Iroquoian enemies in the Piedmont. Their strategies at contact were reactive by necessity, for the English represented either friendly allies with new and powerful technology to better the Algonquians' position or a hostile and lethal "second front." Only after an initial, peaceful period of watchful waiting would the tidewater Algonquians know if the strange intruders were to be friends or foes, offering help or intending harm. Only if the English also determined that their best interests were served by mutually beneficial military and/or trade alliance with the Algonquians could the policy of initial accommodation work in the long term.

In contacts at Roanoke and Jamestown, English colonists—male in composition, military in conception, militant in conduct, and predisposed to make policy by the sword—all too soon provoked hostile responses in kind. Before the founding of Maryland in 1634, there was a direct correlation between the proximity of English and Algonquian settlements and the intensity of hostilities that emerged from their close and constant contact. These "zones of hostility" are rendered diagrammatically as a series of concentric circles radiating outward from core centers of English population in a pattern of greatest to least hostility based on distance (figure 2). Before 1634, only those Algonquian groups both figuratively and literally most removed from English settlements, the political "captials" of the mid-Atlantic chiefdoms, and the intercultural conflicts that erupted, maintained long-term amicable relations with the colonists (see figures 2, 4, 5, and 7).

The English colonists, who altered the cultural, political, economic, and territorial integrity of the aboriginal mid-Atlantic coast and upset the balance of power among several Amerindian groups in the region, embarked upon their American ventures in the late sixteenth and early seventeenth century with strategic military purposes uppermost in their minds. Emerging from a European world torn asunder by religious and dynastic warfare, and influenced by the plots of Spain and the atrocity-ridden Irish rebellions, the early English colonists based their hopes for their nation's success on founding military bases along the mid-Atlantic coast and for their own survival on establishing relations with friendly or pacified native populations there (Fausz 1977).

Figure 2 *The Roanoke Area at Contact, 1584–1590*

Darker tones signify greater degrees of hostility to the English. The arrow indicates the location of the colonists' native allies. (Adapted from figure 1a, Feest 1978c)

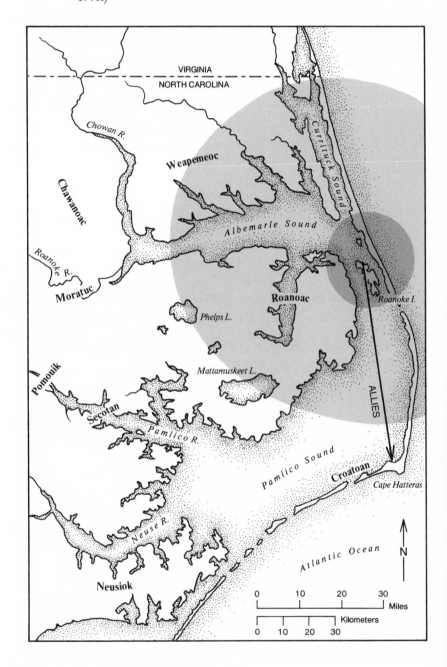

The English, convinced by harsh experience of the dangers inherent in relations with cultural aliens (as with the Spanish and the Irish), sought to make the coastal Algonquians predictable and reliable through the "civilizing" effects of trade, which would "induce Barbarous natures to a likeing and a mutuall society with us" (Peckham 1940:II, 452), and through Christian conversion, considered the "onely course" that could ensure intercultural harmony and "make strangers confide in a new friendship" (Alexander 1624:28). Although the colonizers hoped the Indians would gladly exchange the "pearles of earth" for the "pearles of heaven" (Johnson 1836), they came prepared to subjugate natives who rejected either their physical presence or their cultural "presents." Considering their exalted, albeit precarious, place in a hostile world of Catholic powers, the Protestants from England were determined to have their American outposts either by the gloved hand of peaceful cultural coexistence or by the armored fist of military conquest. Those *mauvais sauvages* who resisted them or threatened their goals would receive a "due reveng of blud and crueltie, to teache them that our kindneses harmd are armed" (Fausz and Kukla 1977:127).

2. Roanoke/Ossomocomuck

Two events between 1584 and 1585 seemed to confirm English opinions about their hated foes in Europe and their potential Indian friends in America. In the summer of 1584, Captains Philip Amadas and Arthur Barlowe explored the North Carolina coast and found the native people there "most gentle, loving, and faithfull, void of all guile and treason . . . [who] lived after the manner of the golden age" (Barlowe 1955:I, 108), which gave rise to the self-confident assurance that they would "honour, obey, feare, and love" the English (Harriot 1955:I, 308). In contrast to this friendly reception, Sir Richard Grenville the next year encountered hostility from Spaniards in the West Indies as he prepared to deliver the first band of colonists to Roanoke Island. The English demanded food from the Spanish by "faire and friendly means," but were determined, if necessary, "to practice force, and to releeve our selves by the sworde." When the Spanish failed to deliver provisions as promised, Grenville "fired the woods" surrounding their fort. Soon after, at Hispaniola, the English obtained the supplies they desired because of "the force that we were of . . .: for doubtlesse if they [the Spanish] had bene stronger than wee, we might have looked for no better curtesie at their handes, then Master John Hawkins received [in his disastrous 1568 defeat] at Saint John de Ullua" ([Anon.] 1955:I, 183, 187).

When the English arrived along the North Carolina outer banks in the mid-1580s, they discovered that the Algonquians' territory of Ossomoco-muck was subdivided into three main enclaves, ruled by separate overlords or *werowances* (figure 2; appendix I). The Secotans occupied villages from the Pamlico River basin to Albemarle Sound, including Roanoke Island. The Roanoacs living on and in the immediate vicinity of the English settlement there were led by Wingina, who may have been the "Lorde of Sequotan" (Barlowe 1955:I, 113; Mook 1944:213–17), and his brother, Granganimeo. The Weapemeocs, situated north of Albermarle Sound under the command of werowance Okisco, constituted a second major territory, while werow-ance Menatonon and the Chawanoacs controlled the upper reaches of the Chowan River basin to the west (Lane 1955:I, 258–65, 270, 279–85; Feest 1978c).

The English reported that Ossomocomuck was the scene of endemic inter-tribal hostilities and that the Roanoacs in 1584 had recently concluded a costly "mortall warre" with Iroquoians to the south—combat that allegedly left them "marvelously wasted and . . . the Countrey [around Roanoke Island] . . . desolate" (Barlowe 1955:I, 113; appendix Ia). Wingina at the same time was still recovering from serious wounds received in yet another "deadlie and terrible warre, with the people and King adjoyning" (Barlowe 1955:1, 101). Thus weakened by war and situated between known Indian enemies on the mainland and unknown aliens along the outer banks, the Roanoacs prudently adopted an accommodationist policy toward the newly arrived Englishmen.

The Roanoacs initially found much to admire in the colonists, believing them to be supernatural creatures or men risen from the dead, because of the terrifying muskets they carried and their ability to live without female com-panionship and to survive the epidemics that soon began to ravage the Indians (Harriot 1955:I, 376, 380). The advantages of having such awe-inspiring aliens as allies was obvious, and the Roanoacs anxiously traded for English axes, hatchets, and knives; "would have given anything for swordes"; and even requested the colonists to attack their enemies to the south (Barlowe 1955:I, 101, 105, 112). "But whether their perswasion be to the ende they may be revenged of their enemies, or for the love they beare us," wrote Captain Barlowe, "we leave that to the triall hereafter" (ibid.,114).

Peaceful accommodation lasted only as long as the English seemed likely to bring the Roanoacs relief from aggression or to offer them some advantage over their traditional enemies, and Wingina and his people quickly shifted to a policy of resistance when the colonists introduced unprecedented amounts of terror and misery to the tribe. Between 1585 and 1586, the English soldiers violently appropriated the meager maize reserves of local werowances (and thereby alienated them by violating tribal custom and chiefly prerogatives); resorted to violence at the slightest provocation (such as burning the village of Aquascogoc for the theft of a silver cup); took hostages (like Menatonon's son, Skiko, and even the werowance himself); and generally threatened to disrupt the balance of power in the area and to dominate its individual polities (Quinn 1955:I, 167–8, 246–9).

Force, applied rather recklessly and ruthlessly by the English against the Carolina Algonquians, certainly justified a hostile response. However, an even greater threat to Indian lives and cultural stability came in the form of killing epidemics transmitted by the alien invaders. Virgin-soil epidemics decimated whole villages in the coastal plain soon after contact with the English, and as Thomas Harriot reported, the Roanoacs were persuaded by this "marvelous accident" that "it was the worke of our God through our meanes and that wee by him might kil and slaie whom wee would without weapons and not come neere them" (Harriot 1955:I, 378–9). Initially awe-struck by what they called the "invisible bullets" that devastated their people, the Roanoacs soon linked hostile English *intent* with this epidemic and concluded that microbes were, like muskets, but one more threatening technology that a foreign god had bestowed on the dangerous invaders. In frantic desperation, Roanoac priests "prophesie[d] that there were more of our [English] generation yet to come, to kill theirs and take their places" (Harriot 1955:I, 380).

Unfortunately for the English, microbes make no distinction between friend and foe, and the epidemic killed off leading accommodationists among the Roanoacs, like Granganimo and Ensenore, a respected advisor, between late 1585 and early 1586. With the death of the last important Roanoac who respected the English and their god, Wingina in the spring took a new name (Pemisapan); fled his village on Roanoke Island; convinced area tribes to withold provisions from the colonists; and attempted to negotiate an ambitious alliance with the Weapemeocs and Chawanoacs, the Moratucs to the west, Chesapeaks to the north, and even his feared Iroquoian enemies, the Mangoaks (Tuscaroras) (Lane 1955:I, 275–84; Fausz 1979a:45–7).

The English under Captain Ralph Lane, a hardened veteran of Irish warfare, feared starvation and a general Indian uprising, which had been communicated to them by the hostage Skiko under threat of death. On 1 June 1586, under the command of "Christ our victory," Lane led his troops against the mainland village of Dasemunkepeuc, routed the Roanoacs, and killed and beheaded Wingina/Pemisapan, whom he claimed had grown in "contempt of us, . . . [and]began to blaspheme . . . that our Lord God was not God" (Lane 1955:I, 277, 287–8). Less than three weeks later, Lane and the Roanoke Island garrison, having little use for either the Indians or the area, abandoned their outpost and returned to England with Sir Francis Drake.

In less than two years of contact, the English managed to kill or alienate the vast majority of Carolina's coastal Algonquians (figure 2). Their actions had prompted the formation of intertribal alliances among traditional enemies to face a common threat, while the armed resistance of the Roanoacs had provided Lane and his overzealous "wylde menn of myne owene naccione" (Lane 1955:I, 204) with an excuse and the opportunity to avenge, in proprietorial fashion, the "*treason* of our *owne* Savages" (Lane 1955:I, 266). Kidnappings, murder, theft, arson, epidemic diseases, and fear, not love, of Christians were the offerings of English "civility" that the Indians of Ossomocomuc remembered. If the Carolina Algonquians by their hostility had ceased to fit the English conception of friendly and guileless natives, so too had the colonists failed to live up to the colonization rhetoric as freedom fighters and positive Christian examples (See Morgan 1975: chps. 1–2).

Neither Thomas Harriot's criticism of Lane's actions as "too fierce" (1955:I, 381) nor the Rev. Richard Hakluyt's outright denunciations of his "crueltie, and outrages" (1955:I,478) could remove the bitter seeds of hatred and mistrust that had been so deeply implanted in the soil and souls of the Roanoacs. Lane's expedient acts of violence bore bitter fruit a year later, for when Governor John White's "Citie of Ralegh" expedition arrived along the Outer Banks in July 1587, the colonists discovered that the fort had been destroyed and that some fifteen soldiers left behind had been slain by Wingina's/Pemisapan's followers ([White] 1955a:II, 524–28). Widespread hostility and armed resistance greeted these new arrivals, and the only Indians who proved hospitable were the loyal Manteo, who had twice been to England, and his fellow Croatoans, who lived on the Outer Banks, far removed from the turmoil near Roanoke Island. In an attempt to salvage a diplomatic triumph of sorts in an otherwise dismal record of Indian relations, the English in 1587 baptized the trusty Manteo and designated him "Lord of Roanoke and Dasemunkepeuc," an empty title fittingly symbolic of the destruction and depopulation that had occurred in the previous two years ([White] 1955a,b:II, 530–1, 598).

The fact that these same Croatoans probably saved and nurtured the "Lost Colony" for several decades after 1588 (thereby achieving a harmonious biracial society that always eluded colonial planners) was never verified by contemporaries and had no positive impact on English attitudes. Instead, the English became preoccupied with their failures at Roanoke Island, while tales of the "Lost Colony" came to epitomize the treacherous nature of hostile Indians and served as the mythopoeic "bloody shirt" for justifying aggressions against the Powhatans years later (Strachey 1953:26; see Quinn 1974: chp. 17).

3. Jamestown/Tsenacommacah

Anglo-Indian relations in Carolina were an important prelude to contact experiences in Virginia two decades later. Long before 1607 both the English and the Powhatans had already formed some definite opinions about each other. In the winter of 1585–86 an expedition dispatched from Roanoke Island lived along the south bank of the James River near its mouth, in the territory of the Algonquian Chesapeaks, Nansamunds, and Kecoughtans— groups jealously independent of Powhatan authority (Quinn 1974:436, 454– 5; Fausz 1977:62–67). The status of those tribes probably accounted for the safe return of the Englishmen, for Captain Lane had been warned by the Chawanoacs, enemies to the Powhatans, that in the area of the James River there lived a wealthy and powerful "king [who] would be loth to suffer any strangers to enter into his Countrey, and . . . [who] was able to make a great many of men into the fielde, which . . . would fight very well" (Lane 1955:I, 2:60–1).

The mid-1580s was precisely when Wahunsonacock/Powhatan was actively engaged in conquering and consolidating Algonquian groups in the Virginia coastal plain, a process that was perhaps at least accelerated by the presence and knowledge of intruding Europeans between 1560 and 1600 (Fausz 1977: chp. 2; Feest 1966:76–79; cf. Turner, this volume). Although there was relatively little direct knowledge of *Englishmen* before 1600, Powhatan or any other Virginia "king" would have been extremely wary of European "strangers" in general on the basis of hostile contacts with the Spanish in the 1560s and 1570s.

The Spanish intrusion into Ajacan (Virginia) in 1561, during which they abducted the Indian "cacique" later known as Don Luis de Velasco, may have unleashed the lethal forces of virgin-soil epidemics. When Don Luis returned to the James and York river basins with an expedition of Spanish Jesuits nine years later, he found "land . . . chastised . . . with six years of famine and death" and that "many have died and many also have moved to other regions to ease their hunger" (Quiros and Segura 1953:89). Deeply concerned that the "land [was] in quite another condition than [he] expected" (ibid.), Don Luis rejoined his people and directed the slaughter of the Jesuit fathers and the desecration of the mission outpost in February 1571 (Carrera 1953:135–37; Ore 1953:181–82).

A year and a half later, in August 1572, the Spanish returned with four ships and 150 men to take *their* revenge. Before their departure from Virginia on 24 August, they slew some twenty Indians in combat and hanged another fourteen (Ore 1953:184–85). "The Country remains very frightened from the chastisement the Governor [Pedro Menendez de Aviles] inflicted," reported a member of the expedition, "for previously they were free to kill any Spaniard who made no resistance. After seeing the opposite of what the Fathers were, they tremble. This chastisement has become famous throughout the land" (Rogel 1953:111; also see 108–9).

Famous indeed. By 1607, after contacts with Europeans in at least each of the previous five decades (Quinn 1974:255–7, 283, 427–30; Feest 1978b:254), Wahunsonacock, with the vital assistance of the strong Pamunkey tribe, had reacted to the prophesies of his priests (that "from the Chesapeack Bay a Nation should arise, which should dissolve and give end to his Empier") and constructed a domain larger and more consolidated than "any of his Predicessors in former tymes" (Strachey 1953:56–7, 104). His subjugation and absorption of independent Algonquian groups lying closest to the bay—in particular the Chesapeaks, Kecoughtans, and Piankatanks— reveal a strategic necessity to control the estuary and its major tributaries, which had already served as "highways" for hostile trans-Atlantic intruders.

When the English landed at Jamestown, Wahunsonacock was the *mamana-towick* (paramount chief) over Tsenacommacah—"densely inhabited land" (Strachey 1953:37; Feest 1966:70) or "the land opposite"—a domain containing more people and administered with greater institutional rigidity and ideological orthodoxy than any Algonquian polity along the Atlantic coast (Fausz 1977: chp. 2; Feest 1978b; Binford 1964; Turner 1982; appendix II). However, as would become apparent during Jamestown's early years, Tsena-commacah, especially in the outlying "fringe" areas along the Potomac River and on the Eastern Shore, was neither as tightly integrated nor as centrally controlled as it needed to be to withstand simultaneous onslaughts by English aliens from the east and increasing pressures from Siouan and Iroquoian enemies to the west and north (appendix IIa; see figure 3).

Anglo-Powhatan relations were friendly enough between spring 1607 and autumn 1609, a probationary period during which each side scrutinized the other's motivations, strengths, and weaknesses. Their lethal muskets and terrifying ships' cannon allowed the small English garrison at Jamestown to maintain a defensive strength that offset the numerical, offensive advantage of the Powhatans, who outnumbered them in fighting men by a ratio of 30 to 1 (Fausz 1977: chp. 4). With limited objectives and meager resources, the English under Captain John Smith were more concerned with obtaining food for survival than with dispossessing the Powhatans of their lands or with launching an Anglican crusade against native beliefs. After testing the fire-arms of the intruders in a bloody attack only twelve days after their arrival, the Powhatans were generally content to stay out of musket range and occasionally to ambush colonists who emerged from James Fort "to doe naturall necessity" ([Archer] 1969:I, 95).

Having tested the firepower of the intruders, Wahunsonacock probably concluded that the pitifully small group of woefully ignorant colonists was not the stuff of conquest prophecies— strong enough to be useful allies but definitely too weak to threaten Tsenacommacah. Feeling superior to these aliens who seemingly came from a land without maize, trees, or women, and who consciously desired to settle on a desolate peninsula of "waste ground," the mamanatowick decided to use the English, not to kill them (Fausz 1977:224–29). When Wahunsonacock adopted Captain Smith into his family and bestowed upon him the rank of a werowance in January 1608, and when the English honored the overlord with a "coronation" ceremony soon after, each group was sending a subtle, symbolic message of superiority to the other. Despite a mutually beneficial trade in corn and copper, a common hatred of the Spanish, and reciprocal pledges to work together as allies to conquer and explore lands beyond the fall line, the Indians regarded the colonists as a weak, inferior "tribe," while the colonists viewed the Indians as easily manipulated, simple "savages" (Fausz 1977: chp. 4).

Symbolic displays of superiority and subsequent efforts by both sides to intimidate and dominate throughout 1608–09 revealed how wary Englishmen and Powhatans were becoming of one another. Each group soon realized that members of the other culture were neither as ignorant nor as inferior as initially believed. The control of trade within each group became increasingly more centralized as Captain Smith and Wahunsonacock alike

Figure 3   *Tsenacommacah and Environs, 1607–1620*

The light tone represents the nucleus of the Powhatan Chiefdom, ca. 1607; the dark zone is the semi-independant Chickahominy enclave. The arrows point to areas of little influence for Powhatans and E marks the locations of the Powhatan's strong enemies. Asterisks (*) indicate areas of greatest Powhatan vulnerability according to prophesy and practice in 1607; while the cross-hatched pattern marks areas dominated by tribes allied with the English in 1612.

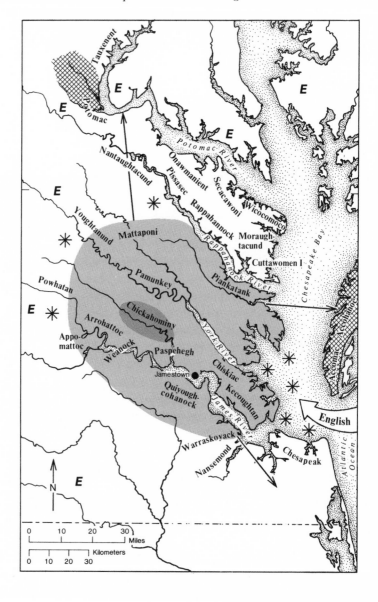

recognized its strategic potential for gaining advantage rather than its capacity for encouraging friendly, reciprocally rewarding, face-to-face contacts between individuals of different cultures. With Jamestown's food supply at stake and the werowances' crucial role as redistributing middlemen/monopolists threatened, Captain Smith and Wahunsonacock moved independently to curtail the hospitable-but-illicit moonlight trade between English mariners and Powhatan tribesmen (Fausz 1982), end their respectful and revealing personal conferences (figure 4), and force one another to obtain the products they needed by theft and coercion (Fausz 1977:239–47). Once again, as at Roanoke, Anglo-Indian relations came to focus more on intimidation than on intimacy, and more on coercion than on commerce.

Although Smith's aggressive actions and his boasts to the Powhatans that "warres" were the "chiefest pleasure" of the English ([Symonds, comp.] 1612:62) purchased short-term survival at an extravagant price in long-term enmity, he, unlike Captain Lane, was a talented, experienced culture-broker who intimidated *selectively* and more to avoid, than to provoke, wholesale slaughter. But Smith, like Lane, had to control growing numbers of unruly "wylde menn" from England who made little distinction between coercion and murder. In the end, he failed. Colonists dispatched to the fall line and the mouth of the James River to live off the land and to avoid the killing summers of Jamestown Island so "tormented" the Indians "by stealing their corne, robbing their gardens, beating them, breaking their houses and keeping some prisoners" (Smith 1624:91) that Powhatan priests began restating their foreboding prophecy of destruction.

Smith was forced to leave Virginia for good on 4 October 1609, wounded by a gunpowder explosion but also wounded by critics who thought his Indian policy too cruel (the Virginia Company) or too lenient (his successors at Jamestown). Almost immediately, the Powhatans "revolted" and began to "murder and spoile all they could incounter." Instead of "corne, provision, and contribution from the Salvages," wrote an English eyewitness, "wee had nothing but mortall wounds," as the "bloody fingers" of the Indians became "imbrued in our bloods" ([Symonds, comp.] 1612:104–05). Launching the initial offensives of what became known as the First Anglo-Powhatan War (1609–14), the Powhatans nearly annihilated the colonists during the winter of 1609–10 by beseiging the starving garrison at James Fort and attacking Englishmen who ventured forth in search of food (Fausz 1983).

As hostility replaced hospitality and threatened to extinguish England's only American colony, Virginia officials grudgingly realized that proximity

Figure 4   *The Powhatan Worldview, 1607*

"The circle of meale signified their [the Powhatans'] Country, the circles of corne, the bounds of the Sea, and the stickes his [John Smith's] Country. They imagined the world to be flat and round, like a trencher, and they in the middest."

—*Captain John Smith's conjuration ceremony among the Pamunkeys, Dec. 1607,* The Generall Historie of Virginia *(1624), p. 48*

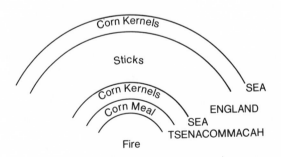

of settlement and close contacts promoted violence, not tolerance, between indigenous and intruding populations that had discovered how irreconcilable were their cultural differences. In 1609 the Virginia Company of London advised the Jamestown garrison that, "if you make friendship with any of these [Virginia Algonquian] nations, as you *must doe, choose to doe it with those that are farthest* from you and enemies unto those amonge whom you dwell, for you shall have least occasion to have differences with them" (Virginia Company 1957:63; my italics; figure 5).

Between 1610 and 1613, the English did manage to establish good relations with the Patawomekes along the south bank of the Potomac River and with the Accomacs and Accohannocs of the Eastern Shore, groups never thoroughly integrated into, or anxious to be separated from, Tsenacommacah (Fausz 1977: Barbour 1969). These groups supplied much-needed maize to the English, acted as informers, and provided other valuable services as amicable allies over several decades. As the English reported in 1613, the "great store of Inhabitants" on the Eastern Shore "seemed very desirous of our love, . . . because they had received good reports from the [Patawomekes] of our courteous usage of them" (Argall 1907:94).

The case was just the opposite for the Powhatans in the James River basin. Reinforced by hundreds of new colonists and soldiers in the spring and summer of 1610, the colony took the offensive against their nearest Indian neighbors in a brutal and atrocity-ridden four-year war of revenge reminiscent of campaigns in Ireland and at Roanoke. With their "forces . . . now such as are able to tame the fury and treachery of the Savages" (Virginia Company 1844:20), the English concentrated their attacks on the Pasbeheghs, Nansamunds, Warraskoyacks, Kecoughtans, and Chickahominies who lived closest to Jamestown, sometimes on a scale out of all proportion to the danger represented by those groups. Between August 1610 and February 1611, for instance, the colonists raided the Pasbeheghs, their nearest but weakest neighbors, on several occasions, bringing total destruction to that village site and killing, in separate incidents, the children of the werowance, the wife of the werowance, and finally the werowance (Wowinchopunk) himself (Fausz 1977:272, 277, 279).

Supported by propaganda that identified Wahunsonacock as the murderer of the "Lost Colonists" and his priests as the dangerous servants of the devil, the English, fighting in full armor and with a crusading fervor "under the banner of Jesus Christ" (Whitaker 1613:44), ravaged the Powhatans with their "Religious Warfare" (Purchase 1907:102) until they controlled the

Figure 5 *Tidewater Virginia at Contact, 1607–1625*
Darker tones indicate greater degrees of hostility to the English. Arrows point toward tribes allied to the English. (Adapted from figure 2, Feest 1978c)

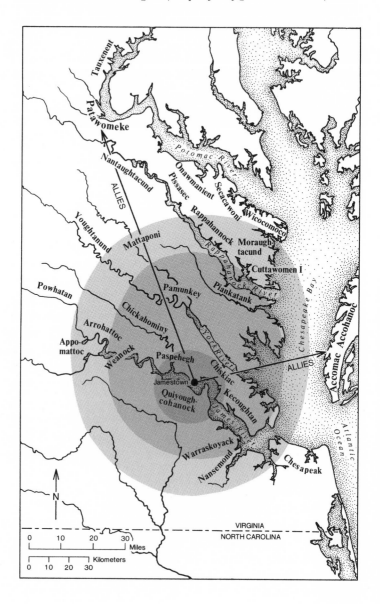

entire length of the James River (Fausz 1977:252–85; Fausz 1981). The colonists had declared that Wahunsonacock was "not able to doe us hurt" (De la Warr 1907:89) by the end of 1611, but he refused to capitulate until after the English had captured Pocahontas in March 1613 (with the vital assistance of the Patawomekes) and delivered a punishing blow against the previously invulnerable Pamunkeys a year later (Fausz 1977:283–85).

With the establishment of peace and the marriage of John Rolfe to the Christianized Pocahontas in early 1614, many Englishmen envisioned a glorious new era of peaceful trade and cooperation between colonists and the Anglican Algonquians they hoped to create (Strachey 1953; Hamor 1615; Fausz 1982), but others, Rolfe among them, became even more enthralled with the prospects for profitable tobacco cultivation. At this crucial crossroads in Anglo-Indian relations, the Virginia Company of London, interested in converts to be won, and the Virginia colonists, much more concerned with lands to be planted, diverged in their goals and divided on policy vis-a-vis the Powhatans. With a conversion-oriented group of Englishmen telling them how they were religiously not in the right way and a tobacco-obsessed group of colonists emphasizing how much they were physically in the way, the Powhatans truly faced a crisis both cultural and territorial in the years between 1614 and 1622.

The English victory in 1614 had effectively ended the rule of Wahunsonacock; aged and lacking credibility, he abdicated in 1617 (the year Pocahontas went to her grave in England) and died the following year. Soon after, Opechancanough, werowance of the still-potent Pamunkeys, assumed authority as paramount chief. While the colonists grew in numbers and prospered through their obsession with tobacco, Opechancanough remained aloof and barely noticed as he reorganized Tsenacommacah, won the allegiance of previously independent groups like the Chickahominies and the Nansamunds, and revitalized the military and cultural traditions of the Powhatans, despite defeat, depopulation, and dispossession (Fausz 1977:305–27; Fausz 1981). Although the Powhatans suffered from lethal epidemics between 1617 and 1619 (Fausz 1977:315), their military capabilities may have actually increased, since land grabs and hostile encroachments by the English helped consolidate Indian strength in the traditionally strong villages along the Mattaponi, Pamunkey, and York rivers. Colonists subsequently reported that "the infinite trade" maintained by the Pamunkeys had allowed Opechancanough "to hyer many auxiliaries which in former times . . . Pohatan was never able to act the like" (Kingsbury 1933:III, 707), and by the early

1620s it would have required an armed and armored force of three hundred Englishmen to dislodge him from his enclave near modern West Point, Virginia (Kingsbury 1935:IV, 12).

In 1619, the colonists noted that Opechancanough and the Pamunkeys had for several years stood "uppon doubtfull termes" and had never "voluntarilie yealded themselves subjects or servants to our Gracious Soveraigne, . . . but to the contrary, whatsoever at any time was done uppon them proceeded from fear without love, for such helpe as we had from them have been procured by sword or trade" (Virginia Colony 1915:35). However, two years later, Opechancanough, with seemingly no less to fear from the English and with certainly no greater reasons for "loving" them, agreed to a "confirmation of a Peace and . . . League" with colony officials. He also informed the Anglican proselytizer George Thorpe that he repudiated the most sacred religious rites of his people, welcomed closer contacts between colonists and Powhatans, and would grant the "English leave to seate themselves anywhere on his Rivers" (Kingsbury 1906:I, 504; 1933:III, 584; Purchas 1907:153).

This, of course, was a ruse to deceive the English, which, considering each colonist's obsessive desire to "planteth himselfe where he pleaseth, and followeth his businesse securely," it did (Smith 1624:138). Opechancanough had worked for some years in concert with Nemattanew, or "Jack of the Feathers"—a charismatic war chief/"prophet" whom the Powhatans allegedly considered invulnerable to bullets—to revitalize native culture and warrior traditions and to embolden the Indians for anticipated combat against muskets (Fausz and Kukla 1977; Fausz 1977:344–52; Fausz 1979b). The Pamunkey werowance told the English what they wanted to hear in 1621—that he was friendly, would give them all the lands they needed for growing tobacco, and wanted Powhatan children to be brought up as Christians, as the Virginia Company so desperately desired—in order to gain their trust and to lull them even further into complacency.

However, at the very time Opechancanough was pledging his good faith, he was preparing an ambitious attack that would remove the hated aliens from Tsenacommacah once and for all (figure 5). He changed his name to Mangopeesomon, in the manner of Winginia some thirty-five years before; tried to procure a vegetable poison available only on the Eastern Shore; and allegedly planned to assemble a large force of warriors at a ceremony for "the takinge upp of Powhatans bones" and to use these troops to "sett upon every Plantatione of the Colonie" (Kingsbury 1933:III, 584; 1935:IV, 10; Waterhouse 1622:21; Fausz and Kukla 1977:117; Fausz 1977:349–50).

Opechancanough, proud of his reputation as "a great Captaine" who "did alwayes fight" (Hamor 1615:54), had obviously determined to attack the colonists years before. Everything the English had done since 1614 increased his power and status; anything they would be likely to do after 1621 could only weaken his position. There was no future in Anglo-Powhatan relations based on peace, for that would only encourage more Englishmen to come to Virginia, to monopolize more territory, to spread more disease, to seize more maize, to Christianize more Indian children, to more thoroughly erode the culture of the Algonquians. What did the Powhatans have to gain by keeping the peace? What could they lose by breaking it?

All was in readiness for a massive uprising against the English, when, in early March 1622, colonists murdered Nemattanew (Smith 1624:144). With his claims of invulnerability to bullets put to a final fatal test, "Jack of the Feathers" played his role to perfection and before dying asked "not to have his men know that he was kild with a Shot" (Fausz and Kukla 1977:108, 117). Opechancanough, too, responded in character and assured the English in public that "he held the peace . . . so firme, as the Skie should sooner fall then it dissolve" (Waterhouse 1622:13), while in private, he reputedly "much grieved and repined [and made] . . . great threats of revenge" (Smith 1624:144).

In the next two weeks Opechancanough was probably occupied with frantic preparations, circulating plans for a concerted, coordinated attack before the true impact of Nemattanew's death eroded tribal solidarity and warrior self-confidence. Falling within the Powhatans' season of Cattapeuk, March was one of the worst times of the year to launch a major offensive, for there was little or no maize surplus from the previous harvest and in only a few weeks a new crop would have to be planted (Fausz 1977:359–60). But Opechancanough had no choice, since his forces could only grow weaker, and those of the colonists stronger, with the passage of time.

On Friday, 22 March 1622, the greatest alliance of Virginia Algonquians ever assembled struck "like violent lightning" (Kingsbury 1935:IV, 73) against dozens of English settlements and farmsteads along both banks of the James River for a distance of over one hundred miles. Infiltrating the homes and fields of their enemies, the warriors bludgeoned to death some 330 English men, women, and children—over a quarter of the colony's population—in hand-to-hand combat, while avoiding almost all contact with musket fire (Fausz 1977:357–403).

Launching the Powhatan Uprising to end the cultural imperialism of the Virginia Company and the territorial encroachment of the colonists, Opechancanough transformed Virginia into a "plantation of sorrowes, . . . plentifull in nothing but want and wanting nothing but plenty" (Kingsbury 1935:IV, 468). But he and his allies had failed to annihilate the English, and the uprising succeeded only in eradicating the impractical, intrusive influence of the Virginia Company, while increasing the power and strengthening the position of the even more threatening Virginia colonists near at hand.

Ironically, the great devastation wrought by Opechancanough's warriors in the James River basin convinced the English survivors and later immigrants how much they needed Indians, especially those living elsewhere in the Chesapeake, for their survival and ultimate success. While the London idealists who had expected the Powhatans' conversion to Christianity now demanded "a vengeful perpetual warre without peace or truce" to "roote out from being any longer a people, so cursed a nation" (Kingsbury 1906:II, 672), the more pragmatic and self-interested leaders in the colony chose to conduct selective and lucrative raids rather than to engage in a genocidal holy crusade against the "cursed race of Cham" (Kingsbury 1906:II, 397; Fausz 1977: chp. 6).

Turning the Second Anglo-Powhatan War (1622–32) to their advantage, members of Virginia's Council of State adopted a practical and purposeful Indian policy that solved many of the colony's most serious and endemic problems: how to defend the colony against hostile natives from without, how to control an unruly servant population within, and how to procure food while concentrating on the cultivation of tobacco for export.

Relying on quick-hitting and mobile militia units, English commanders conducted twice-annual retaliatory raids—"harshe visitts" and "feedfights"—against hostile tribes (Kingsbury 1935:IV, 508; Fausz and Kukla 1977:127). This strategy kept the Indians always on the defensive, inflicted heavy casaulties, deprived them of sustenance for extensive campaigning, and provided the colonists with their main source of maize. English raiders throughout the 1620s transformed their Powhatan enemies into unwittingly subservient "red peasants" by regularly "harvesting" the Indians' crops, while never pursuing their ultimate destruction. Sir George Yeardley, for instance, took "paynes to burne a few of their houses, everie yeare like a Surgion, that wanteth meanes, to keep . . . a patient in hand 3 yeares, that maybee Cured in 3 quarters, or 3 monethes" (Kingsbury 1935:IV, 27). He, and other English commanders who sold captured maize to their hungry countrymen at inflated prices and/or fed it to their own plantation laborers so they could grow tobacco exclusively, functioned as powerful werowances over both peoples and actually came to be known as "Chieftaines" (Smith 1624:155; Fausz 1977: chp. 6).

The colony of Virginia prospered in the 1620s because the war against the Powhatans went well, and that war went well largely because a small oligarchy of English raiders and traders were far-sighted enough to realize that Indians were the keys to their success (figure 6). Through an enlargement of previously beneficial alliances with the Patawomekes, Accomacs, and Accohannocs, the colonists obtained vital military intelligence, secure sources of additional food, safe bases of operation, and, in time, support services for the Chesapeake Bay beaver trade. Following advice from England "to provoke . . . [the Powhatans'] neighboring enimies . . . to the fierce pursuing of them" and to provide bounties for "the bringeing in of theire heades" (Kingsbury 1906:II, 672), the colonists relied upon the Patawomekes to assemble at their main village a large group of Powhatan war chiefs, whom the English then poisoned, ambushed, beheaded and/or scalped in May 1623 (Sackville 1922:507). In 1622 the colonists built a fort adjoining the Patawomeke village and together with them launched a damaging attack against the Nacotchtanks/Anacostans, "mortall enemies" of the Patawomekes living near present-day Washington, D.C. (Smith 1624:153–54).

In November 1623, Sir Francis Wyatt, governor of Virginia, sailed into the Potomac River with over ninety militiamen and boldly assaulted the "Pascoticons [Piscataways] and theire assocyates, beinge the greatest people in those partes of Virginia" and traditional enemies of the Patawomekes (Kingsbury 1935:IV, 450; see figure 6). They "putt many to the swoorde," set fire to the village of Moyaone, and burned "a marvelous quantitie of Corne," because "it was nott possible to bringe it to our boates," as was the usual practice (ibid.; Merrell 1979:554). That Englishmen from the James River would journey so far to scourge their Indian allies' enemy and scorch the earth indicates how important they regarded the alliance with the Patawomekes. In contradiction to the rather ruthless manner in which they dealt with other Indians, the colonists were particularly scrupulous in relations with that tribe. Following the November 1623 raid, Governor Wyatt cautioned his agent trading with the Patawomekes not "to compel by any waies or meanes any Indians whatsoever to trade more than they shalbe willing to trade for, or to offer any violence to any except in his owne defence" (Kingsbury 1935:IV, 448).

By exporting the horrors of the James River conflict to the upper Chesapeake, Governor Wyatt alienated tribes along the north bank of the Potomac

Figure 6 *Maryland Tribes and Major Villages at Contact, ca. 1634
(Adapted from Merrell 1979:551)*

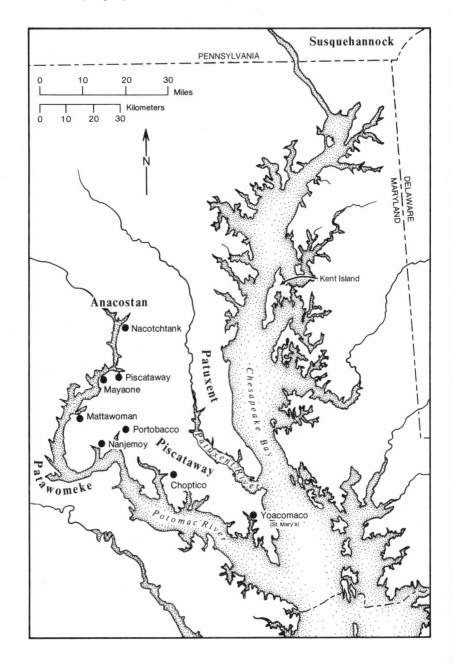

River and created still more allies of Opechancanough. A stunning victory over the colonists in the Potomac River in March 1623 gave hostile Indians access to more muskets and armor than ever before, and the colonists declared that "now the Rogues growe verie bold" and "beinge armed with our Weapons . . . can brave our countrymen at their verie doors" (Kingsbury 1935:IV, 61, 147). The degree to which the Powhatans increasingly relied upon firearms and on an enlarged sphere of alliances in the waging of this war was demonstrated in autumn 1624 (Fausz 1979a).

In the fiercest engagement of the 1620s, Governor Wyatt and sixty muske-teers met a combined force of eight hundred warriors from the Pamunkey tribe and "divers nationes that cam to asiste them" in a two-day pitched battle in open field (Kingsbury 1935:IV, 508). The Pamunkeys fought to defend their extensive maizefields and to preserve their renowned "reputa-tione with the rest of the Salvages," especially since they had allegedly "made greate braggs of what they would doe, Amonge the Northerne nationes." Suffering many casualties (the English admitted that sixteen of their own fell), the Pamunkeys were forced to withdraw, leaving to the colonists enough ripe maize to feed four thousand people for a year while losing face in the presence of allies and interested Indian observers (ibid.).

This was a fitting climax to the most active phase of fighting in the Second Anglo-Powhatan War, for Governor Wyatt himself stated that the battle "shewed what the Indyans could doe. The Indyans were never knowne to shew soe great resolutione" (ibid.:507–08). Although the Powhatans had inflicted and suffered unprecedented casualties between 1622 and 1624 and would continue to threaten and attack English settlements intermittently throughout the decade, by 1625 the colonists, with supplies of powder low and interest in tobacco production high, lost their desire for active campaign-ing and were said to have "worne owt the Skarrs of the massacre" (ibid.: 508; Fausz 1977: chp. 6).

The English commanders who had employed something *less* than "their uttermost and Christian endeavours in prosequtinge revenge against the bloody Salvadges" (Virginia Colony 1915:37) came to believe *in time* that, for self-interest and self-preservation, it was "infinitely better to have no heathen among us, who at best were as thornes in our sides, then to be at peace or league with them" (Wyatt 1926:118). However, these same raiders of the Powhatans in the midst of war proved to be fair and far-sighted traders with friendly tribes, when that strategy was seen to promote self-interest and self-preservation of another kind.

The war with the Powhatans had proven to be "the universal Chirurgion of . . . distempered times" for the English colonists in the 1620s (Alexander 1624:5). The oligarchs who had gained power during crisis conditions were anxious, in Governor Wyatt's words, "to quicken our new springinge hopes" (Kingsbury 1935:IV, 572) by seeking their fortunes in the fur trade once the hostile forces had been pacified. Armed with the knowledge of, and experience with, tribes and territories they had gained in wartime, a handful of intrepid adventurers who already monopolized ships, boats, laborers, interpreters, arms, provision, and capital initiated the Chesapeake beaver trade and thus demonstrated that some Indians could be "good" without being "dead" (Fausz 1982).

Two men, Henry Fleet and William Claiborne, both gentry sons from Kent and veterans of the Second Anglo-Powhatan War, transformed the Chesapeake from a dangerous war zone into a potentially major source of furs for the booming international market. Fleet spent the years between 1623 and 1627 as a captive of the Nacotchtanks (Anacostans), allies and trading partners of the Leaque Iroquois (figure 7; appendix III). Being "better proficient in the Indian language than mine own" made him "more able that way" to initiate contacts with and earn the confidence of Potomac River tribes like the Piscataways and the Patawomekes, as well as distant, unknown inland groups he called the "Usserahaks" and "Herekeenes." Fleet employed Indians as traders in the late 1620s and early 1630s and allegedly "taught the lower Potomac River tribes how to "preserve the furs" they traditionally burned or discarded, convincing them "what benefit may accrue" by selling the beaver pelts to him (Fleet 1876).

Claiborne was an even more ambitious and successful fur trader. As a Virginia councilor, he was granted a monopoly over Indian interpreters, because he had "invented [a method] for safe keeping of any Indians . . . and [found a way] to make them serviceable" (Virginia Colony 1924:111). As colony surveyor, he received several commissions in the late 1620s to explore and trade in the northern reaches of the Chesapeake. Supported by London capital and the fur-rich and friendly Susquehannocks, who desired a safe southern outlet for their beaver pelts, Claiborne established thriving trade posts at Kent and Palmer's islands in the early 1630s (Fausz 1982). The Susquehannocks, who "exceedingly seemed to love . . . Clayborne" and "would sooner trade with . . . [him] then with any other," gave him Palmer's Island at the mouth of their river, helped him clear the land for planting, reconfirmed his title to it as late as 1652, and, in general, remained his loyal and valued allies (Great Britain, High Court of Admiralty 1887).

Figure 7 *Maryland at Contact, ca. 1634*

A and B are zones of hospitality for the Maryland English and their Indian allies. C and D represent areas of hostility for the Maryland and English, i.e., those dominated by the Virginia English and their Susquehannock allies. (Adapted from figure 1, Fausz 1978a)

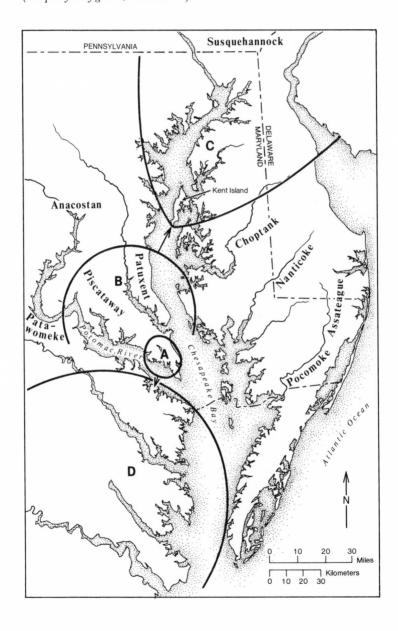

Although the Chesapeake beaver trade was short-lived and its vast potential never fully realized, Fleet and Claiborne offered a lucrative alternative to tobacco (a one-pound beaver pelt was worth twenty-five to a hundred times the price of a pound of "leaf" between 1633 and 1644) and an example of amicable, cooperative Anglo-Indian relations based on trade rather than on cultural and territorial wars (appendix IV). They implicitly discarded the traditional English conception of a "frontier" as the rigid, ethnocentric boundary between "civilized colonists" and "savage Indians" and for a time judged people, irrespective of culture, color, or national origin, as either friendly allies or hostile competitors based on profit potential.

The Chesapeake beaver trade brought Englishmen and Indians together in the most direct and intense form of cultural contact short of war, and yet it allowed—in fact, demanded—that Indians remain Indians, pursuing the skills they knew best without fear of territorial dispossession, and that Englishmen remain Englishmen, performing the services they understood without the need to become Christian crusaders. The quest for the thick and heavy pelts of *Castor canadensis* created a transatlantic network stretching from the beaver dams of America to the docks of London. The crucial point of exchange between *Castor* and the capitalist occurred when the Indian trapper met the English trader, and for at least once a season, they spoke a mutually intelligible language that transcended cultural differences. The fur trade united Englishmen and their Indian allies in a cooperative, symbiotic partnership of mutual benefit across a contact frontier with no territorial or cultural boundaries; ironically, however, the trade divided people of similar culture and common origins in a fiercely competitive struggle for lands, markets, and trade goods.

4. Maryland

As was explained at the beginning of this paper, Anglo-Indian relations in Maryland proceeded from different assumptions and assumed different patterns from those at Roanoke Island and at early Jamestown. The Powhatan Uprising and its aftermath had drawn Nacotchtanks, Piscataways, and Patuxents into the conflict, introduced them to the brutal campaigning of hostile Englishmen, and left them weakened and ever more susceptible to incursions from the aggressive Susquehannocks (Fausz 1982; Merrell 1979; appendix III). Having learned of the fate that befell the Powhatans after almost constant resistance against the Virginia-English and deducing that they had more to gain through trade, Algonquians north of the Potomac River peacefully accommodated themselves to the presence of the Maryland English in 1634.

Lord Baltimore's settlers came to the Chesapeake informed by fifty years of Anglo-Indian contacts, both hostile and hospitable, and their attitudes reflected new and current thinking about the role of native populations in English colonial planning. Considering the tragic failure of policy represented by the Second Anglo-Powhatan War, Sir William Alexander, the royal official who would later grant Claiborne his trading license to Kent Island, in 1624 wrote that Englishmen should "possesse themselves" of American lands "without dispossessing . . . others," for the "ruine" of Indians "could give us neither glory nor benefit" (Alexander 1624:37–38). The very next year, Sir Francis Bacon similarly advocated "plantation in a pure soil; that is, where people are not displanted, . . . for else it is rather an extirpation than a plantation" (Bacon n.d.:72).

In addition to this philosophical change of heart on the part of colonization theorists, the Maryland English more practically conceived of peaceful, cooperative Indian relations based on a profitable trade in furs. The beaver trade pioneered by Fleet and Claiborne was already well known to Lord Baltimore and his Jesuit supporters, and it reportedly became "the main chief encouragement of . . . Lord Proprietarie to undertake the great charge and hazard of planting this Province" (Maryland Colony 1883:I, 43). Within six months of first landing, the Marylanders had shipped over one thousand yards of trading cloth, six hundred axes, forty dozen hawk's bells, three hundred pounds of brass kettles, thirty dozen hoes, forty-five gross of Sheffield knives, and other goods in anticipation of tapping the rich fur market, and had created a joint stock company for that purpose (Stone 1982:26–29).

While some idealistic Marylanders wished that the area Indians would accept Christianity and "live . . . free from covetousnesse" ([Lewger and Hawley] 1910:90), the fur traders, including the Jesuits, counted on that "covetousnesse" for their success. Father White observed that the Piscataways "exceedingly desire civil life and Christian apparell and [would have] long since . . . beene clothed had the covetous English merchants (who would exchange cloath for nought but beaver, which everyone could not get), held them from it (God forbid we should do the like)" (White 1910:44). In their proselytizing among the Potomac and Patuxent river tribes, the Jesuits exchanged trade goods for both furs and converts "to conciliate their affection," and when the Piscataway *tayac* (chief) accepted

Christianity, he "exchanged the skins, with which he was heretofore clothed, for a garment made in our fashion" (Jesuit Letters 1910:127). We do not know if the priests took such fur mantles to market, but there is little doubt that the Jesuits, active sponsors of trading expeditions, reaped temporals while sowing spirituals in their mission work among Indians increasingly denied desirable merchandise from the Susquehannock and Virginia-dominated fur trade (Fausz 1982).

Soon after the arrival of Lord Baltimore's colonists, a local Indian informed them that they "should rather conforme your selves to the Customes of our Countrey, then impose yours upon us" ([Lewgers and Hawley] 1907:90), and it can be argued that Maryland's early success in maintaining amicable relations with the local Algonquian population was attributable to the easy adaptation to such "Customes." Maryland's relations with its nearest Indian neighbors got off to a good start largely through the advice and guidance of Captain Fleet, who attached himself to the new colony because his "hopes and future fortunes depended upon the trade and traffic that was to be had of this river [the Potomac]" (Fleet 1876; Fausz 1982, 1984). Governor Leonard Calvert was, from the first, careful to pay courtesy calls on area werowances, to *purchase* lands from them, and to hold conferences to iron out any difficulties—all of which followed the accepted practices of the Virginia fur traders (Fausz 1984).

The founding of Maryland altered the traditional patterns of Anglo-Indian relations and challenged the accepted wisdom that indigenous populations nearest English settlements would be hostile and more distant ones friendly. There was nothing "miraculous" in the pragmatic acceptance of hard realities: both Marylanders and Piscataways desired trade they found dominated by others and sought mutual protection from much stronger common enemies—the Virginia English and the Susquehannocks. These Anglo-Algonquian neighbors in Maryland sought self-interest and self-preservation through cooperation because neither group could risk competition and alienation in a region with such a precarious balance of power. Forced by circumstances to be less objectionable and more hospitable to each other than parties in earlier contact situations had been, the English and the Indians along the north bank of the Potomac created, through their successful early efforts in accommodation and acculturation, new and important "Customes of the Countrey."

In 1635, promoters of Lord Baltimore's colony enthusiastically declared that "experience hath taught us that by kind and faire usage, the Natives . . .

have upon all occasions performed as many friendly Offices to the English in Maryland . . . as any neighbour . . . in the most Civill parts of Christendome" ([Lewger and Hawley] 1910:84). Unfortunately for all concerned, the seventeenth-century Chesapeake did not qualify as one of "the most Civill parts of Christendome" then or later. Endemic warfare between and among culture groups, coupled with the steady growth of an increasingly territorial-minded English population, soon brought an end to inter-ethnic alliances. When Englishmen and Indians came to realize, especially after 1675, that self-interest and self-preservation were advanced and enhanced by *in-group loyalty* to their cultural brethren, the colonists had an overwhelming advantage. By 1700, Indians along the mid-Atlantic coast—old friends as well as old foes of the English—had all shared a similar fate and were united by the commonality of their harsh experiences with disease, defeat, and dispossession imported and inflicted by aliens from the east.

REFERENCES CITED

Alexander, William
    1624   An Encouragement to Colonies. London.

[Anon.]
    1955   The voyage made by Sir Richard Greenvile, for Sir Walter Ralegh, to Virginia, in the yeere, 1585. *In:* The Roanoke Voyages, 1584–1590. Hakluyt Society, 2nd Series, Nos. 104–105. David Beers Quinn, ed. 1:178–193. London: Cambridge University Press.

[Archer, Gabriel]
    1969   A Relatyon of the Discovery of our River, from James Forte into the Maine. *In:* The Jamestown Voyages Under the First Charter 1606–1609. Hakluyt Society, 2nd Series, Nos. 136–137. Philip L. Barbour, ed. 1:80–98. London: Cambridge University Press.

Argall, Samuel
    1907   A letter of Samuell Argoll touching his Voyage to Virginia and Actions there: Written to Master Nicholas Hawes, June 1613. *In:* Hakluytus Posthumus, or Purchas, His Pilgrimes. Samuel Purchase, ed. 19:90–95. Glasgow: James MacLehose and Sons.

Bacon, Francis
    n.d.   Of Plantations (1625), essay 33. *In:* Essays of Bacon. Henry Morley, ed. pp. 72–74. Cleveland: World Publishing Company.

Barbour, Phillip L.
1969   Pocahontas and Her World. Boston: Houghton Mifflin Company.

[Barlowe, Arthur]
1955   The first voyage made to the coastes of America, with two barkes, wherein were Captaines Master Philip Amadas, and Master Arthur Barlowe, who discovered part of the Countrey now called Virginia, Anno. 1584: Written by one of the said Captaines, and sent to sir Walter Raleigh, knight, at whose charge, and direction, the said voyage was set foorth. *In:* The Roanoke Voyages, 1584–1585. Hakluyt Society, 2nd Series, Nos. 104–105. David Beers Quinn, ed. 1:91–116. London: Cambridge University Press.

Binford, Lewis R.
1964   Archaeological and Ethnohistorical Investigation of Cultural Diversity and Progressive Development Among Aboriginal Cultures of Coastal Virginia and North Carolina. Ph.D. dissertation, Department of Anthropology, University of Michigan.

Carrera, Juan de la
1953   Relation of Juan de la Carrera, 1 March 1600. *In:* The Spanish Mission in Virginia 1570–1572. Clifford M. Lewis and Albert J. Loomie, eds. pp. 123–142. Chapel Hill: University of North Carolina Press.

Del la Warr, Baron (Thomas West]
1907   The Relation of the Right Honorable the Lord De-La-Warre, Lord Governour and Captaine Generall of the Colonie, planted in Virginea, 1611. *In:* Hakluytus Posthumus, or Purchas His Pilgrimes. Samuel Purchas, ed. 19:85–90. Glasgow: James MacLehose and Sons.

Fausz, J. Frederick
1977   The Powhatan Uprising of 1622: A Historical Study of Ethnocentrism and Cultural Conflict. Ph.D. dissertation, Department of History, The College of William and Mary in Virginia.
1979a Fighting "Fire" With Firearms: The Anglo-Powhatan Arms Race in Early Virginia. American Indian Culture and Research Journal 3:33–50.
1979b George Thorpe, Nemattanew, and the Powhatan Uprising of 1622. Virginia Cavalcade 28:110–117.
1981   Opechancanough: Indian Resistance Leader. *In:* Struggle and Survival in Colonial America. David G. Sweet and Gary B. Nash, eds. pp. 21–37. Berkeley: University of California Press.
1982   "By Warre Upon Our Enemies, and Kinde Usage of Our Friends": The Beaver Trade and Interest Group Rivalry in the Development of the Early Chesapeake, 1607–1652. Paper presented at the October 1982 Colloquium

in Colonial American History, Institute of Early American History and Culture, Williamsburg, Virginia. Copy on file at the Institute.

1983 Authority and Opportunity in the Early Chesapeake: The Bay Environment and the English Connection, 1620–1640. Paper presented at 1983 Organization of American Historians Annual Meeting, Cincinnati. Copy on file at Virginia Historical Society, Richmond.

1984 Present at the "Creation": The Chesapeake World That Greeted the Maryland Colonists. Maryland Historical Magazine 79:7–20.

Fausz, J. Frederick, and Jon Kukla
1977 A Letter of Advice to the Governor of Virginia, 1624. The William and Mary Quarterly, 3rd series 34:104–129.

Feest, Christian F.
1966 Powhatan: A Study in Political Organization. Wiener Volkerkundliche Mitteilungen 13:59–83.

1978a Nanticoke and Neighboring Tribes. *In:* Handbook of North American Indians 15:240–252. Washington D.C.: U.S. Government Printing Office.

1978b Virginia Algonquians. *In:* Handbook of North American Indians 15:253–270. Washington, D.C.: U.S. Government Printing Office.

1978c North Carolina Algonquians. *In:* Handbook of North American Indians 15:271–289. Washington, D.C.: U.S. Government Printing Office.

Fleet, Henry
1876 A brief Journal of a Voyage made in the bark Warwick to Virginia and other parts of the continent of America. *In:* The Founders of Maryland As Portrayed in Manuscripts, Provincial Records and Early Documents. The Rev. Edward D. Neill, ed. pp. 19–37. Albany: Joel Munsell.

Great Britain, High Court of Admiralty
1887 Claiborne contra Cloberry et al: Testes Examinati [et jurati] per Allegationen ex parte Will Claiborne. *In:* Archives of Maryland, William Hand Browne, ed. 5:181–239. Maryland Historical Society.

[Hakluyt, Rev. Richard]
1955 The third voyage made by a Ship, sent in the yeere 1586 to the reliefe of the Colonie planted in Virginia, at the sole charges of Sir Walter Raleigh. *In:* The Roanoke Voyages, 1584–1590. Hakluyt Society, 2nd Series, Nos. 104–105. David Beers Quinn, ed. I:477–480. London: Cambridge University Press.

Hamor, Ralph
1615 A True Discourse of the Present Estate of Virginia, and the successe of the

affaires there till the 18 of June 1614. London: John Beale for William Welby.

Harriot, Thomas
1955   A briefe and true report of the newfound land of Virginia, of the commodities and of the nature and manners of the naturall inhabitants. *In:* The Roanoke Voyages, 1584–1590, Hakluyt Society, 2nd Series, Nos. 104–105. David Beers Quinn, ed. I:317–387. London: Cambridge University Press.

Jesuit Letters
1910   Extracts from the Annual Letters of the English Province of the Society of Jesus, 1634, 1638, 1639, 1640, 1642, 1654, 1656, 1681. *In:* Narratives of Early Maryland, 1633–1684. Clayton Colman Hall, ed. pp. 113–144. New York: Charles Scribner's Sons.

Johnson, Robert
1836   A True Declaration of the estate of the Colonie in Virginia (London, 1610). *In:* Tracts . . . Relating . . . to the . . . Settlement . . . of the Colonies in North America, 3:6. Peter Force ed. Washington, D.C.: Peter Force.

Kingsbury, Susan Myra
1906–
1935   Records of the Virginia Company of London. Susan Myra Kingsbury, ed. 1 and 2:1906; 3:1933; 4:1935. Washington, D.C.: U.S. Government Printing Office.

Lane, Ralph
1955   An account of the particularities of the imployments of the English men left in Virginia by Sir Richard Greenevill under the charge of Master Ralfe Lane Generall of the same, from the 17 of August 1585 untill the 18 of June 1586. *In:* The Roanoke Voyages, 1584–1590. Hakluyt Society, 2nd Series, Nos. 104–105. David Beers Quinn, ed. 1:255–294. London: Cambridge University Press.

[Lewger, John, and Jerome Hawley]
1910   A Relation of Maryland; together with a Map of the Countrey, the Conditions of Plantation, with His Majesties Charter to the Lord Baltimore, translated into English. *In:* Narratives of Early Maryland, 1633–1684. Clayton Colman Hall, ed. pp. 65–112. New York: Charles Scribner's Sons.

Maryland, Colony of
1883   Proceedings and Acts of the General Assembly of Maryland, January 1637/ 38–September 1664. *In:* Archives of Maryland, I. William Hand Browne, ed. Maryland Historical Society.

Merrell, James H.
   1979   Cultural Continuity among the Piscataway Indians of Colonial Maryland. The William and Mary Quarterly, 3rd Series, 36:548–570.

Mook, Maurice
   1944   Algonkian Ethno-history of the Carolina Sound. Journal of the Washington Academy of Sciences 34:182–197, 213–228.

Morgan, Edmund S.
   1975   American Slavery, American Freedom: the Ordeal of Colonial Virginia. New York: W. W. Norton and Company.

Ore, Luis Geronimo de
   1953   An account of the Martyrs of the Provinces of Flordia: twelve Religious of the Society of Jesus, who suffered in Jacan (ca. 1617). *In:* The Spanish Jesuit Mission in Virginia, 1570–1572. Clifford M. Lewis and Albert J. Loomie, eds. pp. 179–192. Chapel Hill: University of North Carolina Press.

Peckham, Sir George
   1940   A True Reporte of the late discoveries, and possession, taken in the right of the Crowne of Englande, of the Newfound Landes: By that valiaunt and worthye Gentleman, Sir Humfrey Gilbert Knight (1583). *In:* Voyages and Colonising Enterprises of Sir Humphrey Gilbert. Hakluyt Society, 2nd Series, Nos. 83–84. David Beers Quinn, ed. 2:440–452. London: Cambridge University Press.

Purchas, Rev. Samuel
   1907   Hakluytus Posthumus, or Purchas His Pilgrimes, 19. Samuel Purchas, ed. Glasgow: James MacLehose and Sons.

Quinn, David Beers
   1955   The Roanoke Voyages, 1584–1590. 2 vol. Hakluyt Society, 2nd Series, Nos. 104–105. David Beers Quinn, ed. London: Cambridge University Press.
   1974   England and the Discovery of America, 1482–1620. New York: Alfred A. Knopf.

Quiros, Luis de, and Juan Baptista de Segura
   1953   Letter of Luis de Quiros and Juan Baptista de Segura to Juan de Hinistrosa, 12 September 1570. *In:* The Spanish Jesuit Mission in Virginia, 1570–1572. Clifford M. Lewis and Albert J. Loomie, eds. pp. 85–94. Chapel Hill: University of North Carolina.

Rogel, Juan
  1953   Letter of Juan Rogel to Francis Borgia, 28 August 1572. *In:* The Spanish
         Jesuit Mission in Virginia, 1570–1572. Clifford M. Lewis and Albert J.
         Loomie, eds. pp. 107–114. Chapel Hill: University of North Carolina
         Press.

Sackville, Lionel C.
  1922   Lord Sackville's Papers Respecting Virginia, 1613–1631. *In:* American His-
         torical Review 27:493–538, 738–765.

Smith, Captain John
  1624   The Generall Historie of Virginia, New-England, and the Summer Isles,
         with the names of the Adventurers, Planters, and Governours from their
         first beginning Anno 1584 to this present 1624. London: Printed by J. D.
         and J. H. for Michael Sparkes.

Stone, Garry Wheeler
  1982   Society, Housing, and Architecture in Early Maryland: John Lewger's St.
         John's. Ph.D. dissertation, Department of American Civilization, Univer-
         sity of Pennsylvania.

Strachey, William
  1953   The Historie of Travell into Virginia Britania (1612), Hakluyt Society, 2nd
         Series, No. 103. Louis B. Wright and Virginia Freund, eds. London:
         Cambridge University Press.

[Symonds, William, comp.]
  1612   The Proceedings of the English Colonie in Virginia since their first begin-
         ning from England in the yeare of our Lord 1606, till this present 1612,
         with all their accidents that befell them in their Journies and Discoveries.
         Oxford: Joseph Barnes.

Thorowgood, Cyprian
  1634   A relation of a voyage made by Master Cyprian Thorowgood to the head of
         the baye [1634]. Handwritten original manuscript of two folio pages,
         photostat on file at St. Mary's City Commission, St. Mary's City, Mary-
         land.

Trigger, Bruce G.
  1976   The Children of Aataentsic: A History of the Huron People to 1660. Vol.
         1. Montreal and London: McGill-Queen's University Press.

Virginia, Colony of
  1915   Journals of the House of Burgesses, 1:1619–1658/59. H. R. McIlwaine and
         J. P. Kennedy, eds. Richmond: Virginia State Library.

1924   Minutes of the Council and General Court of Colonial Virginia. Vol. 1. H.R. McIlwaine, ed. Richmond: Virginia State Library.

Virginia Company of London
1844   A true Declaration of the Estate of the Colonie in Virginia (1610). *In:* Tracts and Other Papers, Relating to the Origin, Settlement, and Progress of the Colonies in North America, From the Discovery of the Country to the Year 1776. Vol. 3. Peter Force, ed. Washington, D.C.: Peter Force.
1957   The Three Charters of the Virginia Company of London, With Seven Related Documents, 1606–1621. Samuel M. Bemiss, ed. Williamsburg: Virginia 350th Anniversary Celebration Corporation.

Waterhouse, Edward
1622   A Declaration of the State of the Colony and Affaires in Virginia. With a Relation of the Barbarous Massacre . . . treacherously executed by the Native Infidels upon the English the 22 of March last. London.

Whitaker, Alexander
1613   Good Newes from Virginia. London: Felix Kyngston.

White, Andrew, S. J.
1910   A Briefe Relation of the Voyage Into Maryland (1634). *In:* Narratives of Early Maryland, 1633–1684. Clayton Colman Hall, ed. New York: Charles Scribner's Sons.

[White, John]
1955a   The fourth voyage made to Virginia, with three shippes, in the yeere, 1587. *In:* The Roanoke Voyages, 1584–1590. Hakluyt Society, 2nd Series, Nos. 104–105. David Beers Quinn, ed. 2:515–552. Cambridge University Press, London.
1955b   The fifth voyage of Master John White into the West Indies and parts of America called Virginia, in the yeere 1590. *In:* The Roanoke Voyages, 1584–1590. Hakluyt Society, 2nd Series, Nos. 104–105. David Beers Quinn, ed. 2:598–622. London: Cambridge University Press.

Wyatt, Sir Francis
1926   Letter to [Earl of Southhampton?], summer 1624. *In:* Documents Relating to Sir Francis Wyatt. William and Mary Quarterly, 2nd Series, 6:114–121.

Appendix I:
Roanoke Area Algonquians

Tribe	Werowance	Location
Roanoacs	Wingina (Pemisipan); brother, Granganimeo	Roanoke Is. and mainland opposite (village of Dasemunke-peuc; unknown portion of peninsula between Albermarle Sound to the N. and the Pamlico River to the S.
Weapemeocs	Okisco (subordinate to Chawanoacs)	N. of Albemarle Sound between Chowan River and Curri-tuck Sound.
Chawanoacs	Menatonon; son, Skiko	Upper Chowan River; single largest tribe, with perhaps 18 villages, 2,500 people.
Moratucs	Pooneno	Along Roanoke River roughly between Chawanoac and Roanoac territory.
Croatoans	Manteo? (probably son of the werowance)	Croatoan Is., Outer Banks S. of Roanoke Is. near Cape Hat-teras.
Secotans	Wingina? (sometimes called "Lord of Secotan" by the English. It is not clear if the Secotans constituted a separate tribe, or if the Roanoacs were merely a village segment of the Secotans.)	Unknown portion S. (and N.?) of the Pamlico River.

Total "North Carolina Algonquian" population: 7,000 (Feest 1978c:272)

Appendix IA:
Enemies of the Roanoke Area Algonquians

Tribe	Location
Mangoaks (Mandoags or "rattlesnakes"): threatening and powerful Iroquoian tribe whose "name, and multitude besides their valour is terrible to all the rest of the provinces"; variously identified as Nottoways, Meherrins, or Tuscaroras.	W. of Chawanoacs.
Pomouiks: Iroquoian or Siouan enemies of the Secotans and Roanoacs. Piamacum was Werowance.	Along Pamlico River.
Neusioks: Iroquoian or Siouan tribe; perhaps allies of the Pomouiks.	Along Neuse River.
Chesepians (Chesapeaks): Virginia Algonquian tribe independent of Powhatan before 1600; friendly with Chawanoacs but perhaps hostile to other Carolina Algonquians.	S. bank James River near mouth and along Atlantic Coast.
Tripanicks (probably Nansamunds): Virginia Algonquian tribe, populous and strong, independent of Powhatan before 1614; perhaps hostile to Carolina Algonquians.	S. bank James River between Chesepians and Opossians.
Opossians (probably Warraskoyacks): Virginia Algonquian tribe allied with Powhatan after 1607; perhaps hostile to Carolina Algonquians.	S. bank James River W. of Tripanicks.

Appendix II:
Tsenacommacah, 1607–1612: Principal Tribes and Werowances

Tribe	Werowance
Powhatan's "Inheritance"	
Pamunkey	Opechancanough
	Opitchapam
	Kekataugh
Powhatan	Parahunt
Mattaponi	Werowough
Youghtanund	Pomiscutuck
Appomattoc	Coquonasum & Opuskeno
Arrohattoc	Ashuaquid
Other Loyal Tribes	
Paspahegh	Wowinchopunk
Kiskiack	Ottahotin
Weanoc	Kaquothocum & Ohoroquoh
Kecoughtan (colony)	Pochins
Piankatank (colony)	—
Warraskoyack	Tackonekintaco
Quiyoughcohannock	Oholasc (regent)
Patawomekes*	Matchqueon & Japassus
Other Potomac River Tribes*	—
Rappahannock River Tribes*	—

*Unknown or doubtful loyalty.
Source: William Strachey, *The Historie of Travell into Virginia Britania* (1612), ed. Louis B. Wright and Virginia Freund, Hakluyt Society, 2nd Ser., CIII (London, 1953), 63–69.

Appendix IIA:
Powhatan Enemies, ca. 1607

Tribe	Location
Monacans: seemingly strong Siouan confederacy of 5 tribes, as close as 20 water miles to nearest Powhatan village.	Virginia Piedmont W. of James River fall line, W. to foothills of Blue Ridge Mts.; capital: Rassawek, confluence of Rivanna and James rivers.
Manahoacs: Siouan confederacy of 8 to 12 tribes; allies of Monocans, with combined population of 6,000 +.	Headwaters of Rappahannock and Rapidan rivers, Northern Neck W. of fall line.
Bocootawanaukes ("Pocoughtaonacks"): a "mighty" and "fierce Nation that did eate men" and made "terrible warr" on the Powhatans in annual raids upon the Potomac and Rappahannock river tribes; variously identified as Ottawas or Eries.	Great Lakes?
Massawomekes: a large warlike group, the "most mortall enemies" of the Powhatans (especially the Patawomekes), Susquehannocks, Piscataways, Manahoacs, and Monocans; almost certainly a designation for one or all tribes of the League of the Iroquois.	"beyond the mountains . . . upon a great salt water"
Chawanoacs: at war with Powhatans at some point between 1620 and 1644; also see appendix 1.	
Chickahominies: strong Algonquian tribe of perhaps 2,000 people; warlike and "free" of Powhatan; spoke different dialect and had different political system; remained independent until 1616.	Peninsula between James and York rivers.

Appendix IIA: Continued
Powhatan Enemies, ca. 1607

Tribe	Location
Nansamunds: independent Algonquian tribe of some 800 persons; a "proud warlike Nation" organized as a chiefdom and speaking a different dialect than the Powhatans; remained independent until ca. 1620.	Along Nansemond River, 13 miles from its confluence with the James River.
Accomacs and **Accohannocs:** isolated Eastern Shore tribes with significant cultural differences from the Powhatans; largely independent.	"Virginia" Eastern Shore.

Appendix III:
Maryland Algonquians and Their Enemies

Tribe	Werowance	Location
Algonquians		
Piscataways: confederacy of Algonquian tribes; capital, Moyaone; population, 7,000.	Wannas (d. 1636), Kittamaquund (d. 1641); called "Tayac," or emperor.	N. (and E.) banks of Potomac River, W. of Patuxent R. from Chesapeake Bay to fall line.
Patuxents: closely affiliated with Piscataways culturally and linguistically; independent by 1620s.	Namenacus (as of 1621); brother, Wamanato.	Along E. bank of Patuxent River.
Enemies		
Susquehannocks: very strong Iroquoian tribe of many thousands that annually raided Piscataway territory; well-armed and aggressive.		Susquehanna River, northern Chesapeake Bay.
Anacostans (Nacotchtanks): seemingly strong Iroquoian tribe; raiders of southern Maryland; enemies of Potomac River tribes; unknown relationship with Susquehannocks.		Near site of Washington, D.C.
Other Iroquoian groups, perhaps Eries, Senecas, and/or Mohawks, between 1600 and 1640.		Great Lakes.

Appendix IV:
Beaver and Bead Values in the Chesapeake Relative to Tobacco

Year	Beaver pelts (price per lb.)	Peake (per fathom)	Roanoke (per arms' length)	Tobacco (per lb.)
1633 Va.	7–9s. (84–108d.)	—	—	4–9d.
1634 Va.	10s. (120d.)	10s. (120d.)	—	4–6d.
1636 Va.	6s. 6d.–10s. (78–120d.)	—	—	4–8d.
1638 Md.	7s. 6d.–8s. (90–96d.)	7s. 6d. (90d.)	1s (12d.)	3d.
1643 Md.	12s.–25s. (144–300d.)	—	1s. 8d.–2s. 6d. (20–30d.)	2–3d.
1644 Md.	24s. (288d.)	—	2s. 4d. (28d.)	4d.

Virginia values (all Eastern Shore) are found in Susie M. Ames., *County Court Records of Accomack-Northampton, Virginia 1632–1640* (Washington D.C., 1954), 16–17, 74. Maryland values come from *Archives of Maryland*, III, 67–8, 73, 78; IV, 48, 84–9, 103–5, 214, 227, 274. Tobacco prices are based on Russell R. Menard, "A note on Chesapeake Tobacco Prices, 1618–1660," *Virginia Magazine of History and Biography*, 84 (Oct. 1976), 404–407.

PART IV

The South—Labor, Tribute and Social Policy:

The Spanish Legacy

Commentary on Part IV

William W. Fitzhugh

South of Virginia the course of early European contact took a different turn from that charted in cases from eastern North America. The reasons for this shift in pattern relate to differences in environment, geography, and resources, and with changes in population, economy, and political structure among the resident cultures, but they arose primarily from the policies and methods of Spanish intervention. As an introduction to this section, we will briefly summarize the major contrasts in each of these areas.

The native cultures occupying coastal regions from the Carolinas to the Caribbean islands consisted of a diverse set of cultural and linguistic groups that included Guale, Apalachee, Western and Eastern Timucua, Ais, Tocobaga, Calusa, and Tequesta in the Southeast, and the Ciboney, (Arawak) Lucayo, and Carib in the Caribbean and Bahamas regions (see Deagan, figure 1). Despite the cultural and linguistic diversity of the region, one type of socio-political system was dominent: weakly stratified collecting or food-producing chiefdoms with relatively low, patchy population densities. Still, some of these groups, such as the Taino (Dreyfus 1980–81) and Timucua, may have had high-level chiefdoms with more complex organization and larger population densities than the norm for this region. In many of these areas, aquatic resources contributed importantly to the diet, as did hunting and gathering for groups living in areas with poor agricultural potential. Except for the northernmost groups—the Guale, Timucua, and Apalachee— these cultures occupied peninsular and island environments without extensive hinterlands for reserve populations or environmental barriers to impede the spread of disease or military intervention. These indigenous factors—border vulnerability, geographic isolation, demographic instability, and the absence of regionally integrating political and military institutions—created a different baseline for European contact effects in the Caribbean and the far Southeast, an area that was more culturally fragile and unstable than the central East Coast region. In this regard Florida and the Caribbean cultures had certain biogeographic and cultural similarities with those of the arctic and subarctic.

As we have seen, early European contacts from Greenland to Virginia were dominated by mercantile interests and usually conducted by private groups operating with crown permits or charters giving them rights to trade or exploit resources in a given region. The means by which these projects were undertaken was venture capital, sometimes supplemented by large Crown subsidies or investments. Little control was exercised by the European governments over the actual conduct of activities in the New World, where decisions were made by the companies, the investors, and their agents in the field. Although influenced strongly by political events affecting the European powers, the interactions between Europeans and natives in these northern and central regions of the East Coast were largely entrepreneurial.

South of Virginia, in regions claimed by Spain, an entirely different pattern of European-native contact emerged. Here relations with natives were directed from their very beginnings in 1492 by social and economic policy established by royal decree. Settlement and exploitation of Spanish America was not pursued by private individuals acting on their own or in the interest of commercial concerns, but as servants of the Spanish crown or of the Catholic church. The actors in this arena were not fishermen, traders, and free landholders but priests, military men, and officials who were accountable to higher authorities. Spanish administration operated through the maintenance of colonial enclaves in the midst of native populations. Their goals were to reap maximum economic, military, and spiritual benefit from a minimal investment of personnel and resources. In idealized form, Spain wished to establish a pluralistic empire that reaped glory for the nobles who received commissions as field commanders and governors, jobs and opportunities for the middle class, riches for the crown, and souls for the church. At the same time it was necessary to adopt measures that would insure the survival of native populations on whose shoulders these primary interests rested.

In addition to these different administrative and economic arrangements, Spanish-native history was profoundly influenced by the geography, resources, and cultures that were found in these regions. Unlike many areas of northeastern North America, Florida and the Caribbean did not present the

Spaniards with a physically demanding environment. Permanent settlement was not inhibited by severe winters, sea ice, lack of food, or—to any serious degree in these eastern regions—native unrest. This difference was signalled by the immediate establishment of Spanish colonies in newly discovered areas, beginning with La Isabela in 1493. Moreover, in the Caribbean area the resources important to Spain were not whale oil, fish, or fur pelts—none of which were potential sources of revenues here—but gold, silver, gems, and other precious materials that were already circulating in native societies in the region and that had to be found, expropriated, or mined. The methods needed to acquire this wealth were different from those used to obtain the desired products of northern regions. And in addition, the Spanish colonist population had to be largely self-sufficient in basic commodities, especially food. These needs led rapidly to the imposition of tribute (*repartimiento*) and labor quotas (*encomienda*) exercised through the authority of subjugated native leadership and backed by miliary force. The locus of action was European enclaves established adjacent to native population centers that could provide labor to operate the mines, produce agricultural products (including cattle, sheep, pigs, and horses), and perform the many services needed by the permanently resident, primarily male Spanish population. These conditions led to a host of differences in acculturation history as compared with regions north of the Carolinas. An extremely important figure in the development of these policies was Bartolomé de las Casas, whose concern for the welfare of the Indians led to the formulation of practices designed to protect them from the worst abuses initially imposed upon them. Although these relatively humane policies were by no means always implemented, the Spanish treatment of the Indians was generally better than that of the English and perhaps the French.

The important *differences* in the history of early contact within these eastern portions of Spanish America is the subject of the following essay by Kathleen Deagan. These differences are dramatically underscored by demographic realities. Deagan reports that in the twenty-two years following 1492, 88 percent of the native population of Hispaniola had disappeared, largely as a result of European diseases, and that African slaves had begun to be imported as replacement labor as early as 1510, introducing still other alien diseases. Following the first major New World pandemic in 1519, there were essentially no native peoples left alive in this part of the Caribbean. In northern Florida, where sustained contact with Spanish did not begin until after the 1565 establishment of St. Augustine, Timucuan-speaking populations declined more slowly, but the end result was the same: a population of some thirty-five thousand in the mid-1600s was reduced to extinction by 1728 (see also Dobyns 1983).

The most important differences between the contact histories of "La Florida" (which included Florida and the coastal regions of Georgia and the Carolinas) and the Caribbean resulted from different goals of Spanish policy directed toward them. In the Caribbean, mineral and agricultural exploitation had resulted in military subjugation and the implementation of labor and tribute systems administered through the local native political systems. The rapid decline of native population and its replacement by African slaves soon produced a new syncretism of cultural elements. This is a relatively poorly known period and it is almost completely unexplored archeologically. Deagan's examination of the relationships between the two areas is unique in that Florida and the Antilles are not normally considered as a unit, even though they both were administered from Havana, not New Spain (Mexico City).

In La Florida, Spanish influence was more sporadic and was based on a variety of types of contact, including wreck survivors, discovery expeditions, perhaps unrecorded coastal slaving raids, military ventures, and the establishment of military and mission posts (Quinn 1979). Recent research has greatly expanded the documentary basis for this early Spanish period as well as for French contacts further west. These contacts have been studied extensively from the point of view of history, ethnohistory, and archeology (Brain 1979, 1985; Brown 1980, 1982; Deagan 1974, 1983; DePrater 1983; Deprater and Smith 1980; Dobyns 1983; Foster 1960; Hudson, DePrater, and Smith 1984; McEwan and Mitchem 1984; Mason 1963; Milanich and Fairbanks 1980; Morrell 1965; Neitzel 1965; South 1984; Sturtevant 1962, 1984; Swanton 1939; Thomas 1984; Thomas and Larsen 1979; see also references in Deagan, this volume, papers in Milanich and Proctor 1978, and discussion and references in Swagerty 1984). This strong tradition of research makes European-native contact studies in the greater Southeast one of the better-known subject areas of acculturation in eastern North America.

In contrast to the economic orientation of Spanish contact in the Caribbean, their interest in La Florida was primarily strategic and military, that is, to secure these areas from the English and French, to protect access and exit routes to and from Mexico, Central America, and the Antilles, and to provide bases for missionizing among the Indians. Very little Spanish investment was made in this area, which was turned over to Jesuit and Franciscan friars and a handful of military men scattered in posts along the Georgia and Carolina coasts. Because of their relative poverty, local self-sufficiency required a variety of contacts with the native population, but since few trade goods were available, these posts were not active centers of native activity. Over-emphasis on maintaining strongholds against possible French or English incursion and abortive attempts to convert local Indians in these early sixteenth-century settlements restricted Spanish influence in these areas.

However, following abandonment of these northern outposts and the establishment of St. Augustine in 1565, mission work became more successful and expanded rapidly into much of northern Florida, where it became a strong force of change for the Timucuan Indians of this region (Sturtevant 1962:62–67). The missions were still poor, they offered little in the way of material goods to the Indians, and firearms were strictly forbidden. Because of the poverty of these missions located in an economic backwater of the Spanish Empire, the emphasis on religious rather than economic activity, the collapse of native political and military infrastructure, and the gradual depopulation resulting from the European epidemics, these missions were weakened and fell prey to incursions by Yamasee and Creek Indians and others armed and encouraged by expanding English settlement in the Charleston area. Retreating to the safety of St. Augustine, these remnant groups existed as refugee communities until they were evacuated to other Spanish centers in the Caribbean in 1763. These mission villages would be interesting to compare with mission villages in California and with Indian "praying towns" in New England.

During this long period of Spanish contact Indian institutions were strongly affected by such new subsistence practices as the introduction of livestock and chickens, which began early in the sixteenth century. Village centralization and year-round sedentarism increased, and regional economic interaction and political alliances declined. Mound burial was replaced by Christian burial forms. Major changes in social organization reduced the power and leadership capabilities of chiefs. These changes, combined with population loss, culminated in a marked decline in cultural vitality and the ultimate extinction of these populations and societies due to their inability to defend themselves in the face of external pressure. Some of these changes have been explored to a limited extent through the excavation of Spanish mission sites, but these studies tend to have had Spanish rather than Indian records as their primary focus (e.g., Goggin 1951:186, 1952:60, 72). Future excavations at the sites of Santa Elena (South 1984) and on St. Catherine's Island

(Thomas 1984;) promise to extend our knowledge about Spanish-native interaction at these centers, but there remains a great need for further archeological research on the Spanish impact on Indian cultures in this region.

For the reasons cited above, Spanish activity in Florida and the Caribbean region has produced a diverse record of contact. Although substantial archeological treatment of this record has not yet materialized, historical study has provided large amounts of data suitable for integration with excavated data, and it can be expected that future work in Spanish archives will considerably expand this documentation. The potential for collaborative archeological research is therefore excellent. Because Spanish contact in Florida was largely aimed at religious conversion rather than economic interaction, and because much of this contact was conducted through economically poor religious missions, the pattern of culture change observed in native groups is likely to be different from that found in areas of North America where contacts revolved around the exchange of material goods and their passage through native middlemen and re-distribution systems.

The cases of Spanish-native contact in the Caribbean and Florida offer interesting parallels illustrating differing effects of social, economic, and religious policies on native groups that were geographically bounded and that did not have large populations or complex socio-political development. The areas differ from each other mainly in the relative economic importance given to them by Spanish authorities, a factor that turned out to be inversely proportional to the ultimate longevity of the native populations. The contact history of both cases, Hispaniola and La Florida, also demonstrates clear differences in the role played by European material culture on the development of social and economic institutions. Because trade in material culture was not a major feature of Spanish-Indian contact, the groups engaged in that contact did not experience the kind of competition for resources that developed among other North American groups, and could not use European material culture as a means of display or for gaining advantages from neighboring groups desirous of entering into this trade. This phenomenon, coupled with the strong religious motivation of the Spanish colonists, precipitated the destruction of regional cultural systems that had formerly been operative. What followed was a rapid collapse of native cultures and, for those groups which survived initial disease and attack, acceptance of a subservient role as social and economic vassals of Spanish colonial society until their populations dwindled, disappeared, and eventually were replaced by others.

REFERENCES   CITED

Brain, Jeffrey P.
1979   Tunica Treasure. Papers of the Peabody Museum of Archaeology and Eth-
        nology, Volume 5. Cambridge: Harvard University.
1985   Introduction. *In:* Final Report on the United States De Soto Expedition
        Commission, by John R. Swanton. Reprint edit. Washington, D.C.:
        Smithsonian Institution Press.

Brown, Ian W.
1980   Early 18th Century French-Indian Culture Contact in the Yazoo Bluffs
        Region of the Lower Mississippi Valley. Ph.D. dissertation, Brown Univer-
        sity.
1982   An Archaeological Study of Culture Contact and Change in the Natchex
        Bluffs Region. *In:* LaSalle and His Legacy: Frenchmen and Indians in the
        Lower Mississippi Valley. Patricia Galloway, ed. pp. 176–193. Jackson:
        University Press of Mississippi.

Deagan, Kathleen A.
1974   Sex, Status, and Role in the Mestizaje of Spanish Colonial Florida. Ph.D.
        dissertation, Department of Anthropology, University of Florida.
1983   Spanish St. Augustine: The Archaeology of a Colonial Creole Community.
        New York: Academic Press.

DePrater, Chester
1983   Late Prehistoric and Early Historic Chiefdoms in the Southeastern United
        States. Ph.D. dissertation, University of Georgia.

DePrater, Chester, and Marvin T. Smith
1980   Sixteenth Century European Trade in the Southeastern United States: Evi-
        dence from the Juan Pardo Expeditions (1566–1568). *In:* Spanish Colonial
        Frontier Research. Spanish Colonial Borderlands Research, no. 1. Henry
        Dobyns, ed. pp. 67–78. Albuquerque: Center for Anthropological Studies.

Dobyns, Henry F.
1983   Their Numbers Become Thinned: Native American Population Dynamics
        in Eastern North America. Knoxville: University of Tennessee Press.

Dreyfus, Simone
1980–   Notes sur la chefferie Taino d'Aiti: Capacités productrices, ressources ali-
1981   mentaires, pouvoirs dans une société précolombiénne de forêt tropicale.
        Journal de la Société des Americanistes 67:229–248.

Foster, George
1960 Culture and Conquest: America's Spanish Heritage. Viking Fund Publication in Anthropology 27. New York: Wenner-Gren Foundation for Anthropological Research.

Goggin, John M.
1951 Fort Pupo: a Spanish Frontier Outpost. Florida Historical Quarterly 30(2):139–192.

Hudson, Charles M., Chester DePrater, and Marvin T. Smith
1984 The Hernando de Soto Expedition: From Apalachee to Chiaha. Southeastern Archaeology 3:65–77.

McEwan, Bonnie G., and Jeffrey M. Mitchem
1984 Indian and European Acculturation in the Eastern United States as a Result of Trade. North American Archaeologist 5(4):271–285.

Mason, Carol I.
1963 Eighteenth Century Culture Change among the Lower Creeks. Florida Anthropologist 16(3):65–80.

Milanich, Gerald T., and Charles H. Fairbanks
1980 Florida Archaeology. New York:Academic Press.

Milanich, Gerald T., and Samuel Proctor, eds.
1978 Tacachale: Essays on the Indians of Florida and Southeastern Georgia During the Historic Period. Gainesville: University of Florida Presses.

Morrell, L. Ross
1965 The Wood Island Site in Southeastern Acculturation 1625–1800. Notes in Anthropology 11, Department of Anthropology. Tallahassee: Florida State University.

Neitzel, Robert S.
1965 Archaeology of the Fatherland Site: The Grand Village of the Natchez. Anthropological Papers 51(1). New York: American Museum of Natural History.

Quinn, David Beers, ed.
1979 The New American World. Volume V. The Extension of Settlement in Florida, Virginia, and the Spanish Southwest. New York: Arno Press and Hector Bye, Inc.

South, Stanley
1984 Testing Archaeological Sampling Methods at Fort San Felipe, South Carolina, 1983. Research Manuscript Series 190, South Carolina Institute of Archaeology and Anthropology. Columbia: University of South Carolina.

Sturtevant, William C.
1962 Spanish-Indian Relations in Southeastern North America. Ethnohistory 9(1):41–93.
1984 *Review of* Their Numbers Become Thinned: Native American Population Dynamics in Eastern North America, by Henry F. Dobyns. The American Historical Review 89(5):1380–81.

Swagerty, W. R.
1984 Scholars and the Indian experience: Critical Reviews of Recent Writing in the Social Sciences. Bloomington: Indiana University Press. (Published for the D'Arcy McNickle Center for the History of the American Indian–Newberry Library.)

Swanton, John R.
1939 Final report on the United States De Soto Expedition Commission. House Document 71, 76th Congress, First Session. Washington, D.C.: Government Printing Office.

Thomas, David Hurst
1984 Spanish Santa Catalina: Archaeology in the Active Voice. Paper delivered to the Anthropological Society of Washington, December 18, 1984. Washington: Anthropological Society of Washington/Smithsonian Institution Press.

Thomas, David Hurst, and Clark S. Larsen
1979 The Anthropology of St. Catherines Island: 2. The Refuge-Deptford Mortuary Complex. Anthropological Papers of the American Museum of Natural History 56(1):1–180.

Spanish-Indian Interaction in Sixteenth-Century Florida and Hispaniola

Kathleen A. Deagan

A B S T R A C T

Sixteenth-century Spanish and Indian interaction in the Caribbean and La Florida constitutes one of the most dramatic chapters in the history of European-native American relations, culminating in the complete extinction of the Indians of those areas by the eighteenth century. Interaction was highly patterned, and took place through both formal and informal institutions which were generally subject to official control and organization. The primary spheres of interaction included the organization and exploitation of native labor; the establishment of tribute systems; conversion and missionization; and intermarriage. The mechanisms by which each of these types of interaction brought about changes in American Indian and Euro-American cultures are discussed, and the results of these interaction patterns in Florida and in the Caribbean are compared.

1. Introduction

Interaction between Spaniards and the Indians of Florida and the Caribbean during the sixteenth century constitutes one of the most startling chapters in the history of European-American acculturation. The results of contact in Spanish America ranged variously from the disappearance of American Indian groups to an almost complete retention of pre-Columbian traditional lifeways, to the emergence of a variety of new social configurations (see for example Wagley 1968).

In Florida and the Greater Antilles, however, a combination of economic, ecological, social, and political factors conspired to bring about the eventual and complete extinction of the indigenous peoples of those regions. This process was particularly rapid in the Caribbean, due largely to the disastrous effects of early epidemic disease on an Indian population forced into close proximity with Europeans. The rapidity of population decline among the Antillean groups, as well as the relative absence of archeological data from the early historic period in that area, contribute to the difficulties in documenting the institutional changes that occurred in Caribbean Indian culture prior to its demise. In Florida, however, the disappearance of the native inhabitants was not complete until the eighteenth century. This more gradual decline was due at least in part to modifications in Spanish Indian policy and interaction structures as a result of earlier experiences in the Caribbean, as well as to the very different economic circumstances in the Florida colony.

Through the use of ethnohistorical and archeological sources, it is possible to document some of the processes of interaction and decline among the Florida Indians during the first decades of contact, and to suggest some of the institutional changes that preceded their demise. Because many of the policies governing Spanish-Indian interaction in Florida were based upon experiences in the Caribbean, interaction patterns in both areas will be considered here.

Spanish contact with the New World Indians was initially structured by a set of formal policies designed both to apply Christian principles to the governance of a new state and to help realize the economic potentials of the colonies and meet the needs of the colonists and the crown. Interaction between Spaniards and Indians took place through both formal and informal institutions, including systems of organizations for labor and tribute, religious conversion (both coercive and non-coercive), and intermarriage. In the implementation of all of these interactive processes, however, the Spaniards consistently recognized the social and political structures of the native groups, and effected their policies through the agencies of recognized tribal leaders.

2. Native Cultures at the Time of Contact

2.1. Caribbean

The first sustained contact between Spaniards and American Indians occurred in 1492 with the establishment of Columbus's first settlement, La Navidad, on Haiti's north coast. Thirty-nine crewmembers from the wrecked caravel *Santa Maria* coexisted for nearly a year with the Arawak Indians in the town of the *cacique* (tribal leader) Guacanacaric before their apparently exploitive practices regarding women and gold provoked the Indians to kill the men and destroy their settlement (Jane 1960; Morison 1940). After witnessing the failure of La Navidad, Columbus abandoned the area and established the town of La Isabela near present-day Puerto Plata in the Dominican Republic (Las Casas 1971:47–48). La Isabela was located adjacent to an Arawak town, and interaction with the Indians was immediate and sustained (ibid.:48–52).

The West Indies were inhabited during the time of Columbus's early activities by three major groups—the Arawak, the Ciboney, and the Carib. The Arawak occupied most of the Greater Antilles and the Taino sub-culture of the Arawak group inhabited most of Hispaniola, Puerto Rico, and Cuba at the time of contact (Rouse 1948a:507–546; Cassa 1975; figure 1). The Taino were root crop horticulturalists and fishermen (see Sturtevant 1961) with a chiefdom level of political and social organization. Settlements were sedentary, and ranged from hamlets of a few structures to towns of possibly as many as three thousand people (Rouse 1948a:524). Towns were normally arranged around a ballcourt and chief's house (figure 2).

At least six chiefdoms, organized by a system of ranked matrilineal clans, are documented as having existed in Hispaniola at the time of contact (Vega 1980; Rouse 1948a:532), and interchiefdom warfare was apparently common. Population estimates for the Arawaks on Hispaniola have varied from eight million (Cook and Borah 1971), to three million (Las Casas 1971, vol.2:ch. 18), and to a hundred thousand (Rosenblatt 1954). The highest figure would have reflected a population density of 104.6 people per square kilometer; the lowest, a density of 1.3 persons per square kilometer.

Two other native groups were present in the Caribbean in 1492, the Ciboney and the Carib. The Ciboney, believed to have been the original inhabitants of the Antilles, were distributed in peripheral areas of Cuba and southern Haiti (Rouse 1948b:497). Their economy was based on the hunting and gathering of littoral resources. There was little interaction between the Spaniards and the Ciboney Indians, who apparently disappeared shortly after contact.

The Carib, who are believed to have been relatively recent arrivals in the area (Rouse 1948c; Alegria 1981), inhabited the Lesser Antilles in 1492. The Carib had a reputation for extreme ferocity and cannibalism; they exterminated Arawak men (upon whom they regularly staged attacks) and took Arawak women as wives and slaves. Carib economy was also littoral, and settlement was in small, frequently-moved villages (Rouse 1948c:551). Since the Spaniards did not attempt to settle the Lesser Antilles during the six-

Figure 1 *Locations of Major Indian Groups and Early Spanish Settlement in the Caribbean and Florida (After Rouse 1948a:509)*

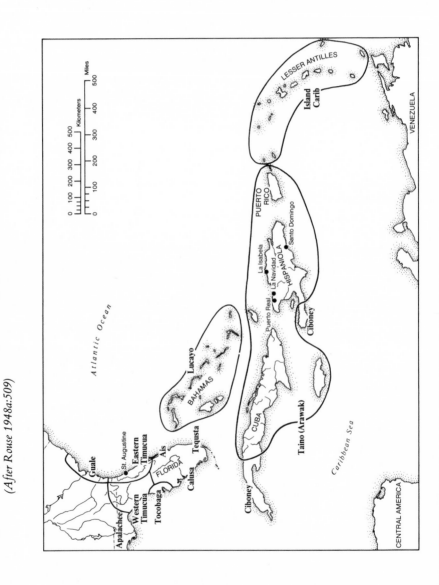

Figure 2 *Taino women of Hispaniola Preparing Manioc Bread (Drawn by Oviedo, pre-1557)*

teenth century, their interaction with the Caribs was sporadic and limited to hostility and slave raids.

2.2. Florida

Although sustained European interaction with Florida Indians did not begin until 1564, these groups had experienced intermittent contact with Spaniards for some forty years prior to initial colonization. Explorations and slaving raids included those of Ponce de Leon (1513), Gordillo (1520), Allyon (1526), Narvaez (1529), De Luna (1559), and Hernando de Soto (1540; see Quattelbaum 1956; Hoffman 1980; Lietch Wright 1981:32–42). Shipwreck victims were also frequently captured by the Florida Indians and some—such as D'Escalante Fontaneda among the Calusa (Smith 1945) and Pedro de Bustincury among the Ais (Lyon 1976:196)—lived among the natives for many years. Although such contact did not result in sustained, institutionally-based interaction between the Indians of Florida and the Spaniards, it did introduce elements of European technology, livestock, and—most important—disease. The latter may have had a particularly profound effect on aboriginal demography and settlement prior to the first colonization efforts. Slaving raids by Antillean colonists undoubtedly also helped to establish a hostile attitude among the Florida Indians.

When Pedro Menendez de Aviles founded St. Augustine in 1565, there were several Indian groups in La Florida (see figure 1). The Timucua and Apalachee groups occupied what is today northern Florida and southeastern Georgia (Milanich 1978; Deagan 1978, n.d.). To the north of the Timucua, along what are now the Georgia and South Carolina coasts, the Spaniards contacted the Guale Indians (Larson 1978, Jones 1978). Southern Florida was occupied by the Calusa (Goggin and Sturtevant 1964; Lewis 1978) and the Tocobaga (Bullen 1978) and southeastern Florida by the Miami, Tequesta, Jororo, Santa Lucia, and Mayaca Indians (Sturtevant 1978).

Spanish settlement and sustained interaction occurred only among the Timucua, the Apalachee, and the Guale, and it is upon data relating to these groups that the following discussion is based. The Timucua were subjected to the earliest and most enduring patterns of interaction with the Spaniards (see Deagan 1978, 1979; Milanich 1978; figure 3). "Timucua" refers to the linguistic affiliation of the tribes first encountered by the French and Spanish in northeastern Florida and southeastern Georgia. They included two major political divisions, those of the Eastern (Deagan 1978) and Western (Milanich

Figure 3 *Timucua Indians with Laudonniere, ca. 1564 Theodore DeBry engraving (1591) of Jacques LeMoyne painting (1565-1586). Facsimiles, University of Florida Library.*

1978) Timucua, each comprising several tribes organized into political confederacies. Intertribal warfare was common among the Timucua, particularly between the confederacies.

The Eastern Timucua were in general adapted to the coastal marshes and barrier islands, and to the St. Johns River and its adjacent coastal pine woods. The Western Timucua occupied the pine oak forests and richer farmlands of the region to the west of the St. Johns River (Milanich 1978:59; Milanich and Fairbanks 1980:216).

The economy of the Timucuan Indians was based on a combination of corn agriculture, hunting, and fishing. Settlements ranged from hamlets of two or three houses to towns of twenty to thirty houses and two hundred to three hundred people (Garcia 1902; Laudonniere 1975; Lowery 1905(1):208; Dobyns and Swagerty 1980:8). Structures were arranged around a central plaza and ballcourt area, which also frequently contained a communal structure and chief's house.

Tribes consisted of from five to twenty villages (Lopez 1605; Swanton 1946:202; Milanich and Sturtevant 1972:3), and the size of Timucua population at the time of contact has been estimated variously at 13,000 Eastern Timucua (Mooney 1928); 20,000 Eastern Timucua (Deagan 1978:94) and between 122,000 and 672,500 for all Timucua speakers (Dobyns and Swagerty 1980). These figures suggest population densities of .819 to 1.3 people per kilometer (based on an area of 15,864 square kilometers) for the Eastern Timucua domain, and 15.9 to 19.05 people per kilometer (based on an area of 35,302 square kilometers) for the entire Timucua region. By 1728 only a single Timucua Indian could be documented as surviving (Deagan 1978:115).

The Apalachee Indians occupied the fertile hilly area between the Apalachicola and Aucilla rivers in northwestern Florida (Deagan n.d.; Tesar 1980:160–250). This powerful centralized chiefdom had a fully horticultural economy, and its predecessors had participated in the late prehistoric Mississippian Ft. Walton cultural tradition (Milanich and Fairbanks 1980:227). Villages were sedentary, and at the time of first Spanish arrival may have had as many as 250 houses (ibid.:229).

Both Panfilo de Narvaez and Hernando de Soto passed through Apalachee territory during their explorations, generating hostility and suspicion among the inhabitants (Bandelier 1972; Smith 1968). They may also have introduced European diseases to the Apalachee and caused the population decline evident between the time of their exploration and the arrival of the early seventeenth-century missionaries (Deagan n.d.; Tesar 1980:193–194; Milanich and Fairbanks 1980:229). Regular contact between Spaniards and Apalachee began with the establishment of the Apalachee mission chain during the early seventeenth century, and continued until the destruction of the missions at the hands of the English in 1702 (Boyd, Smith, and Griffin 1951).

The Guale Indians occupied the coastal region between St. Andrew's and St. Catherine's sounds in South Carolina and Georgia at the time of Spanish contact. The Guale cultivated corn, beans, and pumpkins, but their economy was heavily dependent upon hunting, gathering, and fishing of coastal resources (Larson 1978:122; Jones 1978:192–193). The Guale were apparently not sedentary during the sixteenth century, and spent part of the year away from the coastal villages hunting and gathering forest resources (Larson 1978:123; Jones 1978:191–193). Settlement was in small dispersed villages, which appear to have been even smaller and more dispersed during the winter months (ibid). The Guale had a chiefdom type of political and social organization, with ranked matrilineal clans (Larson 1978:123–125; Jones 1978:196–197, 202–210).

3. The Structure of Spanish-Indian Interaction

During the sixteenth and seventeenth centuries the Indians of Florida and the Caribbean underwent changes in their traditional cultures as a result of Spanish policies in the three major areas of labor and tribute organization, religious conversion, and intermarriage. The former two were governed by official state and church policies, ostensibly intended to protect the Indians by placing them under the guidance of spiritually and politically responsible Spaniards. In exchange, the Indians—as vassals of their Spanish protectors—were to provide tribute of goods and services. Missionary efforts to convert the Indians to Christianity served to further cement the relationship between the church, the crown, and the New World vassal subjects.

The less formal interaction system based on intermarriage operated simultaneously with those of labor and conversion from the earliest years of Spanish colonization. This phenomenon, which had a long-term influence on the development of the Hispanic American cultural tradition, was an important mechanism for change not only in the Indian cultures, but in the Spanish cultures as well. Intermarriage also took place between Indians and African slaves, and tri-racial interaction was a consistent element in the colonial societies of Florida and the Caribbean. This interaction may have played a more important role in provoking changes in historic Indian cultures than has been documented.

3.1. Population Decline and Disease as Factors in Interaction

Obviously the greatest visible impact of contact on the Indians of Florida and particularly of the Caribbean was their decimation and disappearance. The introduction of European disease was a critical factor in this process, and one which has received considerable scholarly attention (Crosby 1972; Sauer 1971; Ashburn 1947; Dobyns 1963; Cook and Borah 1971; Kiple 1983).

Cook and Borah have provided a detailed analysis of the information relevant to the decline of Hispaniola's aboriginal population (1971:376–398). On the basis of the count of Indians made by the Spaniards in 1514, these authors suggest a native population in that year of about 27,800. This represents nearly an 88 percent reduction in number from the estimate and count of 2,260,000 made by the Spaniards in 1496 (Cook and Borah 1971:396). Although the first major pandemic in the New World did not take place until 1519 (Crosby 1972:39), European diseases had clearly made inroads into the Indian population of Hispaniola before that time. Measles, influenza, and respiratory ailments caused large numbers of Indian deaths during the early years of contact, before the introduction of smallpox (Dobyns 1963; Ashburn 1947:chs. 3,6).

After the large-scale introduction of African slaves to the Caribbean in the second decade of the sixteenth century, malaria, hookworm, yaws, leprosy and other diseases believed to be of African origin appeared in the New World and further decimated the aboriginal population, which was still recovering from the first onslaught of European ailments (Kiple 1983; Ashburn 1947:30–41, ch.7). By 1540 fewer than 250 native inhabitants remained in Hispaniola (Cook and Borah 1971:401).

Epidemics of European diseases also ravaged the Indians of Florida during the three centuries of Spanish occupation. Disease was undoubtedly introduced by pre-colonization contact with Europeans through the explorations, shipwreck victims, and slave raids discussed above (see particularly Dobyns 1983:250–274). Indians such as the Eastern Timucua, who lived in close proximity to Spanish occupation sites, appear to have suffered much more severely from the effects of these diseases, although even the Eastern Timucua did not suffer a demographic disaster on the scale of the Arawaks in the Caribbean. Relatively smaller European and African populations, a larger land area for joint occupation, and the comparative dearth of concentrated Spanish population centers probably all functioned to reduce the disastrous impact of European disease in Florida. Epidemics were recorded for the years

1570 and 1591 (Bushnell 1982:13), however, and when Francis Drake sacked St. Augustine in 1586 he apparently introduced a typhus strain which killed many Indians in the vicinity of St. Augustine (Quinn 1955:378). Disease continued to attack the Florida Indians through the seventeenth and eighteenth centuries. Friars claimed that epidemics killed half of the Indians in Florida between 1613 and 1617 (Swanton 1922:338), and others were recorded in 1649, 1659, 1670, and 1672–74 (Swanton 1922:337–338; Bushnell 1982:13). In 1689 there remained only about 550 Eastern Timucuans (Compostela 1689), reduced from a contact period population estimated at as many as 100,000 Indians (see discussion above; Dobyns 1983).

After the establishment of the South Carolina colony by the English in 1670, another factor began to contribute to aboriginal population decline. This was the slave raiding attacks on the Florida Indian settlements by the Carolinians and their Yamassee Indian allies (Lietch Wright 1971:58–73; Fairbanks 1974:18–20), which particularly affected the frontier settlements and missions in north central Florida and in the Guale region. As a result of these attacks and the missions' inability to defend themselves, the mission Indians were gradually consolidated around St. Augustine. After about 1650 the Guale population was moved to Florida (see Deagan 1973; Swanton 1946:136), and continuing attacks on the Apalachee missions resulted in their destruction and abandonment in 1704 (Boyd, Smith, and Griffin 1951). James Moore, who led a major raid, claimed to have killed 1,168 Apalachee and captured 4,325 (Boyd, Smith, and Griffin 1951:14). Some 124 Apalachee moved to St Augustine (Valdes 1729), and others fled to Pensacola (Covington 1972).

During the first decades of the eighteenth century most of the Indian population of Florida was restricted to the vicinity of St. Augustine. Several different tribal groups were consolidated into a number of mission villages and lived in close proximity to one another, an arrangement which parallels that of relocated and consolidated Arawak peoples in sixteenth-century Hispaniola.

The Indian population of St. Augustine in 1689 was 225 (Compostela 1689). By 1714 this had grown to 506 (Crown Cedula 1714), and by 1717 to 942 Indians in ten towns (Escobar 1717). In 1726, 1,011 Indians, including Yamassee, Guale, Chiluca, Timucua, Pojois, Apalachee, Costas, and Macapira groups, were living in sixteen towns around St. Augustine (Valdes 1729). The population peak was reached in 1736, when the number of Indians reached 1,350 in six towns (Benavides 1738). Between that year and

1752, however, the Indian population suffered a drastic decline to 150 adults in five towns (Gelabert 1752), probably as a result of epidemics. This number continued to decline until the end of the Spanish occupation of St. Augustine in 1763. In 1760 fewer than 100 Indians were living in five towns (Scardaville and Belmonte 1979:11), and when the Spaniards departed from Florida in 1763 they were accompanied by the 83 surviving Florida Indians (Puente 1763).

3.2. Labor- and Tribute-Based Interaction

3.2.1. The Caribbean Pattern

The organization of the Caribbean Indians as a labor pool was a matter of immediate and urgent concern for the Spanish colonists. The extremely hard labor necessary for the tasks of construction and subsistence, the unfamiliar and uncomfortable tropical environment, and the Spaniards' abhorrence of physical labor virtually ensured the exploitation of the local population. Such exploitation was effected primarily through two institutions. *Encomienda* was an arrangement by which the inhabitants of a designated region or town were assigned to individual Spaniards as vassals. In exchange for protection and Christian instruction, the Indians were obligated to provide labor and services to their overlord (Kirkpatrick 1939; Gibson 1966:48–50). *Repartimiento* referred to the obligation of Indian caciques or towns to provide a designated tribute of goods or labor to the Spanish officials (ibid.). In some cases, such as in Florida, the Indians who provided labor under the repartimiento were paid a small wage for their work (Bushnell 1983). (See Kirkpatrick 1939 for a fuller discussion of the various definitions and uses of these terms.)

Tribute was established in Hispaniola in 1495 by Christopher Columbus, who required that caciques provide enough gold to fill a small bell every three months (Las Casas, quoted in Cook and Borah 1971:387). By 1499, when the first gold mines were established, the Arawaks were unable to produce sufficient tribute in gold, and thus each chief was required by the Spaniards to send a repartimiento of men to work in the mines as recompense (Floyd 1973:44–45). This was the beginning of the repartimiento system which was to endure as an important tool of exploitation throughout Spanish America.

The encomienda system was formally established in 1509 (Haring 1947:40). *Encomenderos* (overlords) apparently organized the labor of their encomienda vassals through the caciques, who were exempted from labor and often given preferential treatment (Bushnell 1983; Hanke 1964:27). Relocation of Indians for labor in mines, ranches, and farms disrupted and recombined settlements (Haring 1947:39–41). This probably led also to disruption of family structure and lineage residence units, contributing to a general disintegration and breakdown in Hispaniola Arawak society.

As early as 1508 it was necessary for the Spaniards to import Lucayan, Carib, and other Indians from various parts of the Caribbean and from Florida to supplement the labor pool on Hispaniola (Haring 1947:41; Zavala 1938; Cook and Borah 1971(1):385; Lietch Wright 1981:131–132; see also Newson 1976 for a discussion of the phenomenon in Spanish colonial Trinidad). This relocation and recombination of Indian groups must also have disrupted residence and interaction patterns. A major blow to the Hispaniola Arawak population came in 1519, when it was consolidated into towns under the jurisdiction of friars as a result of the Jeronymite Interrogatory (see Hanke 1964:36–38). This coincided with the smallpox epidemic of 1519, which cruelly decimated the weakened and relocated Indian populations (Crosby 1972:46).

After 1519 the Indians of Hispaniola were no longer a significant labor source for the Spaniards' colonization enterprises, and they were superseded by African slaves. The consolidation and devastation of the Arawaks possibly also contributed to the outlawing of encomienda as an inheritable institution in 1520 (Gibson 1966:54), which was largely due to the efforts and influence of New World religious workers headed by Bartolome de las Casas. The encomienda underwent a number of resurrections, changes and eliminations over the subsequent two decades, primarily as the result of conflict between the religious orders and the colonists, who were unable to survive without a large cheap and reliable labor pool. By the mid-1540s, encomienda was so restricted as to be essentially eliminated, except for personal exemptions such as that granted to Pedro Menendez de Aviles in his Florida ventures (Gibson 1966:48–63).

3.2.2. The Florida Pattern

In Florida a system of labor tribute was permitted by an agreement between Pedro Menendez de Aviles, founder of the colony, and the crown of Spain (Lyon 1976:50). During the early years of colonization, however, tribute was extracted only in the form of material commodities (Lyon 1976:118–119).

During the late sixteenth century a system of labor tribute was instituted through the caciques of the Timucua, Apalachee, and Guale, often organized through the missions. Each year Indians from all of these regions were sent to St. Augustine to help build the fortifications, till the fields, and provide miscellaneous services to the Spaniards (Ramirez 1622; Bushnell 1979, 1983:14–15). This practice, which continued through the seventeenth century, resulted in the absence of numbers of adult males from the towns for several months each year, which presumably affected traditional labor and sex role patterns. During one year, nineteen adult men were absent on repartimiento duty from a single Apalachee town (Bushnell 1979:5) which probably did not have an adult male population of many more than fifty.

Encomienda as an institution was never established in Florida. The colony had no economic activities (such as mines or plantations) that required large-scale, intensive labor efforts, and it remained a subsidized military presidio until the end of the Spanish occupation (see Deagan 1983:ch. 3). Large-scale consolidation of Indian populations for purposes of labor organization was unnecessary, and the needs of the garrison at St. Augustine could be met through the annual repartimiento allotment. Both of these factors—the absence of labor-intensive extractive economic activities and the maintenance of the traditional villages apart from the Spanish community—contributed to the less drastic decline in the Florida Indian population as compared to that in the Caribbean.

3.2.3. Technological and Institutional Change: Archeological Aspects

In both Florida and the Caribbean a policy of relocating and consolidating Indian groups appears to have brought about certain poorly understood, but archeologically detectable, changes in aboriginal material culture. Excavations have been conducted at several sites known to have been the locations for repartimiento and encomienda activity involving several culturally distinct groups of Indians living in forced proximity, including Nueva Cadiz, Venezuela (Willis 1976); La Vega Real de la Concepcion, Dominican Republic (Ortega y Fondeur 1978); St. Augustine, Florida (Deagan 1983; Merritt 1977); Yayal, Cuba (Dominguez 1978); and Puerto Real, Haiti (Fairbanks et al. 1981; Marrinan 1982; McEwen 1983; Williams 1983). Preliminary results from work at these sites suggests that the relocation and consolidation of Indian groups is archeologically reflected by the appearance of new and distinct ceramic forms. In Haiti, Cuba and Nueva Cadiz, a thick, crude, hand-molded, and undecorated ceramic ware occurs at the Spanish sites in early sixteenth-century contexts (figure 4). These ceramics are unknown from prehistoric contexts in these areas, and suggest a degradation of indigenous ceramic traditions after contact. This may have been a result of breakdown in the social units responsible for ceramic production or of a disruption in the traditional lines of information and craft transmission.

At Puerto Real this distinct pottery type is spatially isolated into certain areas within the town and has a spatial distribution quite different from either Spanish ceramics or indigenous Arawak ceramics (Williams 1983). At la Vega Real in the Dominican Republic, large quantities of a unique and distinctive pottery type combining Spanish and Indian elements are present in early sixteenth-century contexts. This has been suggested to represent an organized, directed effort by the Spaniards to implement a new craft specialization (Ortega y Fondeur 1978).

In Florida the Spanish colonization era was marked by the appearance not only of new, European-influenced ceramic styles (see Smith 1948), but also by the domination of historic aboriginal material traditions by a ceramic ware known to have been associated with a single group, the Guale. Guale ceramics were almost the only style made and used by Indians in the vicinity of St. Augustine by the end of the seventeenth century, despite the fact that the area was inhabited by several tribal groups (Timucua, Apalachee, Guale, South Florida Indians) each of which possessed a distinctive ceramic tradition at the time of contact (see Milanich and Proctor 1978). Unfortunately the archeological records of these phenomena are at this time too incomplete to do other than suggest that the breakdown and disruption of residence patterns and tribal homogeneity are reflected in the appearance of new or distinct ceramic traditions. It is not possible to identify the specific social mechanisms that brought about this pattern of material change in historic period Indian cultures.

The potential influence of African slaves on Indian culture is another factor that should be considered in the assessment of change brought about through the relocation and consolidation of historic Indians for labor purposes. By 1520 large numbers of Africans were being imported to the Indies to supplement the insufficient Indian labor pool (Haring 1947:204), and black slaves were also part of the Florida colonization effort from the earliest decades. In both areas Africans and Indians undoubtedly sustained regular contact with one another in labor situations. Such contact had several effects on the Indian

Figure 4 *Handmade Non-European Pottery from Sixteenth-Century Puerto Real, Haiti*

groups, one of which was the introduction of the African diseases discussed above. Although these diseases undoubtedly reduced the weakened Indian populations, social interaction and alliances quickly developed between blacks and Indians. Concubinage of Indian women by black slaves apparently occurred regularly, although it was strongly discouraged by Spanish authorities in Florida and in Hispaniola (Hanke 1964:31; Morner 1967:40; Lietch Wright 1981:44). Blacks and Indians joined forces in 1533 on Hispaniola in a decade-long rebellion against the Spaniards (Haring 1947:206), and later in the sixteenth century Florida officials were concerned about the problems caused by escaped slaves (*cimarrones*) living with the Indians of southern Florida (Bushnell 1982:22; Lietch Wright 1981:44).

Interaction between blacks and Indians in labor-related circumstances and other less formal alliances probably involved miscegenation and other kinds of cultural exchanges in such areas as craft production, language, and food preparation (for a discussion of possible interactions between Florida blacks and Indians in the colonial period see Lietch Wright 1981:257–263).

4. Religious Conversion and Social Change

Through the sixteenth century the Catholic church functioned as a counterpoint to the exploitive tendencies in Spanish-Indian relations encouraged by economically motivated colonists. The church missions also provided an alternative structure for Spanish-Indian interaction and, in Florida at least, a mechanism for organizing Indian labor and agricultural production in areas remote from the centers of Spanish control.

From the first days of exploration and colonization the conversion of the New World inhabitants to Catholicism was an important mission in its own right. Church officials, particularly during the first decades of colonization in the Caribbean, had strong crown support in their attempts to convert the American Indians (see Hanke 1964; Gibson 1966:68–70). Thirteen members of religious orders are documented as having reached Hispaniola in 1493 to begin missionary work (Floyd 1973:16). They were shortly followed by the Franciscan friars, and by the Dominican friars in 1510 (Haring 1947:169–171).

The friars also acted to help buffer the Indians from the cruel and exploitive treatment of many Spanish encomenderos. Bartolome de las Casas, the most vocal and famous of these defenders of the Indians, helped to bring about legal changes in the structure of Spanish Indian policy that in theory restricted Spanish exploitation of the Indians (Hanke 1964). The Laws of Burgos, established in 1512, were largely due to Las Casas's and the Dominicans' influence on the Spanish court. The laws provided a code of governance for the management and instruction of the Indians (Hussey 1932). Although the laws sanctioned encomienda, they also contained more sympathetic provisions, such as those that prohibited calling Indians "dogs," reaffirmed that caciques were to be recognized and consulted on tribal matters, and stated that Indians were to be married in the church. They also suggested that any Indian capable of governing himself should be set free of the encomienda and made to pay taxes. Jeronymite friars sent to Hispaniola by the Spanish crown in 1516 to investigate charges of Indian abuse reported that they were able to locate only one Indian capable of governing himself (Hanke 1964:36–37). This was the same interrogatory which brought about the disastrous consolidation of the Hispaniola Arawaks discussed above.

Focusing on the caciques was apparently the most effective method of converting Arawaks, and this became a standard procedure of the Spanish mission effort throughout the region. The children of caciques were removed from the villages and instructed in Spanish and Christianity, after which they returned to their people as missionaries (Hanke 1964:57). Such a system was intended for Florida as well, although it was never successfully implemented (Lewis 1978:25).

4.1. The Florida Mission System

A centralized administration of Indian towns by religious orders was effected somewhat more successfully in Florida. Jesuit missionaries first came to Florida in 1567 and worked among the Indians until 1572, when Indian rebellions forced their departure (Gannon 1965:34; Ore 1936). According to the Jesuit father Rogel, the exploitation of the Indians by the Spanish soldiers was in large part responsible for the failure of the Jesuit mission efforts (Lyon 1976:204–206), although the imposition of stern Catholic precepts of behavior on the unwilling Indians also certainly played a part in the rebellions (Lyon 1976:204–206; Ore 1936:33–38).

The Jesuits were followed in 1577 by the Franciscans who first established missions among the coastal Timucua and Guale groups (Serrano y Saenz 1912:132; Gannon 1965:36-48; Geiger 1937; Matter 1972). By 1610 missions were extended into the interior Timucua areas, and after 1613 to the Apalachee. At the peak of the mission era, there were thirty-eight missions with jurisdiction over some twenty-six thousand Christian Indians (Fairbanks 1974; Gannon 1965:57).

Normally the mission communities consisted of one or two friars living in the mission village with the Indians. Important centers such as St. Catherine's in Guale, San Luis in Apalachee, and San Pedro on Cumberland Island also had small garrisons with a few Spanish soldiers attached. These towns generally each contained a church and a living area for the friars, but otherwise they appear to have maintained their pre-Christian configurations and housing patterns (see Wenhold 1936 for a description of mission Indian culture and technology provided by Bishop Calderon in 1675). The friars' subsistence was provided by their Indian charges, and in addition to giving guidance and instruction to the Indians in the Christian way of life, they also often helped organize the annual repartimiento from the towns to St. Augustine.

In matters of conversion and repartimiento, friars and officials alike worked through the existing aboriginal political structure and the caciques, taking care to recognize Indian status and political distinctions. Failure to do this was in fact a major cause of the 1656 rebellion in the Western Timucua area (see the letter of Don Patricio de Hinachuba as discussed in Boyd, Smith, and Griffin 1951 and in Bushnell 1979). Conversion of the caciques was considered an important priority (Canzo 1598; Meestas 1593), and in at least one case this was effected through marriage between a Spaniard and a cacique, who subsequently extended her conversion to her subjects. Dona Maria Melendez was the chief of Nombre de Dios, the town closest to St. Augustine during the sixteenth century. A Christian married to a Spanish soldier, she was highly praised for her obedience and efforts toward Indian conversion (Canzo 1598). In 1604 this same Dona Maria was installed by the Spaniards as the cacique of the Tacatacuru mission town of San Pedro (on what is today Cumberland Island, Georgia), an event which also suggests direct interference in aboriginal political affairs by Spanish officials (Serrano y Saenz 1912:172; Deagan 1978:103). This was not an isolated incident, since Spanish interference in Guale chiefly succession (to support a more sympathetic Christian candidate) was named as a specific cause of the 1597 Guale rebellion (Canzo 1598; Phillip II 1593; Ore 1936:84).

Other social and sexual practices of the Florida Indians were the subjects of attempted change by the friars. Foremost among these was the exhortation to renounce traditional ritual, religion, and magic in favor of Christianity. The best direct source of information about the specific changes imposed on the Indians by the friars is the 1613 *Confesionario,* written by Fray Francisco Pareja (Milanich and Sturtevant 1972). Rituals relating to hunting, farming, fishing, and gathering were considered sinful, and discouraged, as were many practices related to medicine, sorcery, and the disciplinary and sexual privileges of the caciques. Sexual behavior was especially emphasized in the *Confesionario,* which was intended to prompt the recall and admission of sins by the Indians during confession.

4.2. Archeological Considerations

4.2.1. Status System

The limited archeological information from Florida mission sites suggests that aboriginal status distinctions and manifestations were maintained in the mission towns. The distribution of such scarce commodities as Spanish goods and domestic food items is highly non-random in at least two mission sites, those of St. Catherine's Island, Georgia (David Thomas, personal communication, St. Catherine's Island, 1982), and Baptizing Springs, Florida (Loucks 1979). At the former site ornate religious items were found specifically with Indian burials located near the altar inside the mission church. At the latter site, European trade goods were restricted to a single aboriginal structure in the mission town. These distributions suggest a clearcut pattern of differential access by specific individuals to introduced goods in the Indian mission towns, supporting the documentary suggestions of chiefly privilege during the historic period.

4.2.2. Burial Practices and Monuments

One of the few direct archeological indications of change in aboriginal social and religious institutions through missionary intervention is a shift in burial practices. Among the Timucua and Guale groups burial in earth mounds was customary at the time of contact (Goggin 1952; Milanich and Fairbanks 1980:163–164; Larson 1978:128; figure 5). Excavations at several mission sites in Florida and Georgia have revealed extended Christian-patterned Indian burials in cemeteries and sometimes inside the church (Merritt 1977; Jones 1970; David Thomas, personal communication, St. Catherine's Island, 1982). The distribution of grave goods in the historic burials appears to parallel that found prehistorically in that in both cases only a few individuals

Figure 5 *Timucua Indians Mourning the Death and Burial of a Chief Theodore DeBry engraving (1591) of Jacques LeMoyne painting (1565–1586). Facsimiles, University of Florida Library.*

were accompanied by ornate utilitarian items in the grave. In those areas not subject to successful mission activity, however, mound burial continued into historic times (Deagan 1978:114).

Other implied social changes resulting from religious interaction probably included those related to the attempts to eliminate polygyny (see Ore 1936:73–74, 83–84 for an assessment of the effects of polygyny prohibition); attempts discussed above to manipulate tribal leadership in favor of pro-Christian contenders; and the attempts to prohibit the traditional ballgame (*pelota*) and its attendant ceremonies (Paina 1676; Bushnell 1978).

4.2.3. Settlement, Subsistence, and Economy

A number of settlement and subsistence changes were imposed on the Florida Indians through the mission system. New plant foods—including peaches, peas, garlic, figs, oranges, onions, and wheat—were introduced, as were livestock such as chickens and pigs (Boyd, Smith, and Griffin 1951:175; Smith 1956:57). More instrumental in subsistence and settlement changes were the introductions of iron tools and of intensive farming techniques. Such innovations, particularly the introduction of two yearly plantings in some areas, encouraged a more sedentary agricultural economy (Larson 1978:132; Milanich 1978:82; Bushnell 1979:3; Wenhold 1936). Although hunting continued to play what was probably an important role in the subsistence systems of the Florida Indians, the agricultural innovations of the friars did permit the maintenance of sedentary villages (Pareja 1602; Lopez 1605). According to contemporary descriptions, such as Rene Laudonniere's comment in 1564 that "during the winter they retire for three or four months into the woods where they make small huts of Palm leaves" (Laudonniere 1975:15), this was a change from the Timucua and Guale patterns at initial contact. Agricultural innovation was, of course, particularly effective in areas with suitable agricultural soils, such as the Western Timucua and parts of the Eastern Timucua territories (Milanich 1978:82). In certain coastal areas of the Guale and Timucua regions (to the south of St. Augustine) such sedentarism was never fully attained (Larson 1978:123; Franciscans 1722). Archeological investigation to date has been unable to document specific changes in house size or community configuration from the prehistoric to the historic period.

The Spaniards exploited the labor and products resulting from increased sedentarism through the existing social and economic structures of the Indian towns. By manipulating the caciques, friars and officials were able to gain access to such goods and services through a redistributive structure. Special fields were set aside and communally farmed for the benefit of caciques, friars, and occasionally the garrison in St. Augustine (Wenhold 1936:13, Bushnell 1979:3). Certain prohibitions on Indian activities, such as the restrictions on the ballgame, appear to have had a basis in such economic interests rather than in exclusively religious motives. Missionaries were particularly concerned that fields were neglected and nobody seemed to work during ballgame times (Paina 1676; Bushnell 1978).

Beyond introducing intensive farming methods, some new crops, and increased sedentarism, the mission system does not appear to have brought about major changes in the material and technological aspects of Florida Indian life. Certain European technological elements (tools, clothing, ornaments) appear to have been adopted when available, but changes in aboriginal technology as a result of contact have not yet been clearly documented. Archeological evidence from the mission sites indicates that the major missions were located in areas that already contained concentrated Indian populations in agriculturally suitable settings. San Juan del Puerto (MacMurray 1973); Nombre de Dios (Merritt 1983); the Apalachee missions (Boyd, Smith, and Griffin 1951; Jones 1973; Morrell and Jones 1970); the Guale St. Catherine's mission (Jones 1978; David Thomas, personal communication, St. Catherine's, 1982) and the Tacatacuru mission (Milanich 1971) all contain evidence of pre-mission occupation components. An exception to this pattern seems to be found in parts of the Western Timucua region, where some small mission towns apparently did not have a prehistoric component. These include Baptizing Springs (Loucks 1979) and Fig Springs (Deagan 1972). The assemblages from these sites also contain evidence suggesting that they were occupied by several distinct and non-local Indian groups, including Western Timucua, Apalachee, and Georgia Creek remnants (see Milanich 1978:78–79; Loucks 1979). In these examples of tribal relocation and consolidation, the missionaries do appear to have effected a new settlement and subsistence pattern (Milanich and Fairbanks 1980:170–171).

Religious conversion as a framework for Spanish-Indian interaction seems to have been a relatively weak agent of change in aboriginal cultures of Florida. Certain aspects of religion and ritual behavior were altered, as were certain aspects of social behavior (such as polygyny) incompatible with Christian doctrine. In general, however, these and other changes were implemented through the economic and social institutions existing in Indian societies. The nature of status and trade items was changed, but their distribution in the Indian groups appears to have paralleled that of the pre-mission structure based on ranked clans and redistribution of resources.

5. Intermarriage

Intermarriage and concubinage between Indian women and Spanish men in the New World began immediately as a result of the demographic composition of the earliest Spanish immigrant groups to the Americas. Very few Spanish women were present through the conquest and colonization periods, and in some areas, such as Florida, they were never to be present in significant numbers.

Some of the early Spanish-Indian marriages were at least partly, if not totally, political in nature. These involved unions between female caciques and Spaniards. Priests who arrived in Hispaniola with Columbus's second expedition performed several marriages there between Spaniards and caciques (Floyd 1973:59). This eventually resulted in disputes over who was to have control of the vassal Indians under the cacique's jurisdiction—the husband of the cacique or the Spanish authorities? The question was ultimately resolved in favor of the authorities (see Floyd 1973:59–61).

The crown of Spain soon encouraged such liasons, largely through a misunderstanding of matrilineal succession. The 1516 instruction of Cardinal Cisneros (then regent of Spain) suggested that Spaniards should be encouraged to marry the daughters of caciques, who "were successors of their fathers in the absence of sons" (see Morner 1967:37).

In Florida one of the earliest politically motivated mixed marriages was that of the Adelantado Pedro Menendez de Aviles to the sister of Carlos, chief of the Calusa (Lyon 1976:148; Reilly 1981). The marriage was clearly one of expediency, since Menendez already had a Spanish wife. It served to establish political ties between the Spaniards and the Calusa; however, to obtain Christian instruction, the unfortunate bride was sent with a retinue to Cuba, where she eventually perished. The marriage of Dona Maria Melendez, cacique of Nombre de Dios near St. Augustine, also had the desirable consequence, discussed above, of ensuring the subservience of her subjects to Spain and their conversion to Christianity.

Marriages involving female caciques had the greatest impact on the Indians themselves through the orientation of their leaders toward Spanish concerns. Other, less politically motivated marriages between Indian women and Spanish men also took place throughout Spanish America, and these appear to have had a greater impact on Spanish cultural adaptations than on the Indian groups. The 1514 repartimiento count on Hispaniola indicates that a number of Spaniards had Indian wives not of noble lineage (Floyd 1973:59). Sixty-four of the 171 married men in Santo Domingo were married to Indian women (Morner 1967:26), and presumably a large proportion of the more than one thousand unmarried men had Indian concubines (ibid.).

Initially these marriages were explicitly permitted and even encouraged by the Spanish crown, which indicated in 1503 that Governor Ovando should see to it that some of the inhabitants of Santo Domingo should marry Indian women in order to teach them and thus to bring reason to the Indians (Morner 1967:26). In general, however, such marriages appear not to have been the alliances preferred by the Spaniards (Morner 1967: 26–27).

A similar situation existed in Florida, where only twenty-six of the initial 2,646 persons setting out with Pedro Menendez were married and accompanied by their families (Solis de Meras 1964:77). A year later fourteen women arrived in the colony (Solis de Meras 1964:200), and from that time onward very few Spanish women came to Florida. Between 1594 and 1763 only eight of the 1,705 women married in St. Augustine were not listed as natives of the town, and only two of these were listed as being from Spain (St. Augustine Historical Society n.d.). These circumstances suggest that many of the wives in sixteenth-century St. Augustine were Indians, and that most of the women who married Spaniards in the succeeding centuries had some degree of mixed blood.

The effects of these marriages on Spanish households are evident in the archeological assemblages of St. Augustine's domestic sites from the sixteenth century through the eighteenth century. Subsistence and food preparation activities are dominated by aboriginal elements, while those elements that were more socially visible (ornaments, tablewares, architecture) were predominantly European in character (see Deagan 1983: ch.6). The same pattern has been documented in the archeological assemblage from sixteenth-century Puerto Real, Haiti (McEwen 1983).

Although the visible effects of such intermarriage are evident primarily in the European contexts, they may also have provoked changes in the Indian societies. The marriage of Indian women to Spanish men could presumably have affected sex ratios in the Indian communities, as well as the nature of the relationships between Indian men and women. Sex roles in the Indian communities could theoretically also have been affected by a more intensive

European contact with those communities through women rather than through men. It is also possible that such intermarriage could have influenced attitudes in Indian culture about the desirability of "white" affiliation as contrasted to "Indian" affiliation. The desirability of Europeanization on the part of Indian women is suggested in Oviedo's observations of Indian women bleaching their skin in sixteenth-century Hispaniola (Morner 1967:27).

Concubinage and intermarriage also took place between Indians and blacks, and these did not always involve Indian women and black men. Pareja's *Confesionario* indicates, for example, that Florida caciques took their black slaves and servants as mistresses (Milanich and Sturtevant 1972:34). Magnus Morner suggests that widespread concubinage existed between Indians and blacks, but that marriages were rare and both forms of alliance were strongly opposed by the Spanish authorities (Morner 1967:30,38,40). However, St. Augustine parish records reveal that marriages between both free and slave blacks and Indian men and women took place in Florida with some regularity from the mid-seventeenth century onward. Nineteen of these marriages occurred between 1675 and 1750, accounting for 12.3 percent of all racially mixed marriages during that time (St. Augustine Historical Society n.d.). The effects of these unions on Indian culture have not been documented either archeologically or ethnohistorically, but their presence provides a fertile ground for hypotheses concerning African and Indian cultural exchange in foodways, craft production, medicine, ritual, and magic.

6. Conclusion

Florida and the Caribbean had in common native populations characterized by matrilineal, chiefdom-level social and political organization; economies based on a mixture of horticulture, hunting, and gathering; some degree of sedentarism; and communities of generally fewer than a thousand people. Spanish interaction with the Indians in both areas initially took place through formal policies that balanced the Catholic Church's concern with protection and conversion of the Indians against the desire of the crown and colonists for economic gain through the exploitation of Indian labor. Less formal agents of change, most notably disease and intermarriage, also affected the native groups in both areas.

The changes that occurred in Indian society as a result of this interaction were most visible and dramatic in Hispaniola. There, the need for large numbers of workers in such labor-intensive activities as mining and ranching, coupled with the drastic decimation of the Indians through introduced disease, eventually precipitated the relocation and consolidation of the Hispaniola Indians into centralized and easily controllable communities. This measure, however, brought about increased devastation by diseases probably incurred through closer contact with both Europeans and African slaves. The process not only disrupted traditional Indian community structure, residence patterns, and patterns of social interaction, but resulted by the mid-sixteenth century in the effective disappearance of the Hispaniola Arawaks.

Although the same policies governed Spanish interaction with the Florida Indians, the impact and resulting changes were considerably less drastic in that area. This was largely due to the absence of labor-intensive economic ventures in Florida and the less active program of relocation and consolidation of Florida Indians. Exploitation was largely through tribute and the annual allotment of labor repartimiento from the Indian towns to St. Augustine. Although the repartimiento activities probably disrupted normal community life for the towns involved in it, it was of a temporary nature and far less intensive than in Hispaniola.

The organization of tribute and labor was effected primarily through the existing political and social structures of the Florida Indian societies, which the Spanish authorities explicitly recognized, observed, and used. On more than one occasion, the Spaniards also manipulated Indian political affairs to their own advantage, primarily by supporting or installing pro-Spanish and pro-Christian Indian leaders.

Indian community patterns appear to have remained largely intact, and the initially limited contact of the majority of the Florida Indians with Spaniards and Africans considerably reduced the incidence and impact of foreign pathogens. During the eighteenth century, however, these Indian groups were relocated and consolidated around the Spanish community of St. Augustine, where they consequently suffered rapid disorganization and decline in much the same manner as the consolidated Arawaks in sixteenth-century Hispaniola.

Although the policies of the Catholic church regarding conversion were essentially the same in Florida and in Hispaniola, the implementation of these policies had very different effects. The rapid population decimation of the Hispaniola Indians precluded the emergence of a Christian vassal population. This decline was, in fact, aggravated by the consolidation of the Indians under the supervision of the friars, and the consequent Indian vulnerability to European and African diseases. By contrast, the Florida missionaries went to the Indian population centers to implement their programs of conversion. By 1650 they had a large and flourishing Christian contingent, due at least in part to the absence of competition for the Indians by miners, farmers, or ranchers. The success of the missions in conversion, however, appears from archeological evidence not to have implemented profound changes in either the social organization or the infrastructural elements of Florida Indian communities. Political leadership and social ranking were overtly recognized and used for conversion, and European material elements introduced by the friars accrued primarily to the privileged chiefly group. Although the missionaries introduced more efficient farming methods that led to increased sedentarism in certain parts of La Florida, the benefits resulting from these changes went primarily to the Spaniards through the repartimiento. European elements were added to the aboriginal assemblage when accessible, but few other changes or replacements in Indian material culture as a result of European contact can be documented.

A less formal mode of interaction between the Spaniards and the Indians of Florida and Hispaniola was that of intermarriage. Marriages between Spaniards and caciques were initially encouraged and in this way Indian groups were manipulated to serve Spanish interests by their own leaders. Less politically beneficial marriages also occurred regularly between Spaniards and Indians, but these appear to have brought about more basic changes in the Spanish colonial way of life than in the Indian cultural contexts. The effects of such marriages on Indian attitudes toward race and the relationships between the sexes in Indian society can only be speculated upon.

It would appear that the most severe impact upon Indians of Hispaniola and of Florida, as well as the most evident institutional changes in their societies, were brought about through interaction which involved relocation of Indians from their indigenous settlements and their consolidation in a new area. Although this phenomenon did not occur on a large scale in Florida until more than two hundred years after it was implemented in Hispaniola, the ultimate results for the American Indian inhabitants were the same— depopulation.

REFERENCES CITED

Abbreviations:
  AGI: Archivo General de las Indias, Sevilla
  SCUF: Stetson Collection, University of Florida (P. K. Yonge Library of Florida History)

Alegria, Ricardo
1981   Introduccion a Chronicas Francesas de los Indios Caribes. Manuel Cardenas Ruiz, ed. San Juan: Editorial Universidad de Puerto Rico.

Ashburn, P. M.
1947   The Ranks of Death. New York: Coward McCann, Inc.

Bandelier, Fanny, trans.
1972   The Narrative of Alvar Nunez Cabeza de Vaca. Barre, Mass.: The Imprint Society.

Benavides, Antonio
1738   Governor Benavides to the King of Spain, April 24, 1738. Manuscript. AGI 52-2-16-45. Photostat on file at SCUF.

Boyd, Mark, Hale Smith, and John Griffin
1951   Here They Once Stood: The Tragic Demise of the Apalachee Missions. Gainesville: University Presses of Florida.

Bullen, Ripley P.
1978   The Tocabaga Indians and the Safety Harbor Culture. *In:* Tacachale. J. T. Milanich and S. Proctor, eds. Gainesville: University Presses of Florida.

Bushnell, Amy
1978   That Demonic Game: The Campaign to Stop Indian Pelota Playing in Spanish Florida, 1675–1684. The Americas 35 (July):1–19.
1979   Patricio de Hinachuba: Defender of the Word of God, the Crown of the King and the Little Children of Ivi-tachuco. American Indian Culture and Research Journal 3 (3):1–21.
1982   The King's Coffer. Gainesville: University Presses of Florida.
1983   Cross, Pole and Banner: The Balance of Power in the Provinces of Seventeenth Century, Florida. Paper presented at the Southern Historical Association, Columbia, S.C.

Canzo, Gonzales Mendez de
1598   Letter To The Spanish Crown, Feb. 24, 1598. Manuscript. AGI 54-5-9. On file at the Lowery Collection, University of Florida, Gainesville.

Cassa, Roberto
1975   Los Tainos en la Espanola. Santo Domingo: Universidad Autonima de Santo Domingo.

Compostela, Diego Euclino
1689   Letter of Bishop of Cuba to the Spanish Crown, Sept. 28, 1689. Manuscript. AGI 54-3-2/9. Photostat on file at SCUF.

Cook, Sherburne, and Woodrow Borah
1971   Essays in Population History. Volume 1: Mexico and the Caribbean. Berkeley: University of California Press.

Covington, James
1972   Apalachee Indians: 1704–1763. Florida Historical Quarterly 50 (4):366–384.

Crosby, Alfred
1972   The Columbian Exchange. Westport, Conn.:Greenwood.

Crown Cedula
1714   Royal Cedula to Governor Corcoles y Martinez, Sept. 26, 1714. Manuscript. AGI 54-5-10/87. Photostat on file at SCUF.

Deagan, Kathleen
1972   Fig Springs: The Mid-Seventeenth Century in North-Central Florida. Historical Archaeology 6:23–46.
1973   Mestizaje in Colonial St. Augustine. Ethnohistory 20:55–65.
1978   Cultures in Transition: Assimilation and Fusion Among the Eastern Timucua. *In:* Tacachale. J. T. Milanich and S. Proctor, eds. pp. 89–119. Gainesville: University Presses of Florida.
1979   Timucua 1580: Background Research and Exhibit Plan for a Timucua Village Reconstruction ca. 1580. St. Augustine: St. Augustine Restoration Foundation Inc.
1983   Spanish St. Augustine: The Archeology of a Colonial Creole Community. New York: Academic Press.
n.d.   The Apalachee. *In:* The Southeast, R. Fogelson, ed. Handbook of North American Indians 13. W. Sturtevant, Gen. Ed. Washington, D.C.: Smithsonian Institution.

Dobyns, Henry
1963   An Outline of Andean Epidemic History to 1720. Bulletin of the History of Medicine 37(6):493–515.
1983   Their Numbers Become Thinned: Native American Population Dynamics in Eastern North America. Knoxville: University of Tennessee Press.

Dobyns, Henry and William Swagerty
1980   Timucuan Population in the 1560's. Paper presented at the Southeastern Archaeological Conference, New Orleans, Louisiana.

Dominquez, Lourdes
1978   La Transculturacion en Cuba (s. XVI–XVII). Cuba Arqueologia 33–35.

Escobar, Juan de Ayala
1717   Letter to the Spanish Crown, April 18, 1717. Manuscript. AGI 58-1-30/ 64-65. Photostat on file at SCUF.

Fairbanks, Charles H.
1974   Ethnohistorical Report on the Florida Indians. Commission Findings, Indians Claims Commission. New York: Garland.

Fairbanks, Charles, Rochelle Marrinan, Gary Shapiro, Bonnie MacEwen, and Alicia Kemper
1981   Collected Papers: Puerto Real, Haiti: 1981 Season. Papers presented at Conference on Historic Sites Archeology, 1981. On file at the Florida State Museum, Gainesville.

Floyd, Troy
1973   The Columbian Dynasty in the Caribbean, 1492–1526. Albuquerque: University of New Mexico Press.

Franciscans of Florida
1722   Franciscan Provincial to the Crown of Spain, Dec. 28, 1722. Manuscript. AGI 58-1-301/95. Photostat on file at SCUF.

Gannon, Micheal V.
1965   The Cross in the Sand: The Early Catholic Church in Florida, 1513–1870. Gainesville: University of Florida Press.

Garcia, Genaro
1902   Dos Antiguas Relaciones de la Florida. Mexico: J. Aguilar Vera y Comp.

Geiger, Maynard
1937   The Franciscan Conquest of Florida (1573–1618). Studies in Hispanic American History 1. Washington, D.C.: Catholic University.

Gelabert, Jose
1752   Jose Gelabert to the Crown of Spain, Jan. 10, 1752. Manuscript. AGI 87-1-14/2. Photostat on file at SCUF.

Gibson, Charles
1966   Spain in America. New York: Harper-Colophon.

Goggin, John M.
1952   Space and Time Perspective in Northern St. John's Archaeology. Yale University Publications in Anthropology #47.

Goggin, John M., and William Sturtevant
1964   The Calusa: A Stratified, Non-Agricultural Society (with notes on sibling

marriage). *In:* Explorations in Cultural Anthropology: Essays in Honor of George P. Murdock. Ward Goodenough, ed. New York: McGraw Hill.

Hanke, Lewis
1964   The First Social Experiments in America. Gloucester, Mass.: Peter Smith

Haring, C. H.
1947   The Spanish Empire in America. New York: Harcourt, Brace.

Hoffman, Paul
1980   European Contacts with the Georgia-South Carolina Coast ca. 1515–1566. Paper presented at the Southeastern Archeological Conference, New Orleans, Louisiana.

Hussey, Raymond
1932   Text of the Laws of Burgos Concerning the Treatment of the Indians. Hispanic American Historical Review 12:301–326.

Jane, Cecil, trans.
1960   The Journal of Christopher Columbus. New York Clarkson, Potter, Inc.

Jones, Calvin B.
1970   A 17th Century Spanish Mission Cemetary is Discovered Near Tallahassee. (Florida Department of State) Archives and History News 1(4).
1973   A Semi-Subterranean Structure at Mission San Joseph de Ocuya, Jefferson County, Florida. (Florida Department of State) Bureau of Historic Sites and Properties Bulletin 3:1–50.

Jones, Grant
1978   The Ethnohistory of the Guale Coast Through 1684. *In:* The Anthropology of St. Catherine's Island. Vol. 1: Natural and Cultural History. Anthropological Papers of the American Museum of Natural History. 55(2):178–209.

Kiple, Kenneth
1983   The Epidemiological Dimension to Black Slavery in the Caribbean. Infacto de Espana en la Florida, el Caribe y La Luisiana 1500–1800. Madrid. Centro de Instituto Cooperacion Iberoamericana.

Kirkpatrick, F. A.
1939   Repartimiento-Encomienda. Hispanic American Historical Review 19: 372–379.

Las Casas, Bartolome de
1971   History of the Indies. 2 vols. Andree Collard, trans. New York: Harper and Row.

Larson, Lewis
    1978   Historic Guale Indians of the Georgia Coast and the Impact of the Spanish Mission Effort. *In:* Tacachale, J. T. Milanich and S. Proctor, eds. pp. 120–140. Gainesville: University Presses of Florida.

Laudonniere, Rene
    1975   Three Voyages. Charles Bennett, trans. Gainesville: University Presses of Florida.

Lewis, Clifford
    1978   The Calusa. *In:* Tacachale. J. T. Milanich and S. Proctor, eds. pp. 19–49. Gainesville: University Presses of Florida.

Lietch Wright, J.
    1971   Anglo-Spanish Rivalry in North America. Athens University of Georgia Press.
    1981   The Only Land They Knew. New York: The Free Press.

Lopez, Balthazar
    1605   Balthazar Lopez to the Bishop of Cuba, Sept. 16, 1605. Manuscript AGI 54-5-20. On file in the Lowery Collections, P. K. Yonge Library, University of Florida.

Loucks, L. Jill
    1979   Political and Economic Interactions Between Spaniards and Indians: Archeological and Ethno-historical Perspectives of the Mission System in Florida. Ph.D. dissertation, University of Florida.

Lowery, Woodbury
    1905   The Spanish Settlements Within the Present Limits of the United States, 1513–1561. New York and London.

Lyon, Eugene
    1976   The Enterprise of Florida. Gainesville: University Presses of Florida.

McEwen, Bonnie G.
    1983   Spanish Colonial Adaptations on Hispaniola: The Archeology of Area 35, Puerto Real. M.A. thesis, University of Florida.

MacMurray, Judith
    1973   The Definition of the Ceramic Complex at San Juan del Puerto. M.A. thesis, University of Florida, Gainesville.

Marrinan, Rochelle
    1982   Test Excavations of Building B (Area 2), Puerto Real, Haiti. Report on file at the Florida State Museum, Gainesville.

Matter, Robert
1972 The Spanish Missions of Florida: The Friars Versus the Governors in the "Golden Age" 1606–1690. Ph.D dissertation, University of Washington.

Meestas, Hernando de
1593 Letter of Hernando de Meestas. Manuscript. AGI 14 7–37. Microfilm on file on Reel 3, Lowery Collection, P. K. Yonge Library, University of Florida.

Merritt, J. Donald
1977 Excavation of a Coastal Eastern Timucua Village in Northeast Florida. M.A. thesis, Florida State University.
1983 Beyond the Town Walls: The Indian Element in Colonial St. Augustine. *In:* Spanish St. Augustine, by K. Deagan. New York: Academic Press.

Milanich, J. T.
1971 Surface Information from the Presumed Site of the San Pedro de Mocamo Mission. Conference on Historic Sites Archeology Papers 5:114-121
1972 Excavations at the Richardson Site, Alachua County, Florida: An Early 17th Century Potano Indian Village (Florida Department of State) Bureau of Historic Sites and Properties Bulletin 2:35–61.
1978 The Western Timucua: Patterns of Acculturation and Change. *In:* Tacachale. J. T. Milanich and S. Proctor, eds. pp. 59–88. Gainesville: University of Presses of Florida.

Milanich, J. T., and Charles Fairbanks
1980 Florida Archeology. New York: Academic Press.

Milanich, J. T., and Samuel Proctor, eds.
1978 Tacachale:Essays on the Indians of Florida and Georgia during the Historic Period. Gainesville University Presses of Florida.

Milanich, J. T., and William C. Sturtevant
1972 Francisco Pareja's 1613 Confessionario. Tallahassee: Florida Division of Archives, History and Records Management.

Mooney, James
1928 The Aboriginal Population of America North of Mexico. Washington, D.C.: Smithsonian Institution Miscellaneous Collections 80(7).

Morison, Samuel E.
1940 The Route of Columbus Along the North Coast of Haiti, and the Site of Navidad. Transactions of the American Philosophical Society 31(4):239–285.

Morner, Magnus
  1967 Race Mixture in the History of Latin America. Boston: Little, Brown and
        Co.

Morrell, Ross, and Calvin Jones
  1970 San Juan de Aspalaga. (Florida Department of State) Bureau of Historic
        Sites and Properties Bulletin 1:25–43.

Newson, Linda
  1976 Aboriginal and Spanish Colonial Trinidad. New York: Academic Press.

Ore, Luis Jeronimo de
  1936 The Martyrs of Florida (1513–1616). Maynard Geiger, trans. Franciscan
        Studies 18. New York: Joseph L. Wagner.

Ortega, Elpidio y Carmen Fondeur
  1978 Estudio de la Ceramica del Periodo Indo-Hispano de la Antigua Concepcion
        de la Vega. Fundacion Ortega-Alvarez Serie Cientifica 1. Santo Domingo.

Paina, Juan
  1676 Origin and Beginning of the Ballgame which the Apalachee and Yustega
        Indians have been Playing from Pagan Times up to the Year 1676. Sept 23,
        1676. San Luis, Florida. Manuscript. *Included in:* Expediente relative to the
        visitation of Guale, Timucua and Apalachee, Nov. 29, 1677. AGI Escriba-
        nia de Camara, 156–xxx, fol. 569–83. Translation from notes of John M.
        Goggin. On file at the Department of Anthropology Smithsonian Institu-
        tion.

Pareja, Francisco
  1602 Francisco Pareja to the King of Spain, Sept. 14, 1602. Manuscript. AGI 54-
        5-20/5. On file at the Lowery Collection, P. K. Yonge Library, University
        of Florida.

Phillipe II
  1593 Royal Cedula to the Governor of Florida, Oct. 2, 1593. Manuscript. AGI
        86-5-19. On file at SCUF.

Puente, Elixio
  1763 Plano de la Real Fuerza, Baluarte y Linea de la Plaza de Sn. Agustin de
        Florida. Manuscript and Map. Microfilm on file on Reel 2, Buckingham
        Smith Collection, P. K. Yonge Library, University of Florida.

Quattelbaum, Paul
  1956 The Land Called Chicora: The Carolinas under Spanish Rule with French
        Intrusions, 1520–1670. Gainesville, University of Florida Press.

Quinn, David
1955   The Roanoke Voyages. London: The Hakluyt Society.

Ramirez, Alonso de
1622   Letter to the Crown of Spain, Jan. 15 1622. Manuscript AGI 54-5-17/88.
       Photostat on file at SCUF.

Reilly, Stephen
1981   A Marriage of Expediency: The Calusa Indians and their Relations with
       Pedro Menendez de Aviles in Southeast Florida 1566–1569. Florida Histori-
       cal Quarterly 59(4):395–421.

Rosenblatt, Angel
1954   La Poblacion de America en 1492. Viejos y Nuevos Calculos. Mexico City.

Rouse, Irving
1948a The Arawak. *In:* Handbook of South American Indians. Vol. 4. The Cir-
       cum-Caribbean Tribes. Julian Steward, ed. pp. 507–546. Bureau of Ameri-
       can Ethnology 143.
1948b The Ciboney. *In:* Handbook of South American Indians. Vol 4. The Cir-
       cum-Caribbean Tribes. Julian Steward, ed. pp. 497-506. Bureau of Ameri-
       can Ethnology 143.
1948c The Carib. *In:* Handbook of South American Indians. Vol 4. the Circum-
       Caribbean Tribes. Julian Steward, ed. pp. 547-566. Bureau of American
       Ethnology 143.

St. Augustine Historical Society
n.d.   The Parish Records of the Cathedral of St. Augustine 1594–1763. Photo-
       stat on file at the St. Augustine Historical Society, St. Augustine.

Sauer, Carl. V.
1971   The Early Spanish Main. Berkeley: University of California Press.

Scardaville, Michael, and Jesus Belmonte
1979   Florida in the Late Spanish Period: The 1756 Grinon Report. El Escribano
       16:1–24.

Serrano y Saenz, Manuel, ed.
1912   Documentos Historicos de la Florida y la Luisiana. Siglos xvi al xviii.
       Madrid: Biblioteca de los Americanistas.

Smith, Buckingham, trans.
1945   Memoir of Do. d'Escalante Fontaneda respecting Florida, Written in Spain,
       about the year 1575. Coral Gables: Glade House.

1968 Narratives of de Soto in the Conquest of Florida. (Original translated edition 1866.) Gainesville: Palmetto Books.

Smith, Hale G.
1948 Two Historical Archeological Periods in Florida. American Antiquity 13(4):313–319.
1956 The European and the Indian. Florida Anthropological Society Special Publication 4.

Solis de Mesas, Gonzalo
1964 Pedro Menendez de Aviles. J. T. Connor, trans. Gainesville: University Presses of Florida.

Sturtevant, William C.
1961 Taino Agriculture in the Evolution of Horticultural Systems in Native South America: Causes and Consequences. Antropologia. Supplement 2.
1978 The Last of the South Florida Aborigines. *In:* Tacachale, J. Milanich and S. Proctor, eds. pp. 141–162. Gainesville: University Presses of Florida.

Swanton, John
1922 The Early History of the Creek Indians and Their Neighbors. Bureau of American Ethnology Bulletin 137. Washington: Smithsonian Institution.
1946 Indians of the Southeastern United States. Washington Bureau of American Ethnology Bulletin 137. Washington: Smithsonian Institution.

Symes, M. I. and M. E. Stephens
1965 A-272: The Fox Pond Site. Florida Anthropologist 18:65–72.

Tesar, Louis
1980 An Archeological Survey of Selected Portions of Leon County, Florida. Miscellaneous Project Report Series 49. Tallahassee: Florida Division of Archives, History and Records Management.

Valdez, Juan
1729 Letter of the Bishop of Cuba to the Crown of Spain, Jan 14, 1729. Manuscript. AGI 58-2-8. On file at SCUF.

Vega, Bernardo
1980 Los Casicaszgos de la Hispaniola. Santo Domingo: Museo del Hombre.

Wagley, Charles
1968 The Latin American Tradition. New York: Columbia University Press.

Wenhold, Lucy
1936 A 17th Century Letter of Gabriel Diaz Vara Calderon, Bishop of Cuba, Describing the Indians and Indian Missions of Florida (1675). Smithsonian Miscellaneous Collections 95(1b):1–14.

Williams, Maurice
   1983   Sub-Surface Patterning at 16th Century Puerto Real, Haiti. Project report
          on file at the Florida State Museum, Gainesville.

Willis, Raymond
   1976   The Archaeology of 16th Century Nueva Cadiz. M.A. thesis, Anthropol-
          ogy Department, University of Florida.

Zavala, Silvio
   1938   Los Trabajadores antillanos en el Siglo XVI. Revista de Historia de America
          2 (June):31–67.

CONTRIBUTORS

William W. Fitzhugh is curator of North American archeology at the Smithsonian Institution, where he has served as chairman of the Department of Anthropology. A specialist in the archeology and anthropology of arctic regions, he has conducted fieldwork in Labrador and other northern areas. He has also done research in Scandinavia, Alaska, and the Soviet Union on circumpolar maritime adaptations and prehistoric and historic cultural change in arctic and subarctic regions. His exhibition Inua: Spirit World of the Bering Sea Eskimo recently completed a three-year tour of North America.

Kathleen A. Deagan is chairperson of the anthropology department of the Florida State Museum. Specializing in historical archeology and ethnohistory, particularly of the southeastern United States and the Caribbean, she has conducted excavations in Spanish St. Augustine and at Spanish colonial sites in Haiti and has undertaken collection, site, and documentary research in Honduras, Peru, Cuba, the Dominican Republic, and Puerto Rico.

William Engelbrecht is associate professor and chairperson of the Department of Anthropology, State University College at Buffalo, a director of the New York Archaeological Council, and newsletter editor of the Society of Professional Archeologists. His long-term research interests include Iroquois ceramics and the excavation of the Eaton site, a protohistoric village site south of Buffalo.

J. Frederick Fausz is an associate professor of history at St. Mary's College of Maryland specializing in the ethnohistory of the colonial Chesapeake. His research on seventeenth-century Anglo-Indian relations has appeared in the books *Struggle and Survival in Colonial America* and *Scholars and the Indian Experience* and in a variety of scholarly journals.

Hans Christian Gulløv, a former scientific researcher at the Danish National Museum, is a member of the Institute of Eskimology at the University of Copenhagen. He has conducted archeological fieldwork in Denmark and Greenland since 1967 and ethnological fieldwork in Greenland. His current research interest is the history of the Greenland Eskimo people.

Susan A. Kaplan is director of the Peary-MacMillan Arctic Museum at Bowdoin College and a former guest curator at the National Museum of Natural

History and The University Museum, University of Pennsylvania. An archeologist and anthropologist, she pursues research interests in Labrador and Alaska.

Marc A. Kelley, a specialist in osteopathology in modern and ancient populations, is currently involved in reconstructing health patterns of the northeastern United States and establishing a laboratory for forensic and physical anthropology. He has done extensive fieldwork with the skeletal remains of American Indians and research with Egyptian and Chilean mummies.

Paul A. Robinson is the state archeologist at the Rhode Island Historical Preservation Commission. He has conducted fieldwork in New York State, Rhode Island, and Maine and research on the ecological and ideological strategies with which human groups respond to changing environments and circumstances.

Patrica A. Rubertone is an assistant professor of anthropology at Brown University. She has done fieldwork on historic period sites in New England and Morocco and on prehistoric Pueblo sites in New Mexico and Arizona, and research in urban archeology, rural land use and settlement, and the effects of European expansion on Indian and colonial populations.

Peter A. Thomas is a research assistant professor of anthropology at the University of Vermont and the director of the Consulting Archaeology Program. He has conducted fieldwork in New Zealand, California, New Mexico, Utah, Wisconsin, and the New England states; acted as principal pal investigator for over seventy archeological studies in Vermont and Massachusetts; and published several articles on the contact period in southern New England.

E. Randolph Turner is senior prehistoric archaeologist at the Virginia Research Center for Archaeology, Yorktown, Virginia. An anthropologist by training, he has pursued research interests in the archaeology and ethnohistory of eastern North America, with particular emphasis on Virginia and the evolution of chiefdom societies.